# PENGUIN SHAKESPEARE

*Founding Editor: T. J. B. Spencer*
*General Editor: Stanley Wells*
*Supervisory Editors: Paul Edmondson, Stanley Wells*

T. J. B. SPENCER, sometime Director of the Shakespeare Institute of the University of Birmingham, was the founding editor of the New Penguin Shakespeare, for which he edited both *Romeo and Juliet* and *Hamlet*.

STANLEY WELLS is Emeritus Professor of the University of Birmingham and Chairman of the Shakespeare Birthplace Trust. He is general editor of the Oxford Shakespeare and his books include *Shakespeare: The Poet and His Plays*, *Shakespeare: For All Time*, *Looking for Sex in Shakespeare* and (with Paul Edmondson) *Shakespeare's Sonnets.*

EMRYS JONES was formerly Goldsmiths' Professor of English Literature at the University of Oxford. His publications include *Scenic Form in Shakespeare*, *The Origins of Shakespeare* and *The New Oxford Book of Sixteenth-Century Verse*.

RENÉ WEIS is Professor of English at University College London. He has edited *King Lear* (Longman) and *Henry IV, Part 2* (Oxford) and is the author of *The Yellow Cross* (Penguin). He is currently writing a biography of Shakespeare for John Murray.

*William Shakespeare*

# ANTONY AND CLEOPATRA

*Edited with a Commentary by Emrys Jones*
*Introduced by René Weis*

PENGUIN BOOKS

PENGUIN BOOKS

Published by the Penguin Group
Penguin Books Ltd, 80 Strand, London WC2R 0RL, England
Penguin Group (USA) Inc., 375 Hudson Street, New York, New York 10014, USA
Penguin Group (Canada), 10 Alcorn Avenue, Toronto, Ontario, Canada M4V 3B2
(a division of Pearson Penguin Canada Inc.)
Penguin Ireland, 25 St Stephen's Green, Dublin 2, Ireland (a division of Penguin Books Ltd)
Penguin Group (Australia), 250 Camberwell Road, Camberwell, Victoria 3124, Australia
(a division of Pearson Australia Group Pty Ltd)
Penguin Books India Pvt Ltd, 11 Community Centre, Panchsheel Park, New Delhi – 110 017, India
Penguin Group (NZ), cnr Airborne and Rosedale Roads, Albany, Auckland 1310, New Zealand
(a division of Pearson New Zealand Ltd)
Penguin Books (South Africa) (Pty) Ltd, 24 Sturdee Avenue, Rosebank 2196, South Africa

Penguin Books Ltd, Registered Offices: 80 Strand, London WC2R 0RL, England

www.penguin.com

This edition first published in Penguin Books 1977
Reissued in the Penguin Shakespeare series 2005
1



Set in 11.5/12.5 PostScript Monotype Fournier
Typeset by Palimpsest Book Production Limited, Polmont, Stirlingshire
Printed in England by Clays Ltd, St Ives plc

# *Contents*

# *General Introduction*

Every play by Shakespeare is unique. This is part of his greatness. A restless and indefatigable experimenter, he moved with a rare amalgamation of artistic integrity and dedicated professionalism from one kind of drama to another. Never shackled by convention, he offered his actors the alternation between serious and comic modes from play to play, and often also within the plays themselves, that the repertory system within which he worked demanded, and which provided an invaluable stimulus to his imagination. Introductions to individual works in this series attempt to define their individuality. But there are common factors that underpin Shakespeare's career.

Nothing in his heredity offers clues to the origins of his genius. His upbringing in Stratford-upon-Avon, where he was born in 1564, was unexceptional. His mother, born Mary Arden, came from a prosperous farming family. Her father chose her as his executor over her eight sisters and his four stepchildren when she was only in her late teens, which suggests that she was of more than average practical ability. Her husband John, a glover, apparently unable to write, was nevertheless a capable businessman and loyal townsfellow, who seems to have fallen on relatively hard times in later life. He would have been brought up as a Catholic, and may have retained

Catholic sympathies, but his son subscribed publicly to Anglicanism throughout his life.

The most important formative influence on Shakespeare was his school. As the son of an alderman who became bailiff (or mayor) in 1568, he had the right to attend the town's grammar school. Here he would have received an education grounded in classical rhetoric and oratory, studying authors such as Ovid, Cicero and Quintilian, and would have been required to read, speak, write and even think in Latin from his early years. This classical education permeates Shakespeare's work from the beginning to the end of his career. It is apparent in the self-conscious classicism of plays of the early 1590s such as the tragedy of *Titus Andronicus*, *The Comedy of Errors*, and the narrative poems *Venus and Adonis* (1592–3) and *The Rape of Lucrece* (1593–4), and is still evident in his latest plays, informing the dream visions of *Pericles* and *Cymbeline* and the masque in *The Tempest*, written between 1607 and 1611. It inflects his literary style throughout his career. In his earliest writings the verse, based on the ten-syllabled, five-beat iambic pentameter, is highly patterned. Rhetorical devices deriving from classical literature, such as alliteration and antithesis, extended similes and elaborate wordplay, abound. Often, as in *Love's Labour's Lost* and *A Midsummer Night's Dream*, he uses rhyming patterns associated with lyric poetry, each line self-contained in sense, the prose as well as the verse employing elaborate figures of speech. Writing at a time of linguistic ferment, Shakespeare frequently imports Latinisms into English, coining words such as abstemious, addiction, incarnadine and adjunct. He was also heavily influenced by the eloquent translations of the Bible in both the Bishops' and the Geneva versions. As his experience grows, his verse and prose become more supple, the patterning less apparent, more ready to accommodate the rhythms of ordinary speech, more colloquial in diction, as in the speeches of the Nurse in *Romeo and Juliet*, the characterful prose of Falstaff and Hamlet's soliloquies. The effect is of increasing psychological realism, reaching its greatest heights in *Hamlet*, *Othello*, *King Lear*, *Macbeth* and *Antony and Cleopatra*. Gradually he discovered ways of adapting the regular beat of the pentameter to make it an infinitely flexible instrument for matching thought with feeling. Towards the end of his career, in plays such as *The Winter's Tale*, *Cymbeline* and *The Tempest*, he adopts a more highly mannered style, in keeping with the more overtly symbolical and emblematical mode in which he is writing.

So far as we know, Shakespeare lived in Stratford till after his marriage to Anne Hathaway, eight years his senior, in 1582. They had three children: a daughter, Susanna, born in 1583 within six months of their marriage, and twins, Hamnet and Judith, born in 1585. The next seven years of Shakespeare's life are virtually a blank. Theories that he may have been, for instance, a schoolmaster, or a lawyer, or a soldier, or a sailor, lack evidence to support them. The first reference to him in print, in Robert Greene's pamphlet *Greene's Groatsworth of Wit* of 1592, parodies a line from *Henry VI, Part III*, implying that Shakespeare was already an established playwright. It seems likely that at some unknown point after the birth of his twins he joined a theatre company and gained experience as both actor and writer in the provinces and London. The London theatres closed because of plague in 1593 and 1594; and during these years, perhaps recognizing the need for an alternative career, he wrote and published the narrative poems *Venus and Adonis* and *The Rape of Lucrece*. These are the only works we can be certain that Shakespeare himself was responsible for putting into print. Each bears the author's dedication to Henry Wriothesley, Earl of Southampton (1573–1624), the second in warmer terms than the first. Southampton, younger than Shakespeare by ten years, is the only person to whom he personally dedicated works. The Earl may have been a close friend, perhaps even the beautiful and adored young man whom Shakespeare celebrates in his *Sonnets*.

The resumption of playing after the plague years saw the founding of the Lord Chamberlain's Men, a company to which Shakespeare was to belong for the rest of his career, as actor, shareholder and playwright. No other dramatist of the period had so stable a relationship with a single company. Shakespeare knew the actors for whom he was writing and the conditions in which they performed. The permanent company was made up of around twelve to fourteen players, but one actor often played more than one role in a play and additional actors were hired as needed. Led by the tragedian Richard Burbage (1568–1619) and, initially, the comic actor Will Kemp (d. 1603), they rapidly achieved a high reputation, and when King James I succeeded Queen Elizabeth I in 1603 they were renamed as the King's Men. All the women's parts were played by boys; there is no evidence that any female role was ever played by a male actor over the age of about eighteen. Shakespeare had enough confidence in his boys to write for them long and demanding roles such as Rosalind (who, like other heroines of the romantic comedies, is disguised as a boy for much of the action) in *As You Like It*, Lady Macbeth and Cleopatra. But there are far more fathers than mothers, sons than daughters, in his plays, few if any of which require more than the company's normal complement of three or four boys.

The company played primarily in London's public playhouses – there were almost none that we know of in the rest of the country – initially in the Theatre, built in Shoreditch in 1576, and from 1599 in the Globe, on Bankside. These were wooden, more or less circular structures, open to the air, with a thrust stage surmounted by a canopy and jutting into the area where spectators who paid one penny stood, and surrounded by galleries where it was possible to be seated on payment of an additional penny. Though properties such as cauldrons, stocks, artificial trees or beds could indicate locality, there was no representational scenery. Sound effects such as flourishes of trumpets, music both martial and amorous, and accompaniments to songs were provided by the company's musicians. Actors entered through doors in the back wall of the stage. Above it was a balconied area that could represent the walls of a town (as in *King John*), or a castle (as in *Richard II*), and indeed a balcony (as in *Romeo and Juliet*). In 1609 the company also acquired the use of the Blackfriars, a smaller, indoor theatre to which admission was more expensive, and which permitted the use of more spectacular stage effects such as the descent of Jupiter on an eagle in *Cymbeline* and of goddesses in *The Tempest*. And they would frequently perform before the court in royal residences and, on their regular tours into the provinces, in non-theatrical spaces such as inns, guildhalls and the great halls of country houses.

Early in his career Shakespeare may have worked in collaboration, perhaps with Thomas Nashe (1567–*c.* 1601) in *Henry VI, Part I* and with George Peele (1556–96) in *Titus Andronicus*. And towards the end he collaborated with George Wilkins (*fl.* 1604–8) in *Pericles*, and with his younger colleagues Thomas Middleton (1580–1627), in *Timon of Athens*, and John Fletcher (1579–1625), in *Henry*

*VIII*, *The Two Noble Kinsmen* and the lost play *Cardenio*. Shakespeare's output dwindled in his last years, and he died in 1616 in Stratford, where he owned a fine house, New Place, and much land. His only son had died at the age of eleven, in 1596, and his last descendant died in 1670. New Place was destroyed in the eighteenth century but the other Stratford houses associated with his life are maintained and displayed to the public by the Shakespeare Birthplace Trust.

One of the most remarkable features of Shakespeare's plays is their intellectual and emotional scope. They span a great range from the lightest of comedies, such as *The Two Gentlemen of Verona* and *The Comedy of Errors*, to the profoundest of tragedies, such as *King Lear* and *Macbeth*. He maintained an output of around two plays a year, ringing the changes between comic and serious. All his comedies have serious elements: Shylock, in *The Merchant of Venice*, almost reaches tragic dimensions, and *Measure for Measure* is profoundly serious in its examination of moral problems. Equally, none of his tragedies is without humour: Hamlet is as witty as any of his comic heroes, *Macbeth* has its Porter, and *King Lear* its Fool. His greatest comic character, Falstaff, inhabits the history plays and *Henry V* ends with a marriage, while *Henry VI, Part III*, *Richard II* and *Richard III* culminate in the tragic deaths of their protagonists.

Although in performance Shakespeare's characters can give the impression of a superabundant reality, he is not a naturalistic dramatist. None of his plays is explicitly set in his own time. The action of few of them (except for the English histories) is set even partly in England (exceptions are *The Merry Wives of Windsor* and the Induction to *The Taming of the Shrew*). Italy is his favoured location. Most of his principal story-lines derive from printed writings; but the structuring and translation of these narratives into dramatic terms is Shakespeare's own, and he invents much additional material. Most of the plays contain elements of myth and legend, and many derive from ancient or more recent history or from romantic tales of ancient times and faraway places. All reflect his reading, often in close detail. Holinshed's *Chronicles* (1577, revised 1587), a great compendium of English, Scottish and Irish history, provided material for his English history plays. The *Lives of the Noble Grecians and Romans* by the Greek writer Plutarch, finely translated into English from the French by Sir Thomas North in 1579, provided much of the narrative material, and also a mass of verbal detail, for his plays about Roman history. Some plays are closely based on shorter individual works: *As You Like It*, for instance, on the novel *Rosalynde* (1590) by his near-contemporary Thomas Lodge (1558–1625), *The Winter's Tale* on *Pandosto* (1588) by his old rival Robert Greene (1558–92) and *Othello* on a story by the Italian Giraldi Cinthio (1504–73). And the language of his plays is permeated by the Bible, the Book of Common Prayer and the proverbial sayings of his day.

Shakespeare was popular with his contemporaries, but his commitment to the theatre and to the plays in performance is demonstrated by the fact that only about half of his plays appeared in print in his lifetime, in slim paperback volumes known as quartos, so called because they were made from printers' sheets folded twice to form four leaves (eight pages). None of them shows any sign that he was involved in their publication. For him, performance was the primary means of publication. The most frequently reprinted of his works were the non-dramatic poems – the erotic *Venus and Adonis* and the more moralistic *The Rape of Lucrece*. The *Sonnets*, which appeared in 1609, under his name but possibly without his consent, were less successful, perhaps because the vogue for sonnet sequences, which peaked in the 1590s, had passed by then. They were not reprinted until 1640, and then only in garbled form along with poems by other writers. Happily, in 1623, seven years after he died, his colleagues John Heminges (1556–1630) and Henry Condell (d. 1627) published his collected plays, including eighteen that had not previously appeared in print, in the first Folio, whose name derives from the fact that the printers' sheets were folded only once to produce two leaves (four pages). Some of the quarto editions are badly printed, and the fact that some plays exist in two, or even three, early versions creates problems for editors. These are discussed in the Account of the Text in each volume of this series.

Shakespeare's plays continued in the repertoire until the Puritans closed the theatres in 1642. When performances resumed after the Restoration of the monarchy in 1660 many of the plays were not to the taste of the times, especially because their mingling of genres and failure to meet the requirements of poetic justice offended against the dictates of neoclassicism. Some, such as *The Tempest* (changed by John Dryden and William Davenant in 1667 to suit contemporary taste), *King Lear* (to which Nahum Tate gave a happy ending in 1681) and *Richard III* (heavily adapted by Colley Cibber in 1700 as a vehicle for his own talents), were extensively rewritten; others fell into neglect. Slowly they regained their place in the repertoire, and they continued to be reprinted, but it was not until the great actor David Garrick (1717–79) organized a spectacular jubilee in Stratford in 1769 that Shakespeare began to be regarded as a transcendental genius. Garrick's idolatry prefigured the enthusiasm of critics such as Samuel Taylor Coleridge (1772–1834) and William Hazlitt (1778–1830). Gradually Shakespeare's reputation spread abroad, to Germany, America, France and to other European countries.

During the nineteenth century, though the plays were generally still performed in heavily adapted or abbreviated versions, a large body of scholarship and criticism began to amass. Partly as a result of a general swing in education away from the teaching of Greek and Roman texts and towards literature written in English, Shakespeare became the object of intensive study in schools and universities. In the theatre, important turning points were the work in England of two theatre directors, William Poel (1852–1934) and his disciple Harley Granville-Barker (1877–1946), who showed that the application of knowledge, some of it newly acquired, of early staging conditions to performance of the plays could render the original texts viable in terms of the modern theatre. During the twentieth century appreciation of Shakespeare's work, encouraged by the availability of audio, film and video versions of the plays, spread around the world to such an extent that he can now be claimed as a global author.

The influence of Shakespeare's works permeates the English language. Phrases from his plays and poems – 'a tower of strength', 'green-eyed jealousy', 'a foregone conclusion' – are on the lips of people who may never have read him. They have inspired composers of songs, orchestral music and operas; painters and sculptors; poets, novelists and film-makers. Allusions to him appear in pop songs, in advertisements and in television shows. Some of his characters – Romeo and Juliet, Falstaff, Shylock and Hamlet – have acquired mythic status. He is valued for his humanity, his psychological insight, his wit and humour, his lyricism, his mastery of language, his ability to excite, surprise, move and, in the widest sense of the word, entertain audiences. He is the greatest of poets, but he is essentially a dramatic poet. Though his plays have much to offer to readers, they exist fully only in performance. In these volumes we offer individual introductions, notes on language and on specific points of the text, suggestions for further reading and information about how each work has been edited. In addition we include accounts of the ways in which successive generations of interpreters and audiences have responded to challenges and rewards offered by the plays. The Penguin Shakespeare series aspires to remove obstacles to understanding and to make pleasurable the reading of the work of the man who has done more than most to make us understand what it is to be human.

Stanley Wells

# *The Chronology of Shakespeare's Works*

A few of Shakespeare's writings can be fairly precisely dated. An allusion to the Earl of Essex in the chorus to Act V of *Henry V*, for instance, could only have been written in 1599. But for many of the plays we have only vague information, such as the date of publication, which may have occurred long after composition, the date of a performance, which may not have been the first, or a list in Francis Meres's book *Palladis Tamia*, published in 1598, which tells us only that the plays listed there must have been written by that year. The chronology of the early plays is particularly difficult to establish. Not everyone would agree that the first part of *Henry VI* was written after the third, for instance, or *Romeo and Juliet* before *A Midsummer Night's Dream*. The following table is based on the 'Canon and Chronology' section in *William Shakespeare: A Textual Companion*, by Stanley Wells and Gary Taylor, with John Jowett and William Montgomery (1987), where more detailed information and discussion may be found.

| | |
|---|---|
| *The Two Gentlemen of Verona* | 1590–91 |
| *The Taming of the Shrew* | 1590–91 |
| *Henry VI, Part II* | 1591 |
| *Henry VI, Part III* | 1591 |

| | |
|---|---|
| *Henry VI, Part I* (perhaps with Thomas Nashe) | 1592 |
| *Titus Andronicus* (perhaps with George Peele) | 1592 |
| *Richard III* | 1592–3 |
| *Venus and Adonis* (poem) | 1592–3 |
| *The Rape of Lucrece* (poem) | 1593–4 |
| *The Comedy of Errors* | 1594 |
| *Love's Labour's Lost* | 1594–5 |
| *Edward III* (authorship uncertain, not included in this series) | not later than 1595 (printed in 1596) |
| *Richard II* | 1595 |
| *Romeo and Juliet* | 1595 |
| *A Midsummer Night's Dream* | 1595 |
| *King John* | 1596 |
| *The Merchant of Venice* | 1596–7 |
| *Henry IV, Part I* | 1596–7 |
| *The Merry Wives of Windsor* | 1597–8 |
| *Henry IV, Part II* | 1597–8 |
| *Much Ado About Nothing* | 1598 |
| *Henry V* | 1598–9 |
| *Julius Caesar* | 1599 |
| *As You Like It* | 1599–1600 |
| *Hamlet* | 1600–1601 |
| *Twelfth Night* | 1600–1601 |
| 'The Phoenix and the Turtle' (poem) | by 1601 |
| *Troilus and Cressida* | 1602 |
| *The Sonnets* (poems) | 1593–1603 and later |
| *Measure for Measure* | 1603 |
| *A Lover's Complaint* (poem) | 1603–4 |
| *Sir Thomas More* (in part, not included in this series) | 1603–4 |
| *Othello* | 1603–4 |
| *All's Well That Ends Well* | 1604–5 |
| *Timon of Athens* (with Thomas Middleton) | 1605 |
| *King Lear* | 1605–6 |

| | |
|---|---|
| *Macbeth* (revised by Middleton) | 1606 |
| *Antony and Cleopatra* | 1606 |
| *Pericles* (with George Wilkins) | 1607 |
| *Coriolanus* | 1608 |
| *The Winter's Tale* | 1609 |
| *Cymbeline* | 1610 |
| *The Tempest* | 1611 |
| *Henry VIII* (by Shakespeare and John Fletcher; known in its own time as *All is True*) | 1613 |
| *Cardenio* (by Shakespeare and Fletcher; lost) | 1613 |
| *The Two Noble Kinsmen* (by Shakespeare and Fletcher) | 1613–14 |

# Introduction

*Antony and Cleopatra* is one of Shakespeare's supreme imaginative achievements and its dramatic language may be the most highly wrought and daring in the canon. Samuel Taylor Coleridge noticed 'a giant power in its strength and vigour of maturity' and suggested that the motto for its soaring style should be 'happy valiancy' (*Shakespearean Criticism*). Here, if anywhere, Shakespeare seems to have allowed his imagination and incomparable gift for language to range freely and strain towards poetic sublimity in a historical context and a material world.

The play's rhetoric generates powerful tensions between objective reality and subjective perceptions of it, as in Cleopatra's commemorating the dead 'emperor' Antony. He was, she claims, the soul of generosity in whose bounty there was 'no winter' and who casually dropped from his pocket 'realms and islands' as if they were mere silver coins. His very sensuality inspired wonder at the way in which his pleasures transcended the senses. 'His delights,' she says, were 'dolphin-like' and 'showed his back above | The element they lived in'. When she inquires of her Roman interlocutor Dolabella whether 'there was or might be such a man | As this I dreamt of?' he simply, but not unsympathetically, replies, 'Gentle madam, no' (V.2.76, 87–94).

Critical responses to this play largely depend on whether or not we allow ourselves to be swayed by its rhetorical flights, or whether we give priority to its global politics. It is hardly surprising that *Antony and Cleopatra* has at times been read as a parable about empire and duty conflicting with folly and lust. After all the adulterous love affair of Antony and Cleopatra threatens the commonwealth which, in this play, is nothing less than the empire of the entire world. Nor does Shakespeare mince his words. When Octavius Caesar sneeringly calls Antony an 'old ruffian' (IV.1.4) we do not necessarily disagree. In one sense he is indeed just that, a reckless middle-aged reveller who airily brushes aside pressing matters of state when they present themselves at an inopportune moment. Cleopatra, it seems, is not much better. To the Romans these two are well matched in the land of misrule that is Egypt, a place where Roman soldiers become women. As Caesar points out:

From Alexandria
This is the news: he fishes, drinks, and wastes
The lamps of night in revel; is not more manlike
Than Cleopatra, nor the queen of Ptolemy
More womanly than he . . . (I.4.3–7)

## EXOTIC GENDER-BENDING

That Antony is unmanned in Egypt is clear not only to Octavius and his intelligencers in Alexandria but is cheerfully acknowledged by Cleopatra herself when she recalls one of their transvestite parties:

That time – O times! –
I laughed him out of patience; and that night
I laughed him into patience; and next morn,
Ere the ninth hour, I drunk him to his bed;
Then put my tires and mantles on him, whilst
I wore his sword Philippan. (II.5.18–23)

The 'sword Philippan' here is none other than the one with which Antony overcame Brutus and Cassius at the battle of Philippi (42 BC). It is the ultimate emblem of Roman heroic identity and masculinity. By wearing it Cleopatra, the play's most prolific image-maker, also becomes its greatest iconoclast.

For Antony to surrender his sword to Cleopatra during a nocturnal sex romp constitutes an insult to *Romanitas*, that very particular heroic idealism that was commonly thought to have granted Rome absolute sway over the classical world. Cross-dressing might seem appropriate in comedies like *Twelfth Night* and *As You Like It*, but there the motif serves a restorative strategy. The temporary disguises help heal wounds left in the natural order and form a part of the plays' creative anarchy. Not so in *Antony and Cleopatra* where the lovers' transvestite playing is interpreted, by the Romans if not the dramatist, as exotic and decadent. They may even appear on the public stage in each other's attire. Act I, scene 2 suggests as much: we are at a bawdy Alexandrian party and banquet, with Enobarbus requesting wine to toast Cleopatra while her ladies-in-waiting are discussing where they would ideally like their husband's extra inches to be. 'Not in my husband's nose' (62), Iras replies to Charmian, while the hapless Soothsayer is standing by, knowing that some of his prophecies are as loaded as the weird sisters' equivocations in *Macbeth*. But who cares here?

In the thick of this scene of sexual banter and comedy Cleopatra enters. The play's only source text, the 1623 Folio (which very probably prints Shakespeare's own manuscript), sets out her entry as:

*Enter Cleopatra*

ENOBARBUS

Hush! Here comes Antony.

CHARMIAN Not he; the Queen. (I.2.80)

Modern editions now tend to leave Cleopatra's entrance where the Folio places it, but it has sometimes been sandwiched between Enobarbus' and Charmian's half-lines, or else it was made to follow Charmian's 'the Queen'. The reason for this is clear. The arrangement in the Folio means that Cleopatra enters and Enobarbus claims, against the evidence of his eyes and ours, that Antony has just come in.

This pointed one-line Egyptian scene may indicate that in the Orient the heroic Roman, who claims to be descended from Hercules, dresses in the gender-bending robes of a drag queen; or at least that in Egypt male and female attire are indistinguishable. Of course Enobarbus' admonition to silence is sarcastic, drawing attention to Antony's loss of selfhood, but Charmian's guileless setting him right may intimate that not everybody shares the view that this state of affairs is necessarily a bad thing.

Egypt emasculates, and it does so literally in the case of Mardian the eunuch, a castrated attendant of Cleopatra; in antiquity eunuchs were, paradoxically perhaps, closely associated with Eastern fertility cults. When Mardian encounters Antony after the disastrous battle of Actium his sexless presence reminds Antony of his own loss of manhood. 'O, thy vile lady! | She has robbed me of my sword', he groans, before being reassured by Mardian that, 'No, Antony; | My mistress loved thee, and her fortunes mingled | With thine entirely' (IV.14.22–5). The word 'mingle' is one of many merging and transgressive phrases in the play; here it signals the transcending of the single self for the sake of the other. The same Mardian earlier noted that while he 'can do nothing' in deed (since he is incapable of having sexual intercourse) he nevertheless has 'fierce affections' and thinks of 'What Venus did with Mars' (I.5.15–18). And this particular image connects with others which resonate subliminally in the play and generate a richly ambiguous context for its loss of self and adultery; a morally neutral, androgynous space in which the dilution of the single self becomes a prelude, perhaps, to a more creative shared identity.

## 'SINGLE NATURE'S DOUBLE NAME'

Before the sea-battle of Actium one of Antony's loyal soldiers reminds him that the Romans have traditionally won their battles standing on the earth, the most solid of the four elements. 'Let th'Egyptians | And the Phoenicians go a-ducking' (III.7.63–4), the unnamed soldier urges his commander-in-chief, pleading with Antony to fight on land rather than follow Cleopatra into a sea-battle. But Antony pays no heed and by going 'a-ducking' turns, in Scarus' words, into a 'doting mallard' (III.10.19); the metaphor contrasts Philo's 'dotage' from the first line of the play and the Roman soldier's 'a-ducking'.

That martial Romans disintegrate at sea seems to be the implication of this exchange, and the ensuing defeat proves the point. It is also true, however, that water is the most creative and regenerative of all the elements, and the land of Egypt, as the Greek traveller and historian Herodotus famously wrote in his fifth-century BC *Histories*, was 'a gift of the Nile'. Shakespeare's play exhibits a distinct awareness of the exotic and mysterious cults associated with this most ancient of civilizations. Cleopatra's impassioned desire to be flung stark-naked 'on Nilus' mud' where the waterflies will blow her 'into abhorring' or for her 'country's high pyramides' to become her gibbet show her to have been imagined as an integral part of that world (V.2.58–62). It is for good reasons that she is variously addressed and described as 'Egypt' (III.11.51, 56), 'queen of Ptolemy' (I.4.6) and 'serpent of old Nile' (I.5.25), since such figures of speech and titles ground her in this mysterious world where shapes and gender are only ever constant in flux.

Shakespeare's primary source of information on Egypt was a text by Plutarch, the *Moralia*, which had been 'Englished' in 1603 as the *Morals* by the Elizabethan translator Philemon Holland. Plutarch of Chaeronea (*c.* AD 50–*c.* 120) was a prolific Greek chronicler and biographer whose writings, and particularly his *Lives of the Noble Grecians and Romans*, were Shakespeare's favourite source of information on the worlds of Rome and Ancient Greece. Among the most important mythographic essays in the *Morals* is the 'Of Isis', a text which Edmund Spenser had used several years earlier for *The Faerie Queene* (1590–96). Spenser, like Shakespeare and later John Milton, was intrigued by Egypt and its mystery cults, not least because the writings of Egypt were tantalizingly suggestive and yet indecipherable. The Greeks had called the mysterious script of Egypt 'hieroglyphics', that is divine carvings, and the Renaissance followed suit. In late-fifteenth-century Florence there arose an influential Neoplatonic tradition which held that the sacred writings of Egypt constituted a cabalistic tradition, a kind of Apocrypha; since Moses had grown up at the Egyptian court, he must have included bits of it in the revealed knowledge of the Pentateuch, the first five books of the Bible. The cult of Isis thus inevitably also attracted Judaeo-Christian readings, and this is what Spenser did in his great poem. By aligning the mysteries of the 'church of Isis' in Book V with bisexual images such as *Venus armata* and the figure of Britomart, a disguised young woman bearing male armour in Books III and IV, Spenser set a trend in motion which Shakespeare followed. Spenser's Bower of Bliss, the Garden of Adonis and the Temple of Venus, from *The Faerie Queene* (Books II–IV), all provide analogies to Antony's predicament in Egypt. He is either in the grip of a Circean seductress who turns men into pigs, or he and Cleopatra become 'mysterious' through transcendent love, like John Donne's lovers in his poem 'The Canonization' (published 1633) or Shakespeare's own 'The Phoenix and the Turtle'.

In Plutarch's essay, as in Spenser's poem, Isis is associated with fertility myths and eternal re-creations. Plutarch relates how she pieced together her murdered brother–husband's body from the parts that had been strewn all over the Nile, and how she succeeded in tracing every one of his parts except his penis which she had to remould. For Plutarch this cyclical ritual of dismembering and re-creation symbolizes the periodic floodings of the Nile, a seasonal event during which the excessive swellings of the river water the surrounding banks and deposit on them the fertile mud which provides the seed-beds of Egypt's crops. Does a sense of this also lie behind Cleopatra's 're-membering' of Antony in the last act of the play? In the words of one of the most incisive writers on *Antony and Cleopatra*, 'Like Isis, Cleopatra finds and restores, memorializes and consecrates Antony's male identity: in the womblike receptive space of her female memory, suffused with sexual longing, he can live again' (Janet Adelman, *Suffocating Mothers*).

The play's rhetorical patterning associates Antony with this same watery cycle of flooding and excess through the use of the word 'o'erflows', which is applied to his love for Cleopatra in the second line of the play. In a sense of course *Antony and Cleopatra* is all about a massive swelling of overflowing rhetoric which is answerable only to Shakespeare's imagination. The choice of 'o'er' against 'over' and Enobarbus' similar preference for the elision in 'o'erpicturing' when describing Cleopatra (II.2.205) may be significant. If the manuscript behind the Folio is indeed Shakespeare's, then the elisions are probably authorial. In each case the scansion requires a monosyllable for the line to be perfectly metrical, but the liquid effect resulting from the dropping of the medial 'v' in 'o'er' may have consolidated Shakespeare's choice. Strategies at the micro-levels of scansion and phonology seem to chime with the play's metaphors to render its rhetorical texture ever more fluid. The action moreover flows continuously in such a way that fluidity itself becomes one of its defining features. In the free-wheeling ride that is *Antony and Cleopatra* the stage empties no fewer than forty-two times, more than in any other Shakespearian play. The complete absence of scenic divisions in the Folio (apart from '*Actus Primus. Scæna Prima*') brings this home further.

In the deep structure of Shakespeare's play, as in *The Faerie Queene*, the story of Isis meshes with two other androgynous stories, both of which carry moral as well as mystical burdens: Hercules and Omphale, and Mars and Venus.

Shakespeare's Antony appeals to his legendary pedigree when he exclaims:

> The shirt of Nessus is upon me. Teach me,
> Alcides, thou mine ancestor, thy rage.
> Let me lodge Lichas on the horns o'th'moon,
> And with those hands that grasped the heaviest club
> Subdue my worthiest self. (IV.12.43–7)

Alcides is another name for Hercules, and the reference to the poisoned shirt of the centaur Nessus was familiar to Shakespeare from, among others, *Metamorphoses* IX by Ovid (43 BC–AD 17). Before dying from a wound inflicted by Hercules' arrow, Nessus tricked Deianira into believing that his blood-soaked shirt would secure her husband Hercules' undying love. Instead it killed him by burning itself into his flesh. A few scenes earlier Shakespeare had gone out of his way to align Antony with Hercules: when a mysterious music is suddenly heard under the earth one of Antony's soldiers interprets it as, ''Tis the god Hercules, whom Antony loved, | Now leaves him' (IV.3.17–18).

This beautiful cameo originates in Plutarch's *Lives of the Noble Grecians and Romans*, the main source of the play, but there it was the god Bacchus who abandoned the luckless Antony. Although Antony is the archetypal reveller and a dedicated disciple of Bacchus, Shakespeare changes this to Hercules, because the enslavement of Hercules by the Amazon Omphale was one of the best-known stories in classical mythology. Plutarch uses it in 'The Comparison of Demetrius with Antonius', which rounds off *The Life of Marcus Antonius*: 'as we see in painted tables, where Omphale secretly stealeth away Hercules' club, and took his Lion's skin from him. Even so Cleopatra oftentimes unarmed Antonius . . .' (Geoffrey Bullough, *Narrative and Dramatic Sources of Shakespeare*). After subduing Hercules Omphale punished him by setting him to spin with a distaff and wheel. The image of Hercules at the wheel doing a menial woman's task was emblematic of the unseemly subjugation of masculinity. It also, according to Sir Philip Sidney in *An Apology for Poetry* (1595), 'breedeth both delight and laughter' since 'the representing of so strange a power in love procureth delight and the scornfulness of the action stirreth laughter'. In this unmanned role Antony is indeed the 'triple pillar of the world transformed | Into a strumpet's fool', as the Romans would have it at the very beginning of the play (I.1.12–13).

## ROYAL TROLLOPS AND ROMAN COMMANDERS

The analogy of Antony with Hercules underlines Antony's sexual servitude, and moral opprobrium at first also seems to underpin a complementary story, that of Mars and Venus. Their legendary adultery is related with some gusto by Ovid in *Metamorphoses*, the gist of it being that Mars and Venus conducted a liaison behind her husband Vulcan's back. But he found out about them and created an ingenious, invisible net to ensnare them. When he did so he hoisted them up for all the gods to see as they lay naked in each other's arms. But, instead of joining him in condemning the adulterers, the other gods laughed at Vulcan for thus advertising his own cuckolding; some of them even expressed a desire to be themselves caught with Venus in this fashion. Vulcan's net may well lie behind Cleopatra's welcoming Antony back from the skirmish outside Alexandria with: 'Lord of lords! | O infinite virtue, com'st thou smiling from | The world's great snare uncaught?' (IV.8.16–18). The divine adultery provides the Romans with the perfect image of their commander's fall and is recalled in the acclaimed opening of the play. In their rich and complex use of metaphors and myth these lines reach down to its imaginative core. When we join it two Romans, Philo and Demetrius, are deep in conversation, and Philo begins:

> Nay, but this dotage of our general's
> O'erflows the measure. Those his goodly eyes,
> That o'er the files and musters of the war
> Have glowed like plated Mars, now bend, now turn
> The office and devotion of their view
> Upon a tawny front. His captain's heart,
> Which in the scuffles of great fights hath burst
> The buckles on his breast, reneges all temper,
> And is become the bellows and the fan
> To cool a gypsy's lust. (I.1.1–10)

Philo's lampooning of Antony's affair with Cleopatra cunningly recasts the Ovidian story of Mars and Venus. Its point was after all partly to show up the folly of old men, since the elderly and limping Vulcan (or Hephaistos in Greek) was ill-suited to the beautiful goddess of love. Youth will out in the end, and the dashing god of war provided the perfect match for Venus.

In Philo's application of the story to Antony and Cleopatra there has been considerable slippage. Antony's Mars-like eyes have not, it seems, alighted on the glorious face of a great beauty, but upon 'a tawny front' (I.1.6), a dark face; and far from reaping the pleasurable rewards of Venus, his brave martial (as it were) heart has instead become the 'bellows' fanning the lust of a gypsy. Not even her 'love', but the lascivious cravings of a middle-aged Egyptian siren is what Philo sees this Roman Mars servicing in Cleopatra. According to the Romans, by jeopardizing everything for Cleopatra the Mars-like Antony turns into a foolish Vulcan; and instead of a goddess, he is clutching an ageing trollop in his arms.

Her complexion and age are indeed an issue, as she herself acknowledges when she notes that she is 'with Phoebus' amorous pinches black | And wrinkled deep in time' (I.5.28–9). Acres of difference stretch between the perception of Cleopatra as a middle-aged Nubian courtesan and the queen of Egypt, who attributes her darkness to the loving embraces of Phoebus Apollo. She is no longer in those famous 'salad days' (73) when she was the youthful, alluring mistress of Julius Caesar. She was twenty-eight when she first met Antony (he was then forty-three), and during the action of the play she is in her mid to late thirties. Her love for Antony, she protests, is that much greater since he adores her in spite of her loss of youth and beauty.

Conventionally darkness in Elizabethan England was a flaw, and the audience could be expected, initially at least, to share the Roman view of Antony, and particularly because it is put with such brio by Philo. The word 'dotage' in the opening line is also its first conceptual phrase. In the early seventeenth century it primarily denoted infatuation rather than the foolishness of old age, the lack and loss of sound judgement. Demetrius, Philo's interlocutor, is, however, not so easily swayed, and Philo therefore offers him visual proof: 'Behold and see' (I.1.13). And we join him to witness the world's triple pillar and greatest soldier trade extravagant compliments with his Egyptian paramour.

The Roman view, not surprisingly, focuses on Antony's loss ensuing on his relationship with Cleopatra. Although Shakespeare called his play *Antony and Cleopatra*, it has from time to time been read as if it were instead, as Lord David Cecil suggested, 'the decline and fall of Antony' (*Poets and Story Tellers* (1949)). If this were so, would Shakespeare not have given Antony major soliloquies to consider his predicament? After all, Othello has set pieces which express his anguish at the paralysing effect on the warrior of the collapse of his love for Desdemona. For Othello a mercenary captaincy is at stake, for Antony the dominion of the world. But we rarely see Antony alone, and for him Rome, when compared to his love for Cleopatra, rates as little more than 'Grates me! The sum' (I.1.18).

Heroic interpretations of *Antony and Cleopatra* are the natural corollary of a masculine imperial perspective which allows no scope to the feminine. Educated Elizabethans knew this from reading the most famous imperial poem of them all, the *Aeneid* by Virgil (70–19 BC). When Aeneas longs to remain in Carthage because he loves Dido, its tender-hearted queen, the gods sternly order him, in a dream vision, to resume his quest. This was the founding of a new city in Italy which would eventually pave the way for imperial Rome. When he leaves Dido kills herself, and this death is the price Aeneas has to pay for the empire. When he meets her in the underworld in Book VI he weeps at the thought of her suicide; until that moment he has only heard rumours about it. Dido remains silent and unmoved as 'if she had been hard flint or a standing block of Parian marble' (tr. W. F. Jackson Knight (1956)). Then she flees back into the Elysian shadows where her former husband Sychaeus 'matched his love to hers'.

The encounter of Dido and Aeneas constitutes one of the most acclaimed moments in the poem, and it is therefore particularly striking that Shakespeare allows Antony to rewrite it as he himself prepares for death in Act IV, scene 14. Cleopatra has killed herself, he is told, and she apparently died breaking his name on her lips (29–34). Antony decides to follow her, and vows that in the hereafter he and Cleopatra will meet again:

> Where souls do couch on flowers, we'll hand in hand,
> And with our sprightly port make the ghosts gaze:
> Dido and her Aeneas shall want troops,
> And all the haunt be ours. – Come, Eros, Eros! (51–4)

This is hardly a Shakespearian mistake. Rather, Antony forces a comparison of Cleopatra and himself with that other legendary pairing of a Roman and an African queen from the mythic past whose country Carthage, led by Hannibal, would wage war on Rome one day in the distant future. According to Antony, he and Cleopatra will become love's paragons in the Elysian fields to the point where they will rob even Dido and Aeneas of their retinue.

The comparison underlines the extent of Antony's subjectivity – or should that be delusion? How we react to Antony's invention of a reconciled Dido and Aeneas depends on whether or not we play along with the partisan Roman position in the play. If we do, then Antony's mistake rebounds on him as a fantastical delusion; if, on the other hand, we see it as a shaping fiction, of Antony's dreaming up alternative identities for us to judge, then deeper layers of meaning may yet emerge from it. Antony is either a symbolically castrated Hercules, a pitiable ageing fool, or he and Cleopatra, who shares the title of the play with him after all, add up to something far more complex, rewarding and radical.

What the Romans present us with is a trite morality play that demonstrates that the lustful are punished and the virtuous rewarded; in this case meaning the frigid Octavius Caesar. Moralist critics have at times seriously argued that the play is in the end just that, an elaborate backhanded paean to the Roman empire. They have tended to ignore the fact that Caesar's idea of 'eternity' is to lead Cleopatra in triumph through Rome before having her strangled. 'For her life in Rome | Would be eternal in our triumph', he notes, a mere five lines after promising Cleopatra's messenger that he would use her honourably (V.1.56–66).

The school of thought which in the past confidently aligned Shakespeare with Roman readings was predicated on the notion that law-abiding Elizabethans, including Shakespeare, would naturally identify with Rome and her empire. Or perhaps even her two empires, for when Octavius Caesar, shortly to become the emperor Augustus Caesar, announces that 'The time of universal peace is near' (IV.6.5) we are expected to recognize an allusion to the everlasting empire of Christ.

The Augustinian view, that the Roman empire became the matrix for the reign of Christ, is predicated on the historical fact that Christ was born some thirty-one years after the battle of Actium which ended in the defeat and eventual deaths of Antony and Cleopatra. Tiberius,

Augustus' successor, was emperor during the birth of Christ, and whatever his shortcomings may have been, his dominion was Rome, and Rome was the heart of the universe when BC turned into AD. In Book I of the *Aeneid* Jupiter prophesies that the gods will grant Rome world domination for all eternity; and Juno and Jupiter together will 'foster the nation which wears the toga, the Roman nation, masters of the world'. In the ensuing Christian centuries these Virgilian prophecies were transferred to the empire of Christ whose seat became St Peter's in Rome.

*Did* classical Rome really equate with order and authority in Elizabethan England, notwithstanding the fact that Shakespeare's England hardly acknowledged the spiritual supremacy of that other Rome, the papacy? Even if Elizabethans saw Rome as a role model for power and expansion, it does not follow that Shakespeare writing about Antony and Cleopatra would have automatically endorsed such a view.

## FROM BIOGRAPHICAL HISTORY TO FICTION

Implicit in Roman readings of the play is the questionable assumption that Shakespeare found a homogeneous, ready-made view of Rome in his sources, the most important of which is Plutarch's *Lives*. His use of Plutarch is certainly revealing in this respect, and particularly his telescoping of the *Life of Marcus Antonius*.

Shakespeare read the *Lives* in Sir Thomas North's 1579 translation of Amyot's French version of the original Greek, and he used Plutarch on several occasions before *Antony and Cleopatra*, notably in *Julius Caesar*.

Indeed, at first it may seem as if Shakespeare intended to revisit the Roman world of *Julius Caesar*, from seven years earlier. Although there he portrayed Antony as a Machiavellian demagogue who unleashed the mob against the conspirators, he also associated him already with fertility just as he would in *Antony and Cleopatra*. At the feast of Lupercal Antony's touching of Caesar's barren wife was intended to make her shake off her 'sterile curse', and Caesar noted that Antony, unlike the austere Cassius, loved plays. In *Antony and Cleopatra* the devious Antony has gone, while the reveller and master of rhetoric remain; and now, above all, he is a middle-aged lover who at the start of the play is in his early forties, the same age (coincidentally?) as Shakespeare was when he wrote it.

What rendered Plutarch's *Lives* distinct as well as hugely attractive and accessible was their author's express conviction that history equates with the biography of great men. That is, Antony and Caesar shape the historical events of their time; such is their stature that their times become their biographies. The *Lives* are full of fascinating and colourful vignettes. As Plutarch wrote in *The Life of Alexander*, which is the parallel life of *Julius Caesar*:

> . . . my intent is not to write histories, but only lives. For the noblest deeds do not always show men's virtues and vices; but oftentimes a light occasion, a word, or some sport, makes men's natural dispositions and manners appear more plain than the famous battles won wherein are slain ten thousand men, or the great armies, or cities won by siege or assault.

The most striking of all of Plutarch's chronicles is *The Life of Marcus Antonius*. His fascination with the relationship of the Roman *imperator* and the Egyptian queen is evident from his lively portrayal of the complexity, shifting perspectives, moral ambiguities, riotous behaviour and innocent playfulness of their relationship. But he also castigates Antony. When at Actium Antony turns tail after Cleopatra Plutarch notes censoriously that:

> There Antonius showed plainly that he had not only lost the courage and heart of an Emperor but also of a valiant man, and that he was not his own man, proving that true which an old man spake in mirth: that the soul of a lover lived in another body, and not in his own. He was so carried away with the vain love of this woman, as if he had been glued unto her and that she could not have removed without moving of him also.

Shakespeare echoes Plutarch's image of 'glued' inseparability when he writes:

> Egypt, thou knew'st too well
> My heart was to thy rudder tied by th'strings,
> And thou shouldst tow me after. (III.11.56–8)

While Shakespeare submerges the sprawling ten-year action of Plutarch's *Life* in the eddies of an almost plot-free play, he finds time to linger over some of its more spectacular set pieces.

One of these is Plutarch's account of the meeting of Antony and Cleopatra at Cydnus which, historically, took place in 41 BC. Shakespeare follows the text of North's Plutarch so closely here that this passage affords one of the clearest illustrations of Shakespeare-at-work. Enobarbus' paean, starting with 'The barge she sat in', was clearly written by Shakespeare with the relevant passage from Plutarch open in front of him (II.2.196–231; see Commentary). He rarely stays this loyal even to Holinshed, with the exception of the Salic law speech in *Henry V* which he lifted almost verbatim from the chronicle source, as if to distance himself from it. Whereas in *Henry V* Shakespeare barely tinkers with his original beyond rearranging the words into verse, in *Antony and Cleopatra* the Plutarchan passage is changed from a tableau into a densely conceited and animated dramatic scene. By cutting, adding and inverting, Shakespeare fashions a highly wrought poetic artefact from North's prose. Thus, for example, Plutarch's 'sails of purple' is made to start a new pentameter with 'Purple the sails' immediately after the 'beaten gold' of the barge's poop (197–8). The stressed syllables in the adjacent phrases 'gold' and 'purple' force a pregnant pause in the scansion, as if Enobarbus meant to linger over the visual marvels of the barge as it majestically glides down the river. The colour motif shadows Plutarch as does the harmony of the oars' strokes and flutes. When Plutarch proceeds to elaborate on various instruments of music, however, Shakespeare parts company from him and notes instead how the silver oars 'made | The water which they beat to follow faster, | As amorous of their strokes' (200–202). The image of compliant water enamoured of the pleasurable pain inflicted by the oars of Cleopatra's barge recalls the witty paradoxes of erotically suggestive poems such as John Donne's 'The Bait' (published 1633), in which fish gladly betray themselves to the magnetic beauty of the poet's bathing lover. At Cydnus the water's eager response to the oars' beat carries a similar, if more refined, sensuous charge. It also anticipates the bite of the asp which Cleopatra claims to experience 'as a lover's pinch' while knowing full well that it is the 'stroke of death' (V.2.294). By infusing the natural elements with agency and sense Shakespeare turns Cleopatra's pageant at Cydnus into a distinctly Ovidian scene. The river's infatuation with Cleopatra moreover chimes with the reaction of the winds' surrender to the magic scents exuded by the barge's sails. Their enchanted perfume renders the air itself 'lovesick' (II.2.199) as it wafts across the river to envelop the nearby wharfs where Antony sits alone in the marketplace. Even the vessel's rigging is 'silken' and swells with the touches of the 'flower-soft hands' of women sailors disguised as mermaids (214–15). In the crucible of Enobarbus' rhetoric the boundaries of reality become blurred and we are transported into a world which is no more amenable to reason than the wood near Athens in *A Midsummer Night's Dream*. Whereas Oberon's magic 'translates' Bottom into an ass before he can share the bower of the fairy queen, here Antony is intoxicated by the 'strange invisible perfume' that is borne spore-like on the bewitched winds (217). The mysteries of Egypt are distilled in these nirvana-like images of a seductive Cleopatra and her women at once with a world of the senses that we are invited to see and smell. She is as much of a fiction as Oberon and Titania, and yet Cleopatra's sway, like theirs in Athens, holds in the real world of Rome and Egypt.

She is herself both artefact and life as Shakespeare's rewriting of his source suggests. In Plutarch Cleopatra is said to be 'apparelled and attired like the goddess Venus commonly drawn in picture'. Enobarbus renders this as 'O'erpicturing that Venus where we see | The fancy outwork nature' (II.2.205–6). In the source Cleopatra's outward appearance, and specifically her attire, is compared to generic images of Venus. In Enobarbus' two lines Shakespeare concedes that art outdoes nature in the creation of beauty, but then asks us to consider Cleopatra as a 'real' or natural woman who by being so becomes the ultimate work of art transcending artifice. By analogy, if it is a truth universally acknowledged that no living woman could ever be as beautiful as the Venus figures painted by artists like Botticelli or the madonnas of Bellini, Cleopatra, who is a flesh-and-blood woman, is more attractive still in the fiction of the play.

*Antony and Cleopatra* teems with such paradoxes, and particularly when it comes to its two title characters. Antony is, Cleopatra tells us in his absence, a 'heavenly mingle' whom the excess of sadness and merriment 'becomes' in equal measure: 'So does it no man else' (I.5.59–61). He is a Janus in whom the good nevertheless outstrips the bad each time: 'Though he be painted one way like a Gorgon, | The other way's a Mars' (II.5.116–17). Similarly she in turn provokes a perplexing response from the Romans' man in Alexandria, Enobarbus. He knows her well, and he grants that she is a most intriguing creature of myriad changes:

> Age cannot wither her, nor custom stale
> Her infinite variety. Other women cloy
> The appetites they feed, but she makes hungry
> Where most she satisfies; for vilest things
> Become themselves in her, that the holy priests
> Bless her when she is riggish. (II.2.240–45)

Cleopatra's 'infinite variety' is evoked time and again, and we see her playing many parts and staging different scenes, including, in Act IV, a faked version of her own death which is reminiscent of the love-deaths of Romeo and Juliet. Shortly before her death she acknowledges that 'the fleeting moon' was her planet all along until she prepares to die; only then does she become 'marble-constant' (V.2.240). Her changeability, and indeed mutability, is one of the distinctive traits of her character in Plutarch, although not to the same degree. Nor does he see it as anything other than fickleness: at best the mood swings of an unpredictable romantic woman, at worst the treacherous stratagems of a devious courtesan.

But in the Renaissance mutability assumes other meanings as in the Mutability cantos in Spenser's *The Faerie Queene*, a text that Shakespeare knew and that echoes beneath the surface of the Egyptian material in his play. That mutability was a defining characteristic of humanity had been argued powerfully over a century before *Antony and Cleopatra* by Pico della Mirandola in his influential *Oration on the Dignity of Man* (1486). In it he compared humankind to Proteus, the archetypal changer of shapes in the classical pantheon of the gods: 'Who would not admire this our chameleon? . . . It is man who Asclepius of Athens, arguing from his mutability of character and from his self-transforming nature, on just grounds says was symbolized by Proteus in the mysteries' (*The Renaissance Philosophy of Man*, ed. E. Cassirer, P. O. Kristeller, J. H. Randall Jr. (1948)). Is Shakespeare concerned with such issues in *Antony and Cleopatra* as well – or above all – rather than with writing a Roman history play, notwithstanding William Hazlitt's claim that this was 'the finest of his historical plays' (*Characters of Shakespeare's Plays*)? We should consider the possibility that a much broader concept of identity may be explored here, one which transcends the boundaries of politics and extends to the natural liminality, to the threshold, of male and female and, ultimately, life and death. It is entirely fitting that, as Frank Kermode reminds us in *Shakespeare's Language*, the word 'become' and its derivatives occur seventeen times in *Antony and Cleopatra*, far more often than in any other Shakespeare play. This is the ultimate play of transformation, and the pervasive presence of water here as in *Metamorphoses* further nods towards Ovid's famous poem which Shakespeare preferred before all other works of classical literature.

By political instinct Plutarch was hostile to the empire. For him the heroic age of Rome was the days of the Republic governed by a sovereign Senate and conquering the world through its generals, notably Caesar and Pompey; a Rome, in other words, before the events of the Ides of March of 44 BC which Shakespeare dramatized in *Julius Caesar*. Plutarch was not alone among Shakespeare's classical sources to offer a far from favourable view of imperial Rome. Another text which Shakespeare probably used for *Antony and Cleopatra* was Suetonius' *The Lives of the Twelve Caesars*, a scathing and scandalous account of the degeneracy of the Roman emperors. In *Antony and Cleopatra* Octavius protests that Antony derides him with a particular taunt: 'He calls me boy, and chides as he had power | To beat me out of Egypt' (IV.1.1–2). He is indeed the younger man, but the satiric use of 'boy', which is repeated three times, comes from Suetonius who writes that Octavius alleged that 'some had given it out of him: *That he was a boy . . .*'. Suetonius' *Lives* became available in an English translation in 1606 (by Holland), shortly before Shakespeare started work on *Antony and Cleopatra*, and there is reason for believing that he had read it. Shakespeare had done his homework for *Antony and Cleopatra*, and he found little imperial enthusiasm in either Plutarch or Suetonius. Their writings hardly fostered an austere or particularly authoritarian view of the politics of the play, if they affected Shakespeare's outlook in it at all.

A text which did, however, leave a powerful mark on *Antony and Cleopatra* is *Macbeth*, the play which Shakespeare wrote immediately before. That Shakespeare was planning the next play is suggested by his oddly far-flung comparison of Macbeth and Banquo with Antony and Octavius Caesar:

> There is none but he
> Whose being I do fear; and under him
> My genius is rebuked as, it is said,
> Mark Antony's was by Caesar. (III.1.53–6)

Even the rhetorical structuring of the relationship of Macbeth and Lady Macbeth anticipates the see-saw movement in the language of Antony and Cleopatra. Like the Macbeths, Antony and Cleopatra echo each other again and again, and these echoes, conscious and unconscious, signal the extent of their symbiosis. In *Macbeth* deviations from natural gender signify moral and spiritual corruption. Macbeth asserts that he dares do all that may become a man, and that who 'dares do more is none' (I.7.47); and then he proceeds to do just that, more. Similarly the weird sisters are women with beards and therefore, like Lear's daughters, 'unnatural hags' (*King Lear*, II.4.273). The bias of nature here means that mothers protect their babies and women show compassion; nature as it should be in a benignly Christian world. In *Antony and Cleopatra* the same images and themes resonate but in an imaginative idiom that owes as much to comedy and romance as to tragedy. They are moreover interpreted quite differently, existing no longer in the realm of 'real life' but in the sphere of the imagination which may yet be truer than the world of matter.

It is worth pausing over the alleged confusions of masculine and feminine roles in *Antony and Cleopatra*, when contrasted with *Macbeth* where 'unsexing' spells deeply sinister consequences (I.5.39). Lady Macbeth invokes the powers of darkness to strip her of that very 'milk of human kindness' that feeds and sustains life and which prompted her to remember her father as she saw Duncan asleep. In the Folio text of the play (the only source text) she is only ever called 'Lady' and 'Macbeth's wife', as if Shakespeare meant to foreground her femininity and married status. In the end she goes mad. Her horror at the thought that her husband has become a child-slayer reverberates in the pathos of her jingle: 'The Thane of Fife had a wife; where is she now?' (V.1.41).

In *Antony and Cleopatra* the lovers' children never appear on stage. When Antony claims that he left his pillow 'unpressed in Rome' and forbore 'the getting of a lawful race' for the sake of Cleopatra (III.13.106–7) he is directly contradicting his main source. In Plutarch Antony's wife Octavia returned to Rome after being spurned and there she faithfully kept Antony's house and cared for their children and for those he had by his previous wife Fulvia. Plutarch comments that thus 'thinking no hurt, she did Antonius great hurt. For her honest love and regard to her husband made every man hate him when they saw he did so unkindly use so noble a lady.' Caesar threatens Cleopatra with the murder of her children (V.2.128–33) should she attempt suicide, but these children never feature in her consciousness nor in ours. The lovers' relationship is ruthlessly focused on the two of them, and Shakespeare knew the importance of presenting it that way. John Dryden did not when he rewrote Shakespeare's play in *All For Love, or the World Well Lost* (1678) and introduced the pair's children into it, much to his subsequent chagrin. As he notes in his Preface:

> The greatest error in the contrivance seems to be in the person of Octavia; for, though I might use the privilege of a poet to introduce her into Alexandria, yet I had not enough considered, that the compassion she moved to herself and children was destructive to that which I reserved for Antony and Cleopatra; whose mutual love being founded upon vice, must lessen the favour of the audience to them when virtue and innocence were oppressed by it.

In *Antony and Cleopatra* Octavia's appearances on stage are largely ceremonial. Shakespeare never quite states that the arranged marriage between Antony and Octavia is a deliberate ploy by Caesar (he weeps on parting from his sister, III.2.50–53), but when Menas, one of Sextus Pompey's followers, confides in Enobarbus that the union was brought about by politics rather than 'the love of the parties' Enobarbus concurs: 'I think so too. But you shall find the band that seems to tie their friendship together will be the very strangler of their amity. Octavia is of a holy, cold, and still conversation' (II.6.117–21). Antony, he tells us, 'will to his Egyptian dish again' (124) because he and she are alike. Enobarbus knows. He has a foot in both the Roman and Egyptian camps and is defined largely by his loyalty to Antony, which renders his eventual forsaking of his commander that much more poignant. Enobarbus is the audience's conduit into the play, not least through his semi-choric role as objective commentator and his rhetorical gift for painting in words the magic of the scene at Cydnus for us, among others. After the two lovers and Octavius he is the play's most important figure; perhaps more so than Caesar because of his privileged access to Antony.

It is the play's performance history that reminds us of quite how significant parts such as Enobarbus and Octavius are, not least perhaps because they have at times been done rather more successfully than the lovers; Patrick Stewart as Enobarbus (in 1972 and 1978 Royal Shakespeare Company productions) and Ian Charleson as Caesar (in a 1981 BBC film) suggest themselves, demonstrating that in the theatre the two lovers yield rather more imaginative space to their friends and servants than they do in the study. The play is full of cameo roles, notably Alexas, Dolabella, Agrippa, Thidias, Seleucus, Iras and Charmian, the Soothsayer, Mardian and the Clown, who brings Cleopatra the asp and laces a tragic death scene with pointed sexual comedy; not to mention Philo and Demetrius, who open and close the play's first scene and then do not speak again. The minor parts in the play are variously foils, interlocutors or sounding boards for the lovers or their enemies. Cleopatra's court of women, sexless men and water is a world without hard edges: rounded, cyclical and reminiscent of the circular serpent of the emblematic staff of the god of healing, Asclepius.

The unshakeable loyalty to Cleopatra of Iras and Charmian, who join her in death, contrasts starkly with the way keeping faith is interpreted by the Roman military. At the beginning of Act III the victorious Roman commander Ventidius, who was fleetingly introduced in a stage direction in Act II (II.2.14), appears only to exit after a brief and guarded homily on the dangers of ambition. Warning his comrade-in-arms and deputy Silius against being too zealous, he remarks that Caesar and Antony have always triumphed through their commanders above all but that 'Who does i'th'wars more than his captain can | Becomes his captain's captain' (III.1.21–2). The scene is frequently cut in performance since we never again see any of its characters and they do not seem to leave a mark on anyone else in the play.

Why did Shakespeare put it in here, if not as a reminder perhaps of the real world of Roman power politics, a world that is never far from the heart of the play? The Ventidius scene occurs immediately after the so-called galley scene in which the newly reconciled Roman factions celebrate their diplomatic triumph on board Pompey's galley. Here are not only the three pillars of the world, Antony, Caesar and Lepidus, as well as their followers, but also their host and his lieutenant Menas. The scene is set for a bacchanalian evening as the servants enter '*with a banquet*' (II.7.0). As the wine starts to flow Menas offers Pompey the empire of the world provided he licenses the murder of his guests. Pompey's reply hides under the cloak of Roman honour but his protest rings a shallow and cynical note. He would gladly, he says, have approved the treachery after the event, but his 'honour' prevents him from sanctioning the murder of his guests:

Thou must know
'Tis not my profit that does lead mine honour;
Mine honour, it. Repent that e'er thy tongue
Hath so betrayed thine act. Being done unknown,
I should have found it afterwards well done,
But must condemn it now. (II.7.75–80)

In response Menas, anticipating Enobarbus' desertion, decides that he will 'never follow thy palled fortunes more' (81). The Roman revels, unlike the Eastern ones, echo with treachery and scheming, before turning into song and dance. Enobarbus acts as master of ceremonies and '*places them hand in hand*' (110). After threatening to turn into a tragic bloodbath the galley scene becomes in the end nothing more than a drunken party in which Romans play at being Egyptians. The setting on Pompey's galley and therefore at sea presses home its affinity with the liquid world of Egypt as much as its tributes to Bacchus, dance and song do; with the exception that no women grace this mock-Egyptian scene. Here it is the men who hold hands, and it seems fitting that their fascination with Egypt should revolve primarily around the phallic serpents and crocodiles ('a strange serpent', 48). What, one may wonder, has happened to the Roman *virtus*, that cult of frugality, familial duty and political idealism that rendered Rome great and of which Shakespeare's Brutus was possessed in *Julius Caesar*?

## FOR THINE IS THE KINGDOM?

There may not be a great deal to be said for the Rome of *Antony and Cleopatra*. Even its standard-bearer Octavius Caesar describes the people of Rome as a feckless 'common body' without constancy, likening it to 'a vagabond flag upon the stream', ceaselessly fickle and striving only to 'rot itself with motion' (I.4.44–7).

But what if, instead of reading the play in terms of empire, power and politics, one turned these terms into parts of a far-reaching romantic metaphor? In conventional sixteenth-century love poetry the male lover usually promises his beloved the world, or renounces it for her sake in hyperbolic conceits. Unlike most lovers, however, Antony really *is* in a position to surrender the world; and not just this world, but the next one as well, it seems, for in the linguistic texture of the play imperial and Christian metaphors seamlessly merge.

We encounter in Caesar's 'universal peace' (IV.6.5) a reference to the eternal empire inaugurated by the birth of Christ. This is destined to achieve its apotheosis in the Second Coming, the Day of Judgement which will also be the *hieros gamos* or divine marriage when Christ marries his Church. It may seem rather perverse of Shakespeare to have the adulterous, pleasure-seeking Antony not only allude to this but to cite John's grand vision of the new Jerusalem in Apocalypse. When Cleopatra claims to set a 'bourn' or limit to Antony's love for her he replies, 'Then must thou needs find out new heaven, new earth' (I.1.16–17). The relevant lines (modernized spelling) come from the Book of Revelation 21:1–2 (Bishops' Bible (1568)):

> And I saw a new heaven and a new earth: for the first heaven and the first earth were vanished away, and there was no more sea.
> And I John saw the holy city, new Jerusalem, come down from God out of heaven, prepared as a bride garnished for her husband.

Not only does Antony quote from the Bible, it seems, but the image of the angel bestriding the earth and sea in Revelation 10:1–2 resounds in Cleopatra's vision of a colossus-like emperor Antony:

> And I saw another mighty angel come down from heaven, clothed with a cloud, and the rainbow upon his head, and his

face as it were the sun, and his feet as it were pillars of fire. And he had in his hand a little book open, and he put his right foot upon the sea, and his left foot on the earth.

Such anachronisms rarely worry Shakespeare. After all in *King Lear* Cordelia is twice cast explicitly as a redemptress modelled on Christ, even though the play is set, notionally at least, in a pre-Christian world. There is usually a poetic logic in even Shakespeare's most seemingly outlandish metaphors; and so there may be in the biblical images in *Antony and Cleopatra*.

After his defeat in battle Antony addresses his followers and Enobarbus as they gather around him. He invites them to wait on him and not to 'Scant' his cups:

Tend me tonight.
May be it is the period of your duty.
Haply you shall not see me more; or if,
A mangled shadow. Perchance tomorrow
You'll serve another master. I look on you
As one that takes his leave. Mine honest friends,
I turn you not away, but, like a master
Married to your good service, stay till death.
Tend me tonight two hours, I ask no more,
And the gods yield you for't! (IV.2.21, 24–33)

These words recall Christ's to his disciples in Gethsemane during that last long night of freedom. A traitor, Judas Iscariot, was present then, and when Enobarbus deserts Antony he in turn casts himself as 'A master-leaver and a fugitive' (IV.9.22). The word 'master' here inevitably brings to mind the 'master' of the Gospels. So does Antony's generosity, and he unwittingly breaks

Enobarbus' heart when, as a gesture of forgiveness and understanding, he sends the latter's treasure after him.

The idea of Antony as a Christ figure seems almost bizarre, but the play's rhetorical fabric points in just that direction. So does Cleopatra's leave-taking in Act V, when she prepares to die with 'Immortal longings' in her, anticipating that 'Now no more | The juice of Egypt's grape shall moist this lip' (V.2.280–81). If Antony is made to echo Christ's words from Gethsemane, does Cleopatra's valedictory reference to the grape recall the Last Supper? After breaking the bread, Christ announces that his blood is shed for the remission of sins, and continues: 'But I say unto you, I will not drink henceforth of this fruit of the vine tree, until that day when I shall drink it new with you in my Father's kingdom' (Matthew 26:29).

That in Shakespeare's imaginative conception Antony and Cleopatra are somehow associated with the most exalted images of Christian culture gives pause for thought. Christ famously rose from the dead, and Antony does so too in Cleopatra's vision of him in Act V, which is entirely hers. While the play's metaphors may not be systematically patterned, its various mythopoeic (creation of myths) and biblical analogues share significant common ground. Its three pagan myths, of Hercules–Omphale, Mars–Venus and Osiris–Isis, all involve disintegration of gender boundaries as well as, in the case of the last two, creation (Harmony is the mythic daughter of the union of Mars and Venus) and seasonal re-creation. The Christian story, from Genesis to the birth of Christ, the crucifixion, resurrection and the apocalypse complement strands in this mythic narrative.

The play seems intent on drawing an analogy, albeit obliquely, between Antony and Cleopatra and the greatest Christian story, which, according to the first Bible commentators, is anticipated in the Song of Songs. It is the Song (also known as Canticles or Song of Solomon) which provides another of the play's main imaginative sources, with Cleopatra as the Shulamite (Song 6:13), the exotic queen of Sheba, whose brother, like the historical Cleopatra's, is also her lover: 'I am black, O ye daughters of Jerusalem, but yet fair . . . Marvel not at me that I am so black, for why? the sun hath shined upon me' (Song 1:5–6). It was the Song which provided the Renaissance with a banquet of the senses that was both biblical and Ovidian, and one which since the days of Hippolytus (*c.* AD 170–*c.* 236) has been glossed as an allegory of Christ's bridal hymn to his Church. Egyptian banquets were legendary, the Romans reported back to their countrymen, with 'Eight wild boars roasted whole at a breakfast' after a 'night light with drinking' (II.2.184, 183). In Egypt 'a woman is a dish for the gods, if the devil dress her not' (V.2.272–3), and Cleopatra becomes 'one that looks on feeders', a 'boggler' whom Antony claims to have found 'as a morsel cold upon | Dead Caesar's trencher' (III.13.109–10, 116–17). In this liquid land of wine, women and song the sexes are as indistinguishable as asps and penises. Here, it seems, vilest things indeed 'become' Antony and Cleopatra rather than diminish them as they seem to melt into each other.

## 'NATURE'S PIECE 'GAINST FANCY'

The transgressive gender dualities that Shakespeare played with in some of his comedies translate into transcendent metaphors in *Antony and Cleopatra*. As she prepares to stage her own death Cleopatra for a moment envisages how the Romans will represent her and Antony. It will take the shape of a dramatic farce, she surmises, and she will be forced to watch it as the Romans lead her in triumph:

> The quick comedians
> Extemporally will stage us, and present
> Our Alexandrian revels. Antony
> Shall be brought drunken forth, and I shall see
> Some squeaking Cleopatra boy my greatness
> I'th'posture of a whore. (V.2.216–21)

Her use of 'squeaking' and 'boy' has attracted much comment since in the theatre of the time women were not allowed to act so that Cleopatra was played by a young man or 'boy'; in her case, undoubtedly by one of the more experienced young actors. Shakespeare is taking a chance here since his wayward Cleopatra has repeatedly behaved in ways that have fuelled the hostile Roman view of her and Anthony. At times the idealizing rhetoric that they apply to each other has seemed wholly disproportionate to the enacted reality on stage. George Bernard Shaw famously remarked in *Three Plays for Puritans* (1900) that Shakespeare portrayed Antony and Cleopatra as a feckless womanizer and a courtesan, and then 'finally strains all his huge command of rhetoric and stage pathos to give a theatrical sublimity to the wretched end of the business, and to persuade foolish spectators that the world was well lost by the twain'.

By evoking actual theatrical representation (albeit a partisan one) as a gross travesty of her relationship with Antony, Cleopatra stakes an audacious claim for her subjective interpretation of this love affair which, after his death, can now only exist in the imagination. The long last scene of the play is given over to a rhetorical re-creation in her mind of the relationship that was Antony and Cleopatra. Cleopatra invites us to consider that her vision of 'An Antony' is quite simply true because it is 'nature's piece' rather than the product of fancy; even though she concedes that nature can never quite compete with fancy in the creation of perfect images. But then she is evoking 'An Antony' and not just 'Antony' when she protests that:

> . . . yet t'imagine
> An Antony were nature's piece 'gainst fancy,
> Condemning shadows quite. (V.2.98–100)

The two are quite different: 'An Antony', as Cleopatra has it, denotes an imaginative conception of Antony rather than the 'real' Antony of the first four acts. Cleopatra's memory of Antony differs from the Romans' and from our divided response to the middle-aged reveller. We may have admired his energy, generosity and ability to inspire deep loyalty in followers such as Enobarbus, but we have also witnessed his fits of temper and an unbecoming thraldom to Cleopatra.

In the theatre audiences take these conceptually abstract lines in their stride, but to the student of the play they point in the direction of Shakespeare's concern with wider aesthetic issues. Earlier on Enobarbus had claimed that Cleopatra, whom Plutarch compared to Venus, transcended even fancy's most highly wrought pictures of Venus. In other words, the living reality of the 'wrangling queen' (I.1.48) contains a magic that art cannot replicate. Shakespeare is here engaging in a dialogue with Sidney's *Apology* in which Sidney suggests that 'nature never set forth the earth in so rich tapestry as divers poets have done . . . her world is brazen, the poets only deliver a golden'. To illustrate art's superior claims to history and philosophy Sidney advances the difference between the historical Cyrus (559–529 BC), the magnanimous founder of the Persian empire, and the idea of Cyrus. The real person lived and died, but in poetry the *idea* of 'a Cyrus' lives on for ever and becomes, by example, the inspiration for many Cyruses. The power of art to stir and inspire therefore transcends reality. In *Antony and Cleopatra* Shakespeare both agrees with Sidney and stands his aesthetic theory on its head: the Antony and Cleopatra of the play are, it is suggested, superior by virtue of being real, but they are not of course real, since they are the creatures of Shakespeare's art. They are 'real' only so long as we suspend our disbelief in the theatre and study: they are, one could argue, Shakespeare's supreme fiction.

This degree of imaginative self-consciousness in the play connects intimately with its exploring of the meaning of reality itself. Shakespeare is moving away from the cathartic idiom of the great tragedies, and it is *Antony and Cleopatra* which more than any other work shows him striking out in new directions. Not only do ideas of art, nature and nurture move to the fore in highly stylized and self-conscious works like *The Winter's Tale* and *The Tempest*, but they also explore notions of redemption. In an acclaimed essay on the play, 'Shakespeare's *Antony and Cleopatra*', in *Oxford Lectures on Poetry*, A. C. Bradley remarked that for a tragedy *Antony and Cleopatra* was not painful. The reason is that it is either a tragedy different altogether from the others, or perhaps not a tragedy at all precisely because it seems to explode the conceptual basis of fictional reality itself. If onstage 'reality' is itself called into question, then the characters in the play no longer have the power to draw us in; the empathy which makes us pity Othello and feel for Lear has been supplanted by a different kind of response, one that is more abstract, less direct and more sophisticated in its stylization.

## DYING INTO LIFE

All tragedy ends in death, and so does *Antony and Cleopatra*. Does this render it a tragedy like *Hamlet*, written only a few years earlier and the first work in English openly to confront the reality of death without recourse to Christian salvation? As *Hamlet* ebbs away we are stunned by the waste of human life, and although Horatio appeals to flights of angels to sing Hamlet to his rest we hardly think of him in a heavenly hereafter. Rather we recall the ghost's grim evoking of purgatory, a 'prison house' whose secrets are too horrible to reveal (I.5.14). There may be nothing in the end more frightening existentially than the assumption by man of what had once been the preserve of the divine, but this is what Hamlet has done: taking on the deepest and darkest questions about humankind without recourse to the certainties afforded by religion and the Deity.

Death spells the end of everything in Shakespearian tragedy, but it may not do so in *Antony and Cleopatra*, partly because it is a Roman play. As such it affords Shakespeare imaginative freedoms that were not otherwise available to him. One of the most remarkable differences between the Roman plays and the rest of the canon is their condoning of suicide. Whereas in *Hamlet* or *Cymbeline*, for example, suicide is explicitly recognized to be a mortal sin, in *Antony and Cleopatra* it constitutes a noble act, 'a Roman, by a Roman | Valiantly vanquished' (IV.15.57–8) or, in Cleopatra's phrasing, a deed 'after the high Roman fashion' that makes 'death proud to take us' (86–7). In *Antony and Cleopatra* this extends to the treatment of death itself which, for the lovers, becomes a rite of passage rather than a mark of closure. The play does not allow us to disagree with Cleopatra when, after Antony's death, she muses:

> Patience is sottish, and impatience does
> Become a dog that's mad; then is it sin
> To rush into the secret house of death
> Ere death dare come to us? (IV.15.78–81)

The liminality and re-creation in its large-scale metaphors seamlessly connect with a rhetoric which deconstructs the word 'death'. We know that 'death' in Elizabethan English still preserved the meaning of the French *la petite mort*, that is, sexual climax. No other Shakespeare play exploits the multiple paradoxes of this in the way that *Antony and Cleopatra* does.

Early on Enobarbus alerts us to this in a piece of Roman rhetorical bravado, a soldier's plain talk about women. When Antony feels that his duty summons him out of Egypt after all, Enobarbus replies:

> Under a compelling occasion, let women die. It were pity to cast them away for nothing, though between them and a great cause they should be esteemed nothing. Cleopatra, catching but the least noise of this, dies instantly. I have seen her die twenty times upon far poorer moment. I do think there is mettle in death, which commits some loving act upon her, she hath such a celerity in dying. (I.2.138–45)

To this Antony replies, with a pun on female genitalia, 'She is cunning past man's thought' (146).

What Enobarbus is ostensibly saying is that Cleopatra is a consummate actress who throws melodramatic fainting fits at the slightest provocation. But the 'loving act' clause turns this into a comical reference to her as a lustful, fast-climaxing creature. We are alerted to the fact that in Egypt, it seems, death may not always mean cessation of being. Enobarbus is talking, in the first instance, as a soldier who relishes the fleshpots of Egypt, but his prose also inaugurates an overarching rhetorical pattern which, with increasing intensity, undermines the meaning of the word 'death'.

We have already pointed out that Cleopatra dies twice in the play. The first time is a parody of a love-death after the defeat at Actium; according to Mardian:

The last she spake
Was 'Antony! Most noble Antony!'
Then in the midst a tearing groan did break
The name of Antony; it was divided
Between her heart and lips. She rendered life,
Thy name so buried in her. (IV.14.29–34)

This is of course a lie, but it provokes Antony to respond. He will, he claims, rejoin Cleopatra in Elysium: 'Unarm, Eros. The long day's task is done, | And we must sleep' (35–6).

Sleep is a time-honoured euphemism for death and one which Shakespeare greatly affects. In this play it undermines the finality and horror of death as in the famous image of the dead Cleopatra who, Caesar tells us, 'looks like sleep, | As she would catch another Antony | In her strong toil of grace' (V.2.344–6). Even here the image of Mars caught in a net with Venus reverberates beneath the surface of the flow of the line. We similarly accept the use of the word 'grace' as the most natural phrase in the world since such a quality should naturally accompany the Queen of Egypt displayed to us in her full splendour at this point. And yet 'grace' was in the process of becoming one of the most loaded phrases in the language, as every reader of Milton's *Paradise Lost* (1667) and John Bunyan's *Grace Abounding to the Chief of Sinners* (1666) knows. While nothing could be further from Cleopatra than a Calvinist reading of 'grace', the word's Pauline connotations were well grounded in the language in Shakespeare's time; and Paul seems to be one of the major influences on him in the romances, which can be seen to be imaginatively launched by *Antony and Cleopatra*.

Just before his attempted suicide Antony tells Eros (whose name mirrors Iras) that his own 'visible shape' now resembles 'black vesper's pageants', those fantastical cloud formations which are instantly dislimned and become as 'indistinct | As water is in water' (IV.14.14, 8, 10–11). Antony sees his death as a dissolution in the metamorphic world of Egypt where everything is in flux.

The fact that his attempted suicide turns into a grim farce has been the subject of extensive critical scrutiny. It may reflect rather poorly on a blundering Antony *if*, that is, his role in the play is primarily that of a heroic soldier. Shakespeare inherited this detail of a bungled suicide from Plutarch, but then uses it to underline the way in which our most basic notions of reality are challenged. Foremost among them is the one and only certainty in life, that we all must die: 'a man can die but once; we owe God a death', Feeble states stoically in

*Henry IV, Part II* (III.2.228–9), taking comfort from the fact that this particular calvary we only suffer once. Death is by definition a unique event, but Antony and Cleopatra, flanked by Eros and Iras respectively, die at least twice, and the play deploys a host of euphemisms to cajole us into thinking that death is the gentlest rite of passage, a melting, cloud-like dislimning, and not the stroke of a sword or the venomous bite of an asp.

Moreover, the lovers' dying is mediated through the language of sexual union. As Antony prepares to die he conducts an imaginary conversation with Cleopatra, and then calls out 'Eros! – I come, my queen – Eros! Stay for me' (IV.14.50). Just before falling on his sword he promises that he will be 'A bridegroom in my death, and run into't | As to a lover's bed' (100–101). Similarly Cleopatra claims to hear Antony beckoning to her from beyond the grave:

> Give me my robe; put on my crown; I have
> Immortal longings in me. Now no more
> The juice of Egypt's grape shall moist this lip.
> Yare, yare, good Iras; quick – methinks I hear
> Antony call. I see him rouse himself
> To praise my noble act. I hear him mock
> The luck of Caesar, which the gods give men
> To excuse their after wrath. Husband, I come.
> Now to that name my courage prove my title! (V.2.279–87)

The use of 'Immortal longings', a phrase more commonly associated with romantic yearnings, points to the vivid presence in her mind of an Antony whom she can see and hear, and the use of 'Husband, I come' clearly recalls his 'I come, my queen'. At their first separation in Act I Cleopatra had tried to rationalize Antony's departure and failed to do so: 'Something it is I would –,' she said, but could not remember what it was; then it came to her: 'O, my oblivion is a very Antony, | And I am all forgotten' (I.3.89–91).

Now that he is really gone for ever she will not linger. Death is both a rejoining of the beloved and a coital union as Cleopatra is bound 'again for Cydnus, | To meet Mark Antony' (V.2.228–9). In this world death can be the gentlest of passings, as Cleopatra remarks when her maid Iras '*falls and dies*' of a broken heart after being kissed by Cleopatra: 'The stroke of death is as a lover's pinch, | Which hurts, and is desired' (291, 294–5, but see Commentary, p. 236), and to die is little more than the untying of an 'intrinsicate' knot (303–4). Cleopatra's final words spoken to Charmian are:

> Peace, peace!
> Dost thou not see my baby at my breast,
> That sucks the nurse asleep? (V.2.307–9)

Death has now truly lost its sting, though not perhaps quite in the sense intended by Paul in 1 Corinthians 15. Here it is a mere transition into another phase of being. After the word 'asleep' Cleopatra continues with a kind of lullaby when she murmurs, 'As sweet as balm, as soft as air, as gentle –' The poison is doing its deadly work, and she ceases to be on, 'What should I stay – *She dies*' (312). The serpent of old Nile is finally killed by the most phallic creature alive, and there is no mistaking the sexual undertones of Cleopatra's final union with the killing snake. In case we miss it, the clown who had brought her the asps wishes her 'all joy of the worm' (259).

Cleopatra's description of the asp as a suckling 'baby'

seems almost wilfully to fly in the face of the visual evidence on stage. The most recognizable image of maternity and future life is compressed into this final affirmation by Cleopatra. She is set to rejoin her 'husband' Antony, she tells us. The world's greatest courtesan wishes to be stripped now of all baser elements as she prepares to ascend, phoenix-like, to a reunion with her 'husband'! In that most domestic of words, 'baby', Shakespeare may be hinting at something larger than the political empire. Again and again the play's grand rhetoric turns back in on itself to stake a claim for poignant artlessness, rendered the more effective by the sheer wealth and exuberance of the lovers' rhetoric generally. Antony can be 'the greatest soldier of the world' (I.3.38), a Mars, a Hercules or the colossus of Rhodes, but in her most private and intense moments Cleopatra calls him 'My man of men' (I.5.72). When Antony is finally dead at the end of Act IV Cleopatra rejects Iras' apostrophe, 'Royal Egypt! Empress!', with a proud and defiant 'No more but e'en a woman, and commanded | By such poor passion as the maid that milks | And does the meanest chares' (IV.15.71–4). The power of her response lies in its sheer simplicity: the story of Antony and Cleopatra is just another love story of a man and a woman. It is entirely consistent with this that the greatest tribute that Charmian can pay to her mistress as she reclines, now dead, in her royal robes is to call her a 'lass unparalleled':

> Now boast thee, death, in thy possession lies
> A lass unparalleled. Downy windows, close;
> And golden Phoebus never be beheld
> Of eyes again so royal! (V.2.314–17)

No other play by Shakespeare quite matches the astonishing similes and metaphors of *Antony and Cleopatra*. They demand constantly to be measured against the reality of the two principal characters as we see them on stage. When Cleopatra rapturously exclaims, 'Eternity was in our lips and eyes, | Bliss in our brows' bent; none our parts so poor | But was a race of heaven' (I.3.35–7) we are left wondering not so much about the appropriateness of her hyperboles as about the sheer inventiveness of phrases like 'race of heaven' (but see Commentary, p. 160) . The poetic excess of the play may signal nothing less than 'a sort of impatience at the unexplored resources of the language' (Kermode, *Shakespeare's Language*).

The Elizabethan theatre was a far more oral culture than ours, and audiences were more accustomed to listening and then to conjuring up images from such rhetoric. As David Bevington puts it in his Cambridge edition of the play, 'is Shakespeare asking poetry to do the work of drama?' If so, we may be asked here to agree with Touchstone's statement in *As You Like It* that 'the truest poetry is the most feigning' (III.3.17–18). To that extent *Antony and Cleopatra* is a play in which the audience is actively invited to participate, to envisage the play beyond the play. Bradley noted that in this work it is always the artist and his activity which come to mind first rather than the product itself. Such a position would be unthinkable in the other tragedies where it is 'the product of this activity, the thing presented, that first engrosses us'. And so it is in *King Lear* where it is the searing intensity of the play that we remember above all, what in his celebrated sonnet on *King Lear* John Keats called 'the fierce dispute| Betwixt damnation and impassioned clay' ('On Sitting Down to Read *King Lear* Once Again' (published 1838)).

## TRAGEDY AS SUBLIME COMEDY

*Antony and Cleopatra* is balanced on a knife-edge between tragedy and comedy, sharing with both while being neither. For the audience and Romans the lovers' end will be marked by the high solemnity of a state funeral; for them the play concludes, like most of Shakespeare's comedies, with a sort of postponed wedding. Whereas the other tragedies shroud their action in claustrophobic darkness (*Hamlet*, *Macbeth*, *Othello*) or apocalyptic storms and cold (*King Lear*), this is a Mediterranean play of daylight with Egypt and Italy as its poles. It is not uncommon for Shakespeare to use contrasting locations as he does here, and invariably these are highly charged with meanings. In *Othello*, for example, the stormy crossing from Venice to Cyprus alerts us to the prospect of grave consequences for the cast from the shift of location. As the Venetians head towards this outpost of empire we guess that the constraints of civilization may have been fractured, and so it turns out.

In the end, though, the use of place to structure dramatic action is a defining feature above all of Shakespearian comedy and romance. Here the so-called 'green world' takes on a regenerative function, whether it be a wood near Athens in *A Midsummer Night's Dream*, the forest of Arden in *As You Like It* or Prospero's island in *The Tempest*. Since these locations are not conventionally socialized and regulated the characters enjoy greater freedom to discover who they are and why they act in the way they do. The suspension of authority may involve some necessary turbulence, but it also fosters the birth of a more natural order, one that tends to be both organic and magical. The youthful quartet of

*A Midsummer Night's Dream* emerge changed and reconciled from their sylvan saturnalia; only Demetrius remains 'enchanted' since the love-juice which ties him to Helena stays on his eyes for ever. In *As You Like It* magic similarly aids and abets nature when the courtiers are sorted in the forest by a form of divine intervention. Either way the change is for the better and inextricably linked to a period of anarchy and hostility.

Although Rome and Egypt are real places with antagonistic political configurations quite unlike Oberon's wood or Prospero's island, the Egypt of *Antony and Cleopatra* nevertheless grows recognizably out of the fairy-tale world of the comedies. As if to emphasize the point, Shakespeare has Cleopatra start Act II, scene 5 with a whimsical echo of *Twelfth Night*. 'Give me some music – music, moody food | Of us that trade in love' (1–2), she says, evoking Orsino's languid opening lines.

The way Shakespeare uses Rome and Egypt for pacing the play can be gleaned from just this scene and its place in the wider fabric of the work. Before speaking about music and food Cleopatra last appeared at the end of Act I, when she was preparing to send several greetings a day to Antony who had departed from Egypt for Rome two scenes earlier. Some 350 lines and no fewer than four Roman scenes separate her two appearances. This includes the long scene 2 of Act II which launches the union of Antony and Octavia and which features Enobarbus' elaborate account of Antony and Cleopatra's meeting at Cydnus. Even the fluidity of theatrical performance cannot disguise the fact that history has been made in Rome while Egypt has lingered in stasis, with the *same* characters still on stage in Egypt in Act II, scene 5, Cleopatra, Charmian, Iras, Alexas and Mardian (he enters at line 2). Like Illyria or the forest of Arden in which there is famously no clock, Egypt ignores the notion of time, that linear, progressive and forward-moving concept. The Roman world is that of masculine power politics in which alliances such as that of Antony with Octavia are forged regardless of sentiment, where time and action are of the essence, while the Orient seems an exotic, languid playground, a shapeless muddy space for women, eunuchs and all manner of serpents, including crocodiles. In Roman eyes Egypt is a swamp of iniquity where gallant soldiers founder in a metamorphic land in which the human form itself dissolves metaphorically in water, as Antony's does in Act IV, scene 14 (10–11).

The question of whether dissolution of the self is a necessary prelude to some form of imaginary rebirth or quite simply death itself goes to the heart of the play. Pity and fear hardly enter into the story of two middle-aged lovers who embrace death as a Roman road to freedom and a final reunion; and nothing could be further from the grim and punitive visions of the hereafter afforded by the other tragedies. What Shakespeare imports into *Antony and Cleopatra* is the idea of playing at all levels. Imaginatively it enjoys the freedoms of comedy where anything can, and frequently does, happen. The doubleness of its two-name title, which includes rather than isolates, points in that direction just as surely as its multiple strategies for undercutting the finality of death. So does the prominence accorded Cleopatra who challenges and, in the imagination at least, may overcome the masculine empire of Rome. Her apotheosis may be a delusion, but in the mysterious world of a play which revels in linguistic invention it seems to enjoy a measure of authorial approval. At times the poetry of *Antony and Cleopatra* threatens to cut loose from its own historical fiction which can no longer contain the language used to interpret it. This failure of reality to accommodate the imagination may be partly the point of the play and one of the ways in which it looks ahead to the fantastical world of romances like *The Tempest* in which reality itself becomes the creature of art.

René Weis

# *The Play in Performance*

For a play of its extraordinary stature *Antony and Cleopatra* has a distinctly chequered history in the theatre. Whereas most of the great tragedies boast legendary performances, and sometimes in different media, this play is altogether different. One of its most distinctive features, if not the most important, is a rhetorical inventiveness which turns excess into sheer aesthetic pleasure. Could this be the reason why it has consistently been more successful in the study than on the stage? *Antony and Cleopatra* is the only Shakespearian tragedy not to be performed between 1660 and 1759 when David Garrick produced it. This may well be due, in part at least, to the success of John Dryden's version *All For Love, or the World Well Lost* (1678), but its absence from the stage after that is probably also connected to its blatant flouting of neoclassical conventions. When *Antony and Cleopatra* was revived by Garrick (it only ran for six performances) Edward Capell drastically cut its number of scenes, from forty-two to twenty-seven.

The Jacobean stage for which the play was written was a far more fluid theatrical medium than what succeeded it in the post-Restoration theatre. The scenes in *Antony and Cleopatra* are created above all by dramatic rhetoric, and the play can hence afford to have some one hundred individual or group entrances (Margaret Lamb, *'Antony and Cleopatra' on the English Stage*) and forty-two complete stage clearances, which correspond to the number of scenes in most editions including this one. That the play has no scenic breaks in the 1623 Folio after the initial marking of Act I, scene 1 becomes particularly significant if we accept the commonly held view that behind the Folio lies Shakespeare's authorial draft or holograph. It would appear that Shakespeare imagined the dramatic rhythm of the play to be that of a seamless, see-saw work, and that he trusted the potential of his stage to handle its rapid scenic shifts.

Even so, at first sight the play offers huge scope to the post-Restoration theatre, by virtue of set pieces such as the suicides of the lovers in Acts IV and V, and particularly the theatricality of the famous heaving of the dying Antony into Cleopatra's monument. More perhaps than any other scene this one requires tact and fine-tuning if the stage action is not to deteriorate into farce. Shakespeare's own (almost certainly) stage direction '*They heave Antony aloft to Cleopatra*' (IV.15.37), and indeed the directions implicit in the dialogue, from Cleopatra's 'we must draw thee up' to 'come, come, come' followed by 'And welcome, welcome!' (30, 37–8), indicate the extent to which the scene has been imagined as dramatic spectacle. It chimes with the play's generic split between comedy and tragedy, and its contrasting of masculine weight and a feminine lack of physical prowess links the scene to wider concerns with gender. The spectacle of the heavy warrior Antony being awkwardly hauled up by Cleopatra and her women recalls her wistful reminiscence much earlier, when she sighed 'O happy horse, to bear the weight of Antony!' (I.5.21). There it was an erotic memory, now Antony is a heavy burden whom she is trying to winch up into her monument from which she dare not descend for fear the Romans apprehend her. A clue to how the scene might have been performed at the Globe in 1606–7 may come from Samuel Daniel's *Tragedie of Cleopatra* (1607) in which a profusely bleeding Antony is painfully, haltingly, hoisted up in slings of silk with Iras and Charmian tugging at a pulley (New Variorum, ed. Marvin Spevack (1990)). Since those details are lacking in the 1594 edition of Daniel's play, it has been argued that he added them after seeing a performance of Shakespeare's version. If true, then Daniel's raising up of Antony to the monument would be a thinly disguised eyewitness account of an early Globe production of Shakespeare's play. The issue of theatrical representation and authenticity is complicated further by the fact that the play's text has been thought to look suspect here, because of Antony's striking repetition of the same line about dying: 'I am dying, Egypt, dying; only | I here importune death awhile . . .' he says at IV.15.18–19, and a few lines later, now in Cleopatra's arms aloft, he repeats: 'I am dying, Egypt, dying. | Give me some wine . . .' (41–2). Emrys Jones in the Commentary to IV.15.13–31 takes the sensible view that, rather than signalling a false start, the passage is fully streamlined with this play's characteristic concern with rendering 'the feel of life as it is lived and especially its tendency to untidiness and anticlimax'. It is possible that Cleopatra's monument is intended to recall that same balcony from which Juliet spoke to Romeo all those years ago, since Antony and Cleopatra revisit the earlier play in more ways than one. It is a moot point whether the raising of Antony to the monument elevates him symbolically, rather like an ascending Christ figure (not an impossible reading of the text), or turns him into the ultimately limp, emasculated creature of Cleopatra. When a rather bulky Anthony Hopkins was clumsily hauled up in Peter Hall's 1987 production the audience found the comedy irresistible until they were admonished to silence by one of the guards on stage (Richard Madelaine, *Antony and Cleopatra*).

Cleopatra's death affords less of a spectacle than Antony's, but is no easier to interpret in the theatre. She casts herself as Antony's Isolde or a Juliet about to consummate her marriage in a love-death. The imagery of her with the asps at her breast is perhaps the most striking in the play, not least for its daring since the text clearly indicates that her breast is visible when Dolabella remarks that 'Here, on her breast, | There is a vent of blood, and something blown; | The like is on her arm' (V.2.346–8). In New York in 1889 the glamorous Cora Brown-Potter as Cleopatra boldly bared her breast for the asp to the horror of her husband and to mixed reviews. Nearly a century later Helen Mirren stood briefly naked before surrendering herself to the fangs of the snake, as if the bite were indeed a lover's pinch (Adrian Noble, 1982). In the theatre this scene requires careful imaginative planning, for even a director unsympathetic to her self-glorification would still need to preserve a kind of dignity for the Queen of Egypt. It is precisely Octavius' wounding question 'Which is the Queen of Egypt?' (V.2.112) that Cleopatra now intends to pre-empt, hence her command to Charmian and Iras 'Show me, my women, like a queen. Go fetch | My best attires' (227–8).

Given the global nature of its plot and the struggle for world dominion, interpretations of *Antony and Cleopatra* are bound to be affected by wider historical events. When Marius Goring was cast as a coolly efficient Octavius Caesar in Glen Byam Shaw's post-World War II production (1953) the fact that he had played Hitler in a BBC series made perfect sense since nothing less than the empire of the world is at stake. Generally the play, unlike *Coriolanus* and others, such as *King Lear*, has not lent itself to politically angled or Brechtian, anti-illusionary interpretations, probably because the poetry resists that kind of thing. The failure of Vanessa Redgrave's polemical production at the Riverside Studios in Hammersmith (1995), with herself playing a passion-free queen of Egypt pushing sixty (Cleopatra is twenty-eight at the start), is characteristic: to interpret the play as a parable about the Bosnian war meant squeezing the text into a straitjacket in which the scenery conjured up bleak visions of the besieged city of Sarajevo rather than of the Egypt of Shakespeare's fantasy.

*Antony and Cleopatra* is full of magnificent parts. The roles of Enobarbus and Caesar have attracted some of the best performances over the years. Patrick Stewart as Enobarbus starred in both Trevor Nunn's 1972 Royal Shakespeare Company (RSC) version and Peter Brook's 1978 RSC production, where he played alongside Alan Howard as Antony and Glenda Jackson as Cleopatra. He was as involved in the lovers' story as Emrys James was in the same role in Jonathan Miller's 1981 BBC film where he spoke directly to the camera; and in Hall's 1987 version Michael Bryant put in a great performance as the blunt, plain-dealing fellow who is neither taken in by Egyptian exoticism nor unfairly biased against it. It is Enobarbus who speaks the most famous paean to Cleopatra in the play, and Bryant's delivery of the Cydnus lines invested it with brilliant dramatic life, as if relating the famous meeting made him relive it all over again and succumb to Cleopatra's magic. Highly interesting Caesars in recent years have included a chilling Corin Redgrave (Nunn, 1972), Jonathan Pryce on a learning curve of power (Brook, 1978), Ian Charleson as a tentative and not insensitive empire builder (Miller, 1981) and a calculating Tim Pigott-Smith (Hall, 1987). The reason why Caesars and Enobarbuses have triumphed in the theatre may well be because they are solitary figures. Their performances are simultaneously choric and solipsistic, and these roles do not need to engage directly with others on the stage. They are in fact predicated on not playing off anybody else too closely.

The failure of directors to come up with famous Antonys and Cleopatras cannot be put down to lack of trying. In the twentieth century some of the grandest names in the theatre and cinema have been teamed up, including Edith Evans and Godfrey Tearle (Shaw, 1946), Laurence Olivier and Vivien Leigh (Michael Benthall, 1951), Michael Redgrave and Peggy Ashcroft (Shaw, 1953), Richard Johnson and Janet Suzman (Nunn, 1972), Howard and Jackson (Brook, 1978), Michael Gambon and Helen Mirren (Noble, 1982), Anthony Hopkins and Judi Dench (Hall, 1987), to mention only some British performances from Stratford-upon-Avon and London. The two eponymous characters are equally important and much rides therefore on the chemistry between them. When this is lacking (and it is all too often) the play loses its drive. In the 2002 RSC production, directed by Michael Attenborough, Stuart Wilson played Antony as a middle-aged biker opposite a sensuous, high-maintenance Cleopatra, Sinéad Cusack. The production was energetic enough and fun, but the verse at times eluded the actors, and they never seemed close enough to be close. Even Janet Suzman, one of the greatest

Cleopatras of recent times, struggled opposite Richard Johnson who was widely thought to be too stiff and formal for the role of the middle-aged sensualist Antony. Conversely, in the 1978 Brook production Glenda Jackson played Cleopatra as a mercurial, proto-feminist, crop-haired figure, who lacked, or deliberately forwent, any form of feminine allure. How much sex appeal Cleopatra has in Shakespeare is debatable, but when she exclaims, 'O happy horse, to bear the weight of Antony!' we know that she has experienced that same weight during lovemaking. At the very least there is tenderness in the part. If Jackson was ultimately too cold, and perhaps too shrill, Alan Howard's Antony resembled Henry V and Coriolanus, two roles he made uniquely his own in the 1970s. He starred almost simultaneously in *Coriolanus* and *Antony and Cleopatra*, and his haughty performance in the patrician role of Caius Martius Coriolanus ranks among the greatest ever in that notoriously tough part. While Howard undoubtedly possessed the stature and sheer rhetorical power to make Antony come to life, he seemed to be inhibited by the part throughout. It requires expansive action and the chaotic energy of Falstaff, but Howard was all statuesque dignity. In the end Brook's stripped-down, anti-Romantic production was bleak, tragic and never ran poetically. Its use of translucent screens was intended to set off the intimacy of the lovers' relationship. But in Shakespeare's text the lovers are rarely out of the public view, and Brook's narrowly conceived production appealed to the converted above all. Such was its pace, however, that its sheer length (the text was almost uncut) of nearly four hours hardly registered with the audience.

Why then is it that this galaxy of stars has not, over the years, delivered a performance worthy to set next to the legendary feats of Ian McKellen and Judi Dench as Macbeth and Lady Macbeth at The Other Place in 1978? The issues in *Macbeth* are closer to *Antony and Cleopatra* than may at first appear, and particularly at the level of rhetoric. The Roman play does not of course overtly engage in deep moral searches and its action is far more public than that of *Macbeth*. Notwithstanding the claims to being the greatest love story of all time, a story in which the traditional metaphors and similes of courtly love crystallize into reality, Antony and Cleopatra are rarely glimpsed alone. These two middle-aged heads of state conduct their relationship very much under the public gaze.

While it is almost impossible to get around this in the theatre, cinematic adaptations are a very different matter, and this may explain why of the few television films so far (when compared to theatrical performances) at least two have been well received. Nunn's 1972 RSC production was adapted for television in 1974 and proved an immediate success. His use of a soundtrack to convey an out-of-door Egyptian atmosphere of buzzing flies, crickets, barking dogs and the lapping sounds of the Nile's banks compensates for the small-screen limitations of a medium in which elaborate scenery is not possible. Nunn's camera angles, close-ups and blurring of the lens when filming Egypt to convey a sense of its elusiveness pay tribute rather more effectively perhaps than theatrical production can to the melting world of Shakespeare's script. As the *New York Times* reviewer John J. O'Connor pointed out, its 'visual structure', by relying on 'suggestion' rather than 'literal definition', artfully smoothed the transitions between the many brief scenes in the text.

The camera's ability to turn public moments into

intensely private ones was fully exploited by Miller's 1981 BBC film. Colin Blakely and his Cleopatra, Jane Lapotaire, spoke the verse with poise, but Miller's wariness of the sensuous delights and mad abandon of Egypt resulted in an overly restrained production. While restoring intimacy, Miller arguably gave us the wrong kind, at least if one accepts the view that the play deals with both global issues and great love. Jane Lapotaire was a housewife, more Roman than Egyptian, and the lovers failed to capitalize on the freedoms afforded them by the medium. The camera underlined their apartness and lack of closeness, and instead gave scope to the loners in the play, notably Emrys James's Enobarbus and Ian Charleson's controlled yet charismatic Caesar.

The problems experienced by stage performances seem, almost wilfully, to have been factored into the text of the play. When Cleopatra is left alone on stage at the end she experiences a horrified vision of her relationship with Antony being played in Rome as a farce, with her as an unwilling spectator. The point is that Cleopatra's rejection of this dramatic travesty (as she sees it) stakes a claim for the objective validity of her own superior vision of her relationship with Antony.

Whether or not we accept this will inevitably depend on the power of the play's wider rhetoric to sway us, as well as on the theatrical reality of the first four acts. George Bernard Shaw's scathing view of the lovers in the introduction to *Three Plays for Puritans* (1900) may well be justified from what we have *seen* rather than *heard*. In this play seeing and hearing matter equally and the roles in the play need to be interpreted accordingly. There are very few points of entry into the characters of the two main protagonists, something which is not the case with other tragic figures. This was famously

Olivier's complaint, that the role of Antony lacked characterization and that this was the root cause of his problems with it (Lamb, *'Antony and Cleopatra' on the English Stage*). It is true that we can construct a psychological profile for Macbeth and other tragic heroes and that it is hard to do so for Antony and Cleopatra: 'Grates me! The sum' is a typical response from Antony (I.1.18), and when he has lost everything and Cleopatra bursts into tears he exclaims, 'Fall not a tear, I say; one of them rates | All that is won and lost' (III.11.69–70). Where Othello might try to articulate his loss in a soliloquy, Antony's moods swing with the speed of lightning; and, it seems, with the same lack of premeditation.

A. C. Bradley's shrewd remark in 'Shakespeare's *Antony and Cleopatra*' that in this text we seem always to be dealing with the artistic process rather than the product makes this a hard play to cast and for its roles to be intuited. If the actors concentrate, as readers tend to do, on the transcendent power of the rhetoric they are in danger of becoming like classical Greek actors who spoke from behind masks. As an expressive vehicle for dramatic performance in which characters and dialogue lock into each other *Antony and Cleopatra* may be Shakespeare's most challenging work, if recorded performances to date are a credible guide.

*Antony and Cleopatra* is the least minimalist of Shakespeare's plays, and paring down the parts and its scope is to go against the grain. The Howard–Jackson production suffered from that, and so did Noble's 1982 RSC *Antony and Cleopatra* in which Michael Gambon and Helen Mirren appeared opposite each other. The casting was inspired, but it failed to deliver, this time because the conception had become too small-scale: true, Cleopatra is called a 'wrangling queen' (I.1.48) and vilest things are said to become themselves in her, but even so we think of her as royal and that Mirren never was. Her performance was neurotic and hysterical in its swinging mood shifts; the struggle for empire was here reduced to a squabble.

It is always easier to determine what the parts are not than what they are. When Anthony Hopkins and Judi Dench undertook the roles in Hall's 1987 production they seemed too physically staid to play the lovers. Unlike Noble, Hall consolidated the play's epic vision by extrapolating a lavish and inventive set from the rhetoric, to aid and abet the aural with the visual, as it were. The leisurely pace and length were intended to let the poetry work its elixir, and the production drew plaudits for trusting the language. Hall insisted that Cleopatra never really cared for the Antony of the first four acts, but that she loved the fantastical figure of her dream vision. As Michael Billington perceptively pointed out in the *Guardian*, the production interpreted the play as treating of 'two middle-aged people – carnal, deceitful, often sad – seeking in love a reality greater than themselves'. At the Old Vic ten years earlier (Toby Robertson, 1977) Alec McCowen and Dorothy Tutin had failed for just that reason, for being too comfortably middle-aged and therefore *passé*. At the heart of Shakespeare's play there lie conflicting impulses between, on the one hand, an overwhelming passion which is all-consuming and engenders tragic results, and on the other, an absence of pain as it runs its grand course.

In spite of this and notwithstanding anxieties about an altogether too 'English' manner, Judi Dench put in an electrifying performance. The same charge of Englishness was also levelled against Vivien Leigh's performance opposite her husband Laurence Olivier in

1951. Their relationship onstage lacked fire, and Leigh's interpretation of the role was less Scarlett O'Hara than Blanche Dubois – Leigh starred in the film of *A Streetcar Named Desire* in the same year that she played Cleopatra – and Shakespeare's Cleopatra lies somewhere between the two.

Peggy Ashcroft was similarly thought to be too English for Antony's paramour. She was partnered by a rugged Michael Redgrave in 1953. He was an obvious candidate for the role of Antony, but by his own account he struggled with the division between heroic stature and dissolution. As for Ashcroft, the play's Orientalism rather demands that its queen should be 'tawny' (I.1.6) either through Phoebus' amorous pinches or by virtue of being North African, or both. Ashcroft, who insisted on seeing Cleopatra as a Greek (historically she was the daughter of Ptolemy XII of the Macedonian dynasty that ruled Egypt), was red haired and fair (too English-looking), although that did not stop her from putting in a highly sexed performance. Ashcroft's red hair was presumably meant to conjure up images of Pre-Raphaelite beauty and delicate passions (Janet Achurch had played the first red-haired Cleopatra in 1897), since red hair in the Elizabethan period carried largely negative connotations. The Redgrave–Ashcroft pairing ought to have been a triumph, but like all other productions it ultimately failed to satisfy. Ashcroft was deemed by some reviewers to have put in a rather chilling performance. Kenneth Tynan saw the Redgrave production and clearly wanted something a bit wilder. Remarking that 'the great sluts of world drama' lie beyond the ken of British actresses, he added tartly that 'an English Cleopatra is a contradiction in terms'. With all this talk of Eastern Cleopatras eluding (apparently) thornless English roses, it is worth remembering that the role was written for a male actor. Audiences in London were reminded of this when Mark Rylance directed himself as Cleopatra in the 1999 production at the new Globe Theatre on the South Bank.

With the exceptions of Constance Collier (Herbert Beerbohm Tree, 1906) and Suzman (Nunn, 1972), very few Cleopatras have been dark. When the Talawa Theatre Company (Cleopatra was played by Dona Croll) performed the play at the Bloomsbury Theatre at University College London in 1991 the entire cast was black. The colour-coding of the play is rather different from that of *Othello*, and race is an issue primarily because the Romans choose to make it so. For them the Roman Antony's relationship with a non-white foreign woman is further proof of his dissoluteness. Cleopatra's otherness is a matter of pride to her, and the play (rather than the partisan Romans) seems to see her colour as a badge of honour: the darker and therefore more alien she is the greater Antony's love for her.

The most successful Cleopatra of recorded performance was perhaps the first major one of the nineteenth century, Isabella Glyn, in the 1849 production at Sadler's Wells by Samuel Phelps, with Phelps as Antony. The production cut Shakespeare's text severely, but what was left was all Shakespeare. It was lavish in its uses of spectacle, particularly in the galley scenes and elaborate Egyptian processions. In later productions the stress on grandeur and realism led, logically, to the rhetoric being increasingly smothered by stage shows, such as the spectacular pitched naval battle in Frederick Chatterton's highly pictorial 1873 production at Drury Lane. This show was a popular success, but it was more Gilbert and Sullivan than Shakespeare. Unfortunately for the purists its weakest parts included Act V, which consisted entirely of Shakespeare's text. A distrust of the text or a love of invention, or both, underpinned some of the major productions which followed, including one featuring Lillie Langtry as Cleopatra (directed by Lewis Wingfield) in 1890 and Tree's in 1906, which marked the apogee of grand productions. But the performance had shrunk to a mere eighteen scenes, and Tree ran with the Eastern feel, not least by having his Cleopatra, a queen-of-the-night Constance Collier, appear as Isis, something which Suzman would also do in 1972. From this deeply operatic production, as much *Magic Flute* as *Antony and Cleopatra*, there was no going further down this route, and the reaction that set in was spearheaded by the likes of Harley Granville-Barker, whose important *Prefaces* contributed to the restoration of Shakespeare's play to the stage (*Prefaces to Shakespeare: 'Antony and Cleopatra'* (1930)).

In his 1987 *Antony and Cleopatra* Peter Hall reverted to a full text and included even the odd scene 1 of Act III with Ventidius and Silius. It exists in a vacuum in the play and is sometimes reported rather than played. Arguably the best-loved production of *Antony and Cleopatra* since the Second World War was Trevor Nunn's in 1972. It formed part of a cycle of plays called 'The Romans', and Nunn cast his lot in with the Egyptians whose world was lavishly represented as a festive, multi-coloured, drowsy nirvana pitted against a brutal, darkly monochrome Rome. Nunn's production coincided with the Tutankhamun exhibition at the British Museum in London which revived interest in ancient Egypt just as fifty years earlier Howard Carter's discovery of the Tutankhamun tomb had enhanced the prestige of Egypt in the Western imagination. Under the circumstances Janet Suzman's wily Cleopatra may have been played rather oddly against the grain since she came across as a manipulative and mercenary creature whose love for Antony was inextricably linked to a lust for power. The queen of Egypt *is* Egypt in Shakespeare's text; to uncouple her from the magic of her land seems a Roman thing to do. Nunn's impeccable sense of timing and his sheer inventiveness turned his script into great theatre, but his decision to interpret the polarities of Rome and Egypt politically rather than metaphorically, and to put them at the heart of the play, ran up against radical views of *Antony and Cleopatra* that were beginning to emerge at just around that time.

René Weis

# *Further Reading*

There were four major editions of *Antony and Cleopatra* in the 1990s: New Variorum, edited by Marvin Spevack (1990); New Cambridge Shakespeare, edited by David Bevington (1990); Oxford Shakespeare, edited by Michael Neill (1994); and Arden 3, edited by John Wilders (1995). The New Variorum (published by the Modern Language Association) includes an analysis of textual variants and substantial sections on the play's sources, critical history, reception, themes, characters and fortunes on the stage. This excellent MLA volume should be the first port of call for all serious students. The New Cambridge edition is sound throughout, and its introduction even-handed, although Bevington, like most modern readers of the play, leans towards a 'romantic' interpretation of Shakespeare's lovers. The Oxford edition devotes much of Neill's finely tuned introduction to the play's performance history, which is usually thought to be its Achilles heel. The notes and introduction of John Wilders's Arden 3 offer useful guidance to the first-time student of the play. Where Neill and Bevington declare their hands enthusiastically with regard to the tremendous poetry of *Antony and Cleopatra*, Wilders retains a sober distance and proceeds with cool reason, and may be rather more in the Roman camp.

In the preface to his 1765 edition of Shakespeare Samuel Johnson baulked at what he thought were the structural flaws: 'events . . . are produced without any art of connexion or care of disposition'. Such strictures did not trouble the Romantics unduly. It was they who rediscovered this maverick play with its quicksands of shifting scenes which defy the logic of the neoclassical unities of time, place and action. The question of decorum cuts to the core of *Antony and Cleopatra*. William Hazlitt (*Characters of Shakespeare's Plays* (1817)) and Samuel Taylor Coleridge (1819; *Shakespearean Criticism*, ed. T. M. Raysor (1907)) chose to ignore its alleged structural deficiencies and responded instead to its magical verse line and grandeur.

In an incisive essay, 'Shakespeare's *Antony and Cleopatra*', published in his *Oxford Lectures on Poetry* (1909), A. C. Bradley noted that in *Antony and Cleopatra* we are constantly aware of the play's artifice and that for a tragedy it was not 'painful'. He excluded it from his great study *Shakespearean Tragedy* (1904), not least because he felt that its structure and a catastrophe divided between Act IV (Antony's death) and Act V are characteristic features of comedy and tragicomedy. Bradley also noted that Antony, like Richard II, 'sees his own fall with the eyes of a poet, but a poet much greater than the young Shakespeare, who could never have written Antony's marvellous speech about the sunset clouds'. Moreover, Bradley stressed that the global politics of the play need to be measured against the way in which it explores the relationship of the two lovers; both do feature in its title.

The polarizing of two different mindsets in *Antony and Cleopatra* has led some critics to read the play as a moral parable predicated on the notion that Rome stands for *virtus* or *Romanitas*, while Egypt is a Spenserian bower of bliss where heroes are turned into pigs by a Circean Cleopatra. The classic statement of this position is F. M. Dickey's *Not Wisely But Too Well: Shakespeare's Love Tragedies* (1957; 1966), which ultimately endorses an arid moralistic view of the lovers by privileging Rome and empire. Dickey's reading chimes with the view expressed by Shakespeare's contemporary Sir Francis Bacon who, in the 'Essay of Love' (*Essays* 1597, 1625), wrote that the historic Antony stood out among all past great men for losing an empire because he was 'a voluptuous man, and inordinate'. Dickey remains impervious to what Frank Kermode has called 'the unanswerable argument of poetry' (*Shakespeare's Language* (2000)) and stresses its political and moral imperatives. In *Some Shakespearean Themes* (1959) L. C. Knights had, in moralistic, Leavisite fashion, similarly refused to be intoxicated by the play's heady rhetorical brew. Noting that the lovers' views of each other in Acts IV and V hardly correspond to ours, he suggests that 'Shakespeare gives the maximum weight to an experience that is finally "placed"' and that it is 'perhaps this that makes the tragedy so sombre in its realism, so little comforting to the romantic imagination'.

At the other extreme from Dickey is G. Wilson Knight's chapter 'The Transcendental Humanism of *Antony and Cleopatra*', in *The Imperial Theme* (1954). His rhapsodic praise of the lovers and the sublimity of the poetry plays down the importance of Roman claims. Knight's reading is to some extent consolidated by T. J. B. Spencer who in 'Shakespeare and the Elizabethan Romans' (*Shakespeare Survey 10* (1957)) notes that 'in spite of literary admiration for Cicero, the Romans in the imagination of the sixteenth century were Suetonian and Tacitian rather than Plutarchan'. In other words,

Shakespeare may have been wary of the Roman empire, and therefore of Octavius Caesar, because his sources Suetonius and Tacitus both inclined towards the Republic; his track record in *Julius Caesar*, where Brutus not only kills Caesar but also steals his play, points in this direction.

Shakespeare found his capricious couple in Plutarch's famous *Lives of the Noble Grecians and Romans*. The historian's biographical account of Antony and Cleopatra is a masterpiece in its own right. Few texts left their mark as profoundly or as creatively on a Shakespeare play. The extent of Shakespeare's debt to it can be gleaned from a number of source studies, including T. J. B. Spencer's *Shakespeare's Plutarch* (1964) and volume V of Geoffrey Bullough's *Narrative and Dramatic Sources of Shakespeare* (1964). Bullough reproduces Sir Thomas North's 1579 translations of Plutarch, including the important comparison of Antony and Demetrius, and he also conveniently identifies Shakespeare's major borrowings from Plutarch. Bullough's introductory essay to the section on *Antony and Cleopatra* offers illuminating analyses of the way in which Shakespeare worked with this and other sources.

In '*Antony and Cleopatra*: The Limits of Mythology' (*Shakespeare Survey 23* (1970)), Harold Fisch connects the play's mythopoeia to its wider concerns with fertility and transcendence, as Michael Lloyd had done earlier in 'Cleopatra as Isis' (*Shakespeare Survey 12* (1959)). Lloyd moreover pointed out the importance of Apuleius' second-century fable *The Golden Ass* for this play and also the role of *The Faerie Queene*, which Shakespeare undoubtedly drew on for the church of Isis as well as, quite probably, its explorations of bisexuality. Shakespeare's imaginative use of mythic images is brilliantly tackled by Frank Kermode in his synoptic introduction in the *Riverside Shakespeare* (1974), the best short piece to date on the play.

Of the many studies of Shakespeare's Rome, M. W. MacCallum's *Shakespeare's Roman Plays and their Background* (1910; reissued with a new introduction by T. J. B. Spencer in 1967) remains one of the most important for its scope, intellectual elegance and sheer authority. Arguably the most influential book-length study of *Antony and Cleopatra* since the Second World War is Janet Adelman's *The Common Liar: An Essay on 'Antony and Cleopatra'* (1973). Following on from scholars such as John F. Danby, Eugene Waith, Maurice Charney and Ernest Schanzer, Adelman argues that Shakespeare draws on well-known mythopoeic images from classical literature to underpin the play's interest in gender-crossing and identity. Her account is the fullest yet of liminality and Egyptian metamorphoses in *Antony and Cleopatra*, including Shakespeare's use of the Isis story in Plutarch's *Moralia*. She developed her ideas on the play in a more feminist idiom in *Suffocating Mothers: Fantasies of Maternal Origin in Shakespeare's Plays* (1992). The lovers' transvestite blending together is the subject of a searching article by Phyllis Rackin, 'Shakespeare's Boy Cleopatra, the Decorum of Nature, and the Golden World of Poetry' (*PMLA* 87 (1972), pp. 201–12), in which she links the play's interest in symbiosis to the transsexual nature of the Elizabethan stage.

The play's use of the Bible and especially the Book of Revelation to signal a desire to transcend boundaries and death itself is studied by Ethel Seaton in '*Antony and Cleopatra* and the *Book of Revelation*' (*Review of English Studies* (1946), pp. 219–24). In an important essay called 'Shakespeare and Dürer's Apocalypse' (*Shakespeare*

*Studies* 4 (1968)) Helen Morris points out that the passages from Revelation which Shakespeare echoes 'are very often those which are vividly illustrated' in the Bishops' Bible of 1568. The Angel with a face like the sun, feet like pillars of fire, a booming voice and straddling the earth and the sea while holding open the book (Revelation 10), originates in Albrecht Dürer's famous woodcuts to accompany Apocalypse. Cleopatra's vision of a thundering Antony who bestrides the ocean comes to mind, and the dolphin in the Dürer woodcut behind the emblematic illustration in the Bishops' Bible may have prompted Cleopatra's image of the dolphin-like Antony.

The divine marriage of Apocalypse is linked backwards to the Song of Songs, and the analogy between Cleopatra and the biblical 'beloved' has been foregrounded by a number of writers on the play, notably by S. L. Bethell in *Shakespeare and the Popular Dramatic Tradition* (1944), who writes that just as 'the exotic and sensual *Song of Songs* may be understood allegorically of the marriage of Christ and his Church' so it is quite possible that this sensual love story 'might also yield its hidden meaning to an audience simultaneously aware of the two levels of story and significance'. The case for Antony's sensuousness actively connecting with the spiritual, or directly leading to it, is also argued by, among others, P. J. Traci, *The Love Play of 'Antony and Cleopatra': A Critical Study of Shakespeare's Play* (1970).

One of the subtlest essays on *Antony and Cleopatra* is Emrys Jones's introduction to the 1977 New Penguin Shakespeare edition of the play. Jones is instructive on Shakespeare's extensive use of Plutarch, and his discussion of the structure and pace of the play and of the way it aims to 'imitate disorder and formlessness as they manifest themselves in life' is invaluable. Also useful is

Anne Barton's 1973 essay on the generic and structural challenges of the play, 'Nature's Piece 'Gainst Fancy: The Divided Catastrophe in *Antony and Cleopatra*', which is included in her collection *Essays, Mainly Shakespearean* (1994). In a seminal study, *Literary Transvaluation: From Vergilian Epic to Shakespearean Tragi-comedy* (1984), Barbara Bono charts the trajectory of Shakespeare's re-creation of one of the most famous love stories of all time in ways which are suggestive and often fascinating. More recently Heather James has studied ways in which the play 'resists' the *Aeneid* in *Shakespeare's Troy* (1997).

Three collections of essays should be noted. Mark Rose edited *Twentieth Century Interpretations of 'Antony and Cleopatra'* (1977), and John Russell Brown oversaw the Macmillan Casebook on the play (1968; reissued 1991). Between them they anthologize some of the most influential writing on the play, to which should be added the New Casebook Series volume, edited by John Drakakis (1994), which includes critical work on *Antony and Cleopatra* with a more theoretical, political and cultural history slant.

In *Vision and Rhetoric in Shakespeare: Looking Through Language* (2000) Alison Thorne approaches the play as a highly stylized work which is read most fruitfully against the backdrop of Renaissance theories of the imagination, and especially Sir Philip Sidney's *Apology for Poetry* (1595). Thorne's discussion of the play's reflexivity and of Cleopatra's self-deification in Act V ranks among the most interesting to date of that strand.

The play's afterlife on the stage is discussed in all of the 1990s editions mentioned above as well as in a number of studies specifically dedicated to it. Margaret Lamb's *'Antony and Cleopatra' on the English Stage* (1980) provides a useful survey of some of the play's main performances, and in *Peter Hall Directs 'Antony and Cleopatra'* (1990) Tirzah Lowen discusses the National Theatre production of 1987 with Judi Dench and Anthony Hopkins. These should be supplemented by the volume on *Antony and Cleopatra* (1998), edited by Richard Madelaine for the Cambridge series Shakespeare in Production, which offers an instructive and interesting survey of the problems and challenges posed by the play in recorded performances. The section on the Jacobean theatre is outstanding, not least as regards the kind of boy or youth required to play the part of Cleopatra, and on whether or not the play was written as an early Blackfriars production rather than for the Globe. After a substantial introduction, Madelaine reproduces the text of the play with a full set of theatrical annotations.

Also useful is Barbara Hodgdon's essay '*Antony and Cleopatra* in the Theatre', in *The Cambridge Companion to Shakespearean Tragedy* (ed. Claire McEachern (2002)), and further guidance on film and television adaptations of the play is provided by *Shakespeare on Television* (ed. J. C. Bulman and H. R. Coursen (1988)), *Shakespeare and the Moving Image* (ed. Anthony Davies and Stanley Wells (1994)), *Shakespeare the Movie* (ed. Lynda E. Boose and Richard Burt (1997)) and Joan Lord Hall's *'Antony and Cleopatra': A Guide to the Play* (2002), which contains a thoughtful fifty-page discussion of the play's performance history.

# THE TRAGEDY OF ANTONY AND CLEOPATRA

## *The Characters in the Play*

| | |
|---|---|
| Mark ANTONY<br>Octavius CAESAR<br>LEPIDUS | triumvirs |
| DEMETRIUS<br>PHILO<br>Domitius ENOBARBUS<br>VENTIDIUS<br>SILIUS<br>EROS<br>CANIDIUS<br>SCARUS<br>DECRETAS | Antony's friends and followers |
| MAECENAS<br>AGRIPPA<br>TAURUS<br>DOLABELLA<br>THIDIAS<br>GALLUS<br>PROCULEIUS | Caesar's friends and followers |

Sextus POMPEY

MENECRATES }
MENAS } Pompey's friends
VARRIUS }

CLEOPATRA, Queen of Egypt

CHARMIAN }
IRAS }
ALEXAS }
MARDIAN } Cleopatra's attendants
DIOMEDES }
SELEUCUS }

OCTAVIA, Caesar's sister

MESSENGERS
SOOTHSAYER
ATTENDANTS
SERVANTS
SOLDIERS
BOY
A schoolmaster, Antony's AMBASSADOR
CAPTAIN
SENTRY and WATCH
GUARDS
EGYPTIAN
CLOWN

Cleopatra's ladies, eunuchs, servants, soldiers, captains, officers

*Enter Demetrius and Philo* I.1

PHILO

Nay, but this dotage of our general's
O'erflows the measure. Those his goodly eyes,
That o'er the files and musters of the war
Have glowed like plated Mars, now bend, now turn
The office and devotion of their view
Upon a tawny front. His captain's heart,
Which in the scuffles of great fights hath burst
The buckles on his breast, reneges all temper,
And is become the bellows and the fan
To cool a gypsy's lust.

*Flourish. Enter Antony, Cleopatra, her ladies Charmian and Iras, the train, with eunuchs fanning her*

Look where they come.
Take but good note, and you shall see in him
The triple pillar of the world transformed
Into a strumpet's fool. Behold and see.

CLEOPATRA

If it be love indeed, tell me how much.

ANTONY

There's beggary in the love that can be reckoned.

CLEOPATRA

I'll set a bourn how far to be beloved.

ANTONY
Then must thou needs find out new heaven, new earth.
*Enter a Messenger*

MESSENGER
News, my good lord, from Rome.

ANTONY
Grates me! The sum.

CLEOPATRA
Nay, hear them, Antony.
Fulvia perchance is angry; or who knows
If the scarce-bearded Caesar have not sent
His powerful mandate to you: 'Do this, or this;
Take in that kingdom, and enfranchise that.
Perform't, or else we damn thee.'

ANTONY
How, my love?

CLEOPATRA
Perchance? Nay, and most like.
You must not stay here longer. Your dismission
Is come from Caesar. Therefore hear it, Antony.
Where's Fulvia's process? Caesar's I would say! Both!
Call in the messengers. As I am Egypt's Queen,
Thou blushest, Antony, and that blood of thine
Is Caesar's homager; else so thy cheek pays shame
When shrill-tongued Fulvia scolds. The messengers!

ANTONY
Let Rome in Tiber melt, and the wide arch
Of the ranged empire fall! Here is my space.
Kingdoms are clay. Our dungy earth alike
Feeds beast as man. The nobleness of life
Is to do thus – when such a mutual pair
And such a twain can do't, in which I bind,
On pain of punishment, the world to weet
We stand up peerless.

CLEOPATRA
Excellent falsehood!
Why did he marry Fulvia, and not love her?

I'll seem the fool I am not. Antony
Will be himself.

ANTONY But stirred by Cleopatra.
Now for the love of Love and her soft hours,
Let's not confound the time with conference harsh.
There's not a minute of our lives should stretch
Without some pleasure now. What sport tonight?

CLEOPATRA
Hear the ambassadors.

ANTONY Fie, wrangling queen!
Whom everything becomes – to chide, to laugh,
To weep; whose every passion fully strives
To make itself, in thee, fair and admired.
No messenger but thine; and all alone
Tonight we'll wander through the streets and note
The qualities of people. Come, my queen;
Last night you did desire it. (*To the Messenger*) Speak
not to us.

*Exeunt Antony and Cleopatra with the train*

DEMETRIUS
Is Caesar with Antonius prized so slight?

PHILO
Sir, sometimes, when he is not Antony,
He comes too short of that great property
Which still should go with Antony.

DEMETRIUS I am full sorry
That he approves the common liar, who
Thus speaks of him at Rome; but I will hope
Of better deeds tomorrow. Rest you happy! *Exeunt*

## I.2

*Enter Charmian, Iras, and Alexas*

CHARMIAN Lord Alexas, sweet Alexas, most anything
Alexas, almost most absolute Alexas, where's the sooth-

sayer that you praised so to th'Queen? O that I knew this husband, which you say must charge his horns with garlands!

ALEXAS Soothsayer!

*Enter a Soothsayer*

SOOTHSAYER Your will?

CHARMIAN Is this the man? Is't you, sir, that know things?

SOOTHSAYER
In Nature's infinite book of secrecy
A little I can read.

ALEXA Show him your hand.

*Enter Enobarbus*

ENOBARBUS
Bring in the banquet quickly; wine enough
Cleopatra's health to drink.

CHARMIAN (*to Soothsayer*) Good sir, give me good fortune.

SOOTHSAYER I make not, but foresee.

CHARMIAN Pray then, foresee me one.

SOOTHSAYER
You shall be yet far fairer than you are.

CHARMIAN He means in flesh.

IRAS No, you shall paint when you are old.

CHARMIAN Wrinkles forbid!

ALEXAS Vex not his prescience; be attentive.

CHARMIAN Hush!

SOOTHSAYER
You shall be more beloving than beloved.

CHARMIAN I had rather heat my liver with drinking.

ALEXAS Nay, hear him.

CHARMIAN Good now, some excellent fortune! Let me be married to three kings in a forenoon and widow them all. Let me have a child at fifty, to whom Herod of

Jewry may do homage. Find me to marry me with Octavius Caesar, and companion me with my mistress.

SOOTHSAYER
You shall outlive the lady whom you serve.

CHARMIAN O, excellent! I love long life better than figs.

SOOTHSAYER
You have seen and proved a fairer former fortune
Than that which is to approach.

CHARMIAN Then belike my children shall have no names. Prithee, how many boys and wenches must I have?

SOOTHSAYER
If every of your wishes had a womb,
And fertile every wish, a million.

CHARMIAN Out, fool, I forgive thee for a witch.

ALEXAS You think none but your sheets are privy to your wishes.

CHARMIAN Nay, come, tell Iras hers.

ALEXAS We'll know all our fortunes.

ENOBARBUS Mine, and most of our fortunes, tonight shall be drunk to bed.

IRAS There's a palm presages chastity, if nothing else.

CHARMIAN E'en as the o'erflowing Nilus presageth famine.

IRAS (*to Charmian*) Go, you wild bedfellow, you cannot soothsay.

CHARMIAN Nay, if an oily palm be not a fruitful prognostication, I cannot scratch mine ear. Prithee, tell her but a workyday fortune.

SOOTHSAYER Your fortunes are alike.

IRAS But how, but how? Give me particulars.

SOOTHSAYER I have said.

IRAS Am I not an inch of fortune better than she?

CHARMIAN Well, if you were but an inch of fortune better than I, where would you choose it?

IRAS Not in my husband's nose.

CHARMIAN Our worser thoughts heavens mend! Alexas – come, his fortune, his fortune! O, let him marry a woman that cannot go, sweet Isis, I beseech thee, and let her die too, and give him a worse, and let worse follow worse till the worst of all follow him laughing to his grave, fiftyfold a cuckold! Good Isis, hear me this prayer, though thou deny me a matter of more weight; good Isis, I beseech thee!

IRAS Amen. Dear goddess, hear that prayer of the people! For, as it is a heart-breaking to see a handsome man loose-wived, so it is a deadly sorrow to behold a foul knave uncuckolded. Therefore, dear Isis, keep decorum, and fortune him accordingly!

CHARMIAN Amen.

ALEXAS Lo now, if it lay in their hands to make me a cuckold, they would make themselves whores but they'd do't.

*Enter Cleopatra*

ENOBARBUS
Hush! Here comes Antony.

CHARMIAN Not he; the Queen.

CLEOPATRA
Saw you my lord?

ENOBARBUS No, lady.

CLEOPATRA Was he not here?

CHARMIAN
No, madam.

CLEOPATRA
He was disposed to mirth; but on the sudden
A Roman thought hath struck him. Enobarbus!

ENOBARBUS
Madam?

CLEOPATRA
Seek him, and bring him hither. Where's Alexas?

ALEXAS
Here at your service. My lord approaches.

*Enter Antony with a Messenger and Attendants*

CLEOPATRA
We will not look upon him. Go with us.

*Exeunt all but Antony, Messenger, and Attendants*

MESSENGER
Fulvia thy wife first came into the field.

ANTONY
Against my brother Lucius?

MESSENGER
Ay.
But soon that war had end, and the time's state
Made friends of them, jointing their force 'gainst
Caesar,
Whose better issue in the war from Italy
Upon the first encounter drave them.

ANTONY
Well, what worst?

MESSENGER
The nature of bad news infects the teller.

ANTONY
When it concerns the fool or coward. On.
Things that are past are done, with me. 'Tis thus:
Who tells me true, though in his tale lie death,
I hear him as he flattered.

MESSENGER
Labienus –
This is stiff news – hath with his Parthian force
Extended Asia; from Euphrates
His conquering banner shook, from Syria

To Lydia and to Ionia,
Whilst –

ANTONY Antony, thou wouldst say –

MESSENGER O, my lord.

ANTONY
Speak to me home; mince not the general tongue.
Name Cleopatra as she is called in Rome.
Rail thou in Fulvia's phrase, and taunt my faults
With such full licence as both truth and malice
Have power to utter. O, then we bring forth weeds
When our quick winds lie still, and our ills told us
Is as our earing. Fare thee well awhile.

MESSENGER
At your noble pleasure. *Exit*

ANTONY
From Sicyon, ho, the news? Speak there!

FIRST ATTENDANT
The man from Sicyon – is there such an one?

SECOND ATTENDANT
He stays upon your will.

ANTONY Let him appear.
(*aside*) These strong Egyptian fetters I must break,
Or lose myself in dotage.

*Enter another Messenger, with a letter*

What are you?

MESSENGER
Fulvia thy wife is dead.

ANTONY Where died she?

MESSENGER
In Sicyon.
Her length of sickness, with what else more serious
Importeth thee to know, this bears.

*He gives him the letter*

ANTONY Forbear me.

*Exit Messenger*

There's a great spirit gone! Thus did I desire it.
What our contempts doth often hurl from us,
We wish it ours again. The present pleasure,
By revolution lowering, does become
The opposite of itself. She's good, being gone;
The hand could pluck her back that shoved her on.
I must from this enchanting queen break off.
Ten thousand harms, more than the ills I know,
My idleness doth hatch. How now, Enobarbus!

*Enter Enobarbus*

ENOBARBUS What's your pleasure, sir?

ANTONY I must with haste from hence.

ENOBARBUS Why, then we kill all our women. We see how mortal an unkindness is to them. If they suffer our departure, death's the word.

ANTONY I must be gone.

ENOBARBUS Under a compelling occasion, let women die. It were pity to cast them away for nothing, though between them and a great cause they should be esteemed nothing. Cleopatra, catching but the least noise of this, dies instantly. I have seen her die twenty times upon far poorer moment. I do think there is mettle in death, which commits some loving act upon her, she hath such a celerity in dying.

ANTONY She is cunning past man's thought.

ENOBARBUS Alack, sir, no; her passions are made of nothing but the finest part of pure love. We cannot call her winds and waters sighs and tears; they are greater storms and tempests than almanacs can report. This cannot be cunning in her; if it be, she makes a shower of rain as well as Jove.

ANTONY Would I had never seen her!

ENOBARBUS O, sir, you had then left unseen a wonderful

piece of work, which not to have been blessed withal would have discredited your travel.

ANTONY Fulvia is dead.

ENOBARBUS Sir?

ANTONY Fulvia is dead.

ENOBARBUS Fulvia?

ANTONY Dead.

ENOBARBUS Why, sir, give the gods a thankful sacrifice. When it pleaseth their deities to take the wife of a man from him, it shows to man the tailors of the earth; comforting therein that when old robes are worn out there are members to make new. If there were no more women but Fulvia, then had you indeed a cut, and the case to be lamented. This grief is crowned with consolation: your old smock brings forth a new petticoat; and indeed the tears live in an onion that should water this sorrow.

ANTONY

The business she hath broachèd in the state
Cannot endure my absence.

ENOBARBUS And the business you have broached here cannot be without you; especially that of Cleopatra's, which wholly depends on your abode.

ANTONY

No more light answers. Let our officers
Have notice what we purpose. I shall break
The cause of our expedience to the Queen
And get her leave to part. For not alone
The death of Fulvia, with more urgent touches,
Do strongly speak to us, but the letters too
Of many our contriving friends in Rome
Petition us at home. Sextus Pompeius
Hath given the dare to Caesar and commands
The empire of the sea. Our slippery people,

Whose love is never linked to the deserver
Till his deserts are past, begin to throw
Pompey the Great and all his dignities
Upon his son; who, high in name and power,
Higher than both in blood and life, stands up
For the main soldier; whose quality, going on,
The sides o'th'world may danger. Much is breeding
Which, like the courser's hair, hath yet but life
And not a serpent's poison. Say our pleasure,
To such whose place is under us, requires
Our quick remove from hence.

ENOBARBUS I shall do't. *Exeunt*

## I.3

*Enter Cleopatra, Charmian, Alexas, and Iras*

CLEOPATRA
Where is he?

CHARMIAN I did not see him since.

CLEOPATRA (*to Alexas*)
See where he is, who's with him, what he does.
I did not send you. If you find him sad,
Say I am dancing; if in mirth, report
That I am sudden sick. Quick, and return.
*Exit Alexas*

CHARMIAN
Madam, methinks, if you did love him dearly,
You do not hold the method to enforce
The like from him.

CLEOPATRA What should I do I do not?

CHARMIAN
In each thing give him way. Cross him in nothing.

CLEOPATRA
Thou teachest like a fool: the way to lose him.

CHARMIAN

Tempt him not so too far. I wish, forbear.
In time we hate that which we often fear.

*Enter Antony*

But here comes Antony.

CLEOPATRA I am sick and sullen.

ANTONY

I am sorry to give breathing to my purpose –

CLEOPATRA

Help me away, dear Charmian! I shall fall.
It cannot be thus long; the sides of nature
Will not sustain it.

ANTONY Now, my dearest queen –

CLEOPATRA

Pray you, stand farther from me.

ANTONY What's the matter?

CLEOPATRA

I know by that same eye there's some good news.
What says the married woman – you may go?
Would she had never given you leave to come!
Let her not say 'tis I that keep you here.
I have no power upon you. Hers you are.

ANTONY

The gods best know –

CLEOPATRA O, never was there queen
So mightily betrayed! Yet at the first
I saw the treasons planted.

ANTONY Cleopatra –

CLEOPATRA

Why should I think you can be mine, and true –
Though you in swearing shake the thronèd gods –
Who have been false to Fulvia? Riotous madness,
To be entangled with those mouth-made vows
Which break themselves in swearing!

ANTONY Most sweet queen –

CLEOPATRA

Nay, pray you seek no colour for your going,
But bid farewell, and go. When you sued staying,
Then was the time for words. No going then!
Eternity was in our lips and eyes,
Bliss in our brows' bent; none our parts so poor
But was a race of heaven. They are so still,
Or thou, the greatest soldier of the world,
Art turned the greatest liar.

ANTONY How now, lady!

CLEOPATRA

I would I had thy inches. Thou shouldst know
There were a heart in Egypt.

ANTONY Hear me, Queen.
The strong necessity of time commands
Our services awhile; but my full heart
Remains in use with you. Our Italy
Shines o'er with civil swords. Sextus Pompeius
Makes his approaches to the port of Rome.
Equality of two domestic powers
Breed scrupulous faction; the hated, grown to strength,
Are newly grown to love. The condemned Pompey,
Rich in his father's honour, creeps apace
Into the hearts of such as have not thrived
Upon the present state, whose numbers threaten;
And quietness, grown sick of rest, would purge
By any desperate change. My more particular,
And that which most with you should safe my going,
Is Fulvia's death.

CLEOPATRA

Though age from folly could not give me freedom,
It does from childishness. Can Fulvia die?

ANTONY

She's dead, my queen.
Look here,
(*he gives her the letter*)
and at thy sovereign leisure read
The garboils she awaked. At the last, best,
See when and where she died.

CLEOPATRA O most false love!
Where be the sacred vials thou shouldst fill
With sorrowful water? Now I see, I see,
In Fulvia's death, how mine received shall be.

ANTONY

Quarrel no more, but be prepared to know
The purposes I bear; which are, or cease,
As you shall give th'advice. By the fire
That quickens Nilus' slime, I go from hence
Thy soldier-servant, making peace or war
As thou affects.

CLEOPATRA Cut my lace, Charmian, come.
But let it be. I am quickly ill and well,
So Antony loves.

ANTONY My precious queen, forbear,
And give true evidence to his love, which stands
An honourable trial.

CLEOPATRA So Fulvia told me.
I prithee turn aside and weep for her;
Then bid adieu to me, and say the tears
Belong to Egypt. Good now, play one scene
Of excellent dissembling, and let it look
Like perfect honour.

ANTONY You'll heat my blood; no more.

CLEOPATRA

You can do better yet; but this is meetly.

ANTONY
Now by my sword –
CLEOPATRA And target. Still he mends.
But this is not the best. Look, prithee, Charmian,
How this Herculean Roman does become
The carriage of his chafe.
ANTONY I'll leave you, lady.
CLEOPATRA
Courteous lord, one word.
Sir, you and I must part, but that's not it.
Sir, you and I have loved, but there's not it.
That you know well. Something it is I would –
O, my oblivion is a very Antony,
And I am all forgotten.
ANTONY But that your royalty
Holds idleness your subject, I should take you
For idleness itself.
CLEOPATRA 'Tis sweating labour
To bear such idleness so near the heart
As Cleopatra this. But, sir, forgive me,
Since my becomings kill me when they do not
Eye well to you. Your honour calls you hence.
Therefore be deaf to my unpitied folly,
And all the gods go with you! Upon your sword
Sit laurel victory, and smooth success
Be strewed before your feet!
ANTONY Let us go. Come.
Our separation so abides and flies
That thou residing here goes yet with me,
And I hence fleeting here remain with thee.
Away! *Exeunt*

## 1.4

*Enter Octavius Caesar, reading a letter, Lepidus, and their train*

CAESAR

You may see, Lepidus, and henceforth know
It is not Caesar's natural vice to hate
Our great competitor. From Alexandria
This is the news: he fishes, drinks, and wastes
The lamps of night in revel; is not more manlike
Than Cleopatra, nor the queen of Ptolemy
More womanly than he; hardly gave audience, or
Vouchsafed to think he had partners. You shall find there
A man who is the abstract of all faults
That all men follow.

LEPIDUS

I must not think there are
Evils enow to darken all his goodness.
His faults, in him, seem as the spots of heaven,
More fiery by night's blackness, hereditary
Rather than purchased, what he cannot change
Than what he chooses.

CAESAR

You are too indulgent. Let's grant it is not
Amiss to tumble on the bed of Ptolemy,
To give a kingdom for a mirth, to sit
And keep the turn of tippling with a slave,
To reel the streets at noon, and stand the buffet
With knaves that smells of sweat. Say this becomes him –
As his composure must be rare indeed
Whom these things cannot blemish – yet must Antony
No way excuse his foils when we do bear
So great weight in his lightness. If he filled
His vacancy with his voluptuousness,
Full surfeits and the dryness of his bones
Call on him for't. But to confound such time
That drums him from his sport and speaks as loud

As his own state and ours, 'tis to be chid
As we rate boys who, being mature in knowledge,
Pawn their experience to their present pleasure
And so rebel to judgement.

*Enter a Messenger*

LEPIDUS Here's more news.

MESSENGER
Thy biddings have been done; and every hour,
Most noble Caesar, shalt thou have report
How 'tis abroad. Pompey is strong at sea,
And it appears he is beloved of those
That only have feared Caesar; to the ports
The discontents repair, and men's reports
Give him much wronged.

CAESAR I should have known no less.
It hath been taught us from the primal state
That he which is was wished until he were;
And the ebbed man, ne'er loved till ne'er worth love,
Comes deared by being lacked. This common body,
Like to a vagabond flag upon the stream,
Goes to and back, lackeying the varying tide,
To rot itself with motion.

MESSENGER Caesar, I bring thee word
Menecrates and Menas, famous pirates,
Makes the sea serve them, which they ear and wound
With keels of every kind. Many hot inroads
They make in Italy. The borders maritime
Lack blood to think on't, and flush youth revolt.
No vessel can peep forth but 'tis as soon
Taken as seen; for Pompey's name strikes more
Than could his war resisted.

CAESAR Antony,
Leave thy lascivious wassails. When thou once
Was beaten from Modena, where thou slew'st

Hirtius and Pansa, consuls, at thy heel
Did famine follow, whom thou fought'st against,
Though daintily brought up, with patience more
Than savages could suffer. Thou didst drink
The stale of horses and the gilded puddle
Which beasts would cough at. Thy palate then did deign
The roughest berry on the rudest hedge.
Yea, like the stag when snow the pasture sheets,
The barks of trees thou browsèd'st. On the Alps
It is reported thou didst eat strange flesh,
Which some did die to look on. And all this –
It wounds thine honour that I speak it now –
Was borne so like a soldier that thy cheek
So much as lanked not.

LEPIDUS 'Tis pity of him.

CAESAR
Let his shames quickly
Drive him to Rome. 'Tis time we twain
Did show ourselves i'th'field; and to that end
Assemble we immediate council. Pompey
Thrives in our idleness.

LEPIDUS Tomorrow, Caesar,
I shall be furnished to inform you rightly
Both what by sea and land I can be able
To front this present time.

CAESAR Till which encounter,
It is my business too. Farewell.

LEPIDUS
Farewell, my lord. What you shall know meantime
Of stirs abroad, I shall beseech you, sir,
To let me be partaker.

CAESAR Doubt not, sir;
I knew it for my bond. *Exeunt*

I.5

*Enter Cleopatra, Charmian, Iras, and Mardian*

CLEOPATRA
Charmian!

CHARMIAN
Madam?

CLEOPATRA (*yawning*)
Ha, ha.
Give me to drink mandragora.

CHARMIAN
Why, madam?

CLEOPATRA
That I might sleep out this great gap of time
My Antony is away.

CHARMIAN
You think of him too much.

CLEOPATRA
O, 'tis treason!

CHARMIAN
Madam, I trust, not so.

CLEOPATRA
Thou, eunuch Mardian!

MARDIAN
What's your highness' pleasure?

CLEOPATRA
Not now to hear thee sing. I take no pleasure
In aught an eunuch has. 'Tis well for thee
That, being unseminared, thy freer thoughts
May not fly forth of Egypt. Hast thou affections?

MARDIAN
Yes, gracious madam.

CLEOPATRA
Indeed?

MARDIAN
Not in deed, madam; for I can do nothing
But what indeed is honest to be done.
Yet have I fierce affections, and think
What Venus did with Mars.

CLEOPATRA
O, Charmian,

Where think'st thou he is now? Stands he, or sits he?
Or does he walk? Or is he on his horse?
O happy horse, to bear the weight of Antony!
Do bravely, horse, for wot'st thou whom thou mov'st?
The demi-Atlas of this earth, the arm
And burgonet of men. He's speaking now,
Or murmuring 'Where's my serpent of old Nile?'
For so he calls me. Now I feed myself
With most delicious poison. Think on me,
That am with Phoebus' amorous pinches black
And wrinkled deep in time. Broad-fronted Caesar,
When thou wast here above the ground, I was
A morsel for a monarch; and great Pompey
Would stand and make his eyes grow in my brow;
There would he anchor his aspect, and die
With looking on his life.

*Enter Alexas*

ALEXAS Sovereign of Egypt, hail!

CLEOPATRA
How much unlike art thou Mark Antony!
Yet, coming from him, that great medicine hath
With his tinct gilded thee.
How goes it with my brave Mark Antony?

ALEXAS
Last thing he did, dear Queen,
He kissed – the last of many doubled kisses –
This orient pearl. His speech sticks in my heart.

CLEOPATRA
Mine ear must pluck it thence.

ALEXAS 'Good friend,' quoth he,
'Say the firm Roman to great Egypt sends
This treasure of an oyster; at whose foot,
To mend the petty present, I will piece
Her opulent throne with kingdoms. All the East,

Say thou, shall call her mistress.' So he nodded,
And soberly did mount an arrogant steed,
Who neighed so high that what I would have spoke
Was beastly dumbed by him.

CLEOPATRA What was he, sad or merry?

ALEXAS

Like to the time o'th'year between the extremes
Of hot and cold, he was nor sad nor merry.

CLEOPATRA

O well-divided disposition! Note him,
Note him, good Charmian, 'tis the man; but note him!
He was not sad, for he would shine on those
That make their looks by his; he was not merry,
Which seemed to tell them his remembrance lay
In Egypt with his joy; but between both.
O heavenly mingle! Be'st thou sad or merry,
The violence of either thee becomes,
So does it no man else. Met'st thou my posts?

ALEXAS

Ay, madam, twenty several messengers.
Why do you send so thick?

CLEOPATRA Who's born that day
When I forget to send to Antony
Shall die a beggar. Ink and paper, Charmian.
Welcome, my good Alexas. Did I, Charmian,
Ever love Caesar so?

CHARMIAN O, that brave Caesar!

CLEOPATRA

Be choked with such another emphasis!
Say 'the brave Antony'.

CHARMIAN The valiant Caesar!

CLEOPATRA

By Isis, I will give thee bloody teeth
If thou with Caesar paragon again

My man of men.

CHARMIAN By your most gracious pardon,
I sing but after you.

CLEOPATRA My salad days,
When I was green in judgement, cold in blood,
To say as I said then. But come, away,
Get me ink and paper.
He shall have every day a several greeting,
Or I'll unpeople Egypt. *Exeunt*

*

## II.I

*Enter Pompey, Menecrates, and Menas, in warlike manner*

POMPEY
If the great gods be just, they shall assist
The deeds of justest men.

MENECRATES Know, worthy Pompey,
That what they do delay they not deny.

POMPEY
Whiles we are suitors to their throne, decays
The thing we sue for.

MENECRATES We, ignorant of ourselves,
Beg often our own harms, which the wise powers
Deny us for our good; so find we profit
By losing of our prayers.

POMPEY I shall do well.
The people love me, and the sea is mine;
My powers are crescent, and my auguring hope
Says it will come to th'full. Mark Antony
In Egypt sits at dinner, and will make
No wars without doors. Caesar gets money where
He loses hearts. Lepidus flatters both,

Of both is flattered; but he neither loves,
Nor either cares for him.

MENAS
Caesar and Lepidus
Are in the field. A mighty strength they carry.

POMPEY
Where have you this? 'Tis false.

MENAS
From Silvius, sir.

POMPEY
He dreams. I know they are in Rome together,
Looking for Antony. But all the charms of love,
Salt Cleopatra, soften thy waned lip!
Let witchcraft join with beauty, lust with both!
Tie up the libertine in a field of feasts;
Keep his brain fuming. Epicurean cooks
Sharpen with cloyless sauce his appetite,
That sleep and feeding may prorogue his honour
Even till a Lethe'd dullness –

*Enter Varrius*

How now, Varrius?

VARRIUS
This is most certain that I shall deliver:
Mark Antony is every hour in Rome
Expected. Since he went from Egypt 'tis
A space for farther travel.

POMPEY
I could have given less matter
A better ear. Menas, I did not think
This amorous surfeiter would have donned his helm
For such a petty war. His soldiership
Is twice the other twain. But let us rear
The higher our opinion, that our stirring
Can from the lap of Egypt's widow pluck
The ne'er lust-wearied Antony.

MENAS
I cannot hope
Caesar and Antony shall well greet together.

His wife that's dead did trespasses to Caesar.
His brother warred upon him – although, I think,
Not moved by Antony.

POMPEY I know not, Menas,
How lesser enmities may give way to greater.
Were't not that we stand up against them all,
'Twere pregnant they should square between themselves,
For they have entertainèd cause enough
To draw their swords. But how the fear of us
May cement their divisions and bind up
The petty difference, we yet not know.
Be't as our gods will have't! It only stands
Our lives upon to use our strongest hands.
Come, Menas. *Exeunt*

## II.2

*Enter Enobarbus and Lepidus*

LEPIDUS
Good Enobarbus, 'tis a worthy deed,
And shall become you well, to entreat your captain
To soft and gentle speech.

ENOBARBUS I shall entreat him
To answer like himself. If Caesar move him,
Let Antony look over Caesar's head
And speak as loud as Mars. By Jupiter,
Were I the wearer of Antonio's beard,
I would not shave't today.

LEPIDUS 'Tis not a time
For private stomaching.

ENOBARBUS Every time
Serves for the matter that is then born in't.

LEPIDUS
But small to greater matters must give way.

ENOBARBUS
Not if the small come first.
LEPIDUS Your speech is passion;
But pray you stir no embers up. Here comes
The noble Antony.
*Enter Antony and Ventidius*
ENOBARBUS And yonder Caesar.
*Enter Caesar, Maecenas, and Agrippa*
ANTONY
If we compose well here, to Parthia.
Hark, Ventidius.
CAESAR I do not know,
Maecenas; ask Agrippa.
LEPIDUS (*to Caesar and Antony*) Noble friends,
That which combined us was most great, and let not
A leaner action rend us. What's amiss,
May it be gently heard. When we debate
Our trivial difference loud, we do commit
Murder in healing wounds. Then, noble partners,
The rather for I earnestly beseech,
Touch you the sourest points with sweetest terms,
Nor curstness grow to th'matter.
ANTONY 'Tis spoken well.
Were we before our armies, and to fight,
I should do thus.
*Flourish*
CAESAR
Welcome to Rome.
ANTONY
Thank you.
CAESAR
Sit.
ANTONY
Sit, sir.

CAESAR
Nay then.
*They sit*

ANTONY
I learn you take things ill which are not so,
Or, being, concern you not.

CAESAR I must be laughed at
If, or for nothing or a little, I
Should say myself offended, and with you
Chiefly i'th'world; more laughed at that I should
Once name you derogately, when to sound your name
It not concerned me.

ANTONY My being in Egypt, Caesar,
What was't to you?

CAESAR
No more than my residing here at Rome
Might be to you in Egypt. Yet if you there
Did practise on my state, your being in Egypt
Might be my question.

ANTONY How intend you – practised?

CAESAR
You may be pleased to catch at mine intent
By what did here befall me. Your wife and brother
Made wars upon me, and their contestation
Was theme for you. You were the word of war.

ANTONY
You do mistake your business. My brother never
Did urge me in his act. I did inquire it,
And have my learning from some true reports
That drew their swords with you. Did he not rather
Discredit my authority with yours,
And make the wars alike against my stomach,
Having alike your cause? Of this, my letters
Before did satisfy you. If you'll patch a quarrel,

As matter whole you have to make it with,
It must not be with this.

CAESAR You praise yourself
By laying defects of judgement to me, but
You patched up your excuses.

ANTONY Not so, not so;
I know you could not lack, I am certain on't,
Very necessity of this thought, that I,
Your partner in the cause 'gainst which he fought,
Could not with graceful eyes attend those wars
Which fronted mine own peace. As for my wife,
I would you had her spirit in such another;
The third o'th'world is yours, which with a snaffle
You may pace easy, but not such a wife.

ENOBARBUS Would we had all such wives, that the men might go to wars with the women.

ANTONY
So much uncurbable, her garboils, Caesar,
Made out of her impatience – which not wanted
Shrewdness of policy too – I grieving grant
Did you too much disquiet. For that you must
But say I could not help it.

CAESAR I wrote to you
When, rioting in Alexandria, you
Did pocket up my letters, and with taunts
Did gibe my missive out of audience.

ANTONY Sir,
He fell upon me, ere admitted, then.
Three kings I had newly feasted, and did want
Of what I was i'th'morning; but next day
I told him of myself, which was as much
As to have asked him pardon. Let this fellow
Be nothing of our strife; if we contend,
Out of our question wipe him.

CAESAR You have broken
The article of your oath, which you shall never
Have tongue to charge me with.

LEPIDUS Soft, Caesar!

ANTONY
No, Lepidus; let him speak.
The honour is sacred which he talks on now,
Supposing that I lacked it. But on, Caesar:
The article of my oath –

CAESAR
To lend me arms and aid when I required them,
The which you both denied.

ANTONY Neglected rather;
And then when poisoned hours had bound me up
From mine own knowledge. As nearly as I may,
I'll play the penitent to you; but mine honesty
Shall not make poor my greatness, nor my power
Work without it. Truth is that Fulvia,
To have me out of Egypt, made wars here,
For which myself, the ignorant motive, do
So far ask pardon as befits mine honour
To stoop in such a case.

LEPIDUS 'Tis noble spoken.

MAECENAS
If it might please you to enforce no further
The griefs between ye: to forget them quite
Were to remember that the present need
Speaks to atone you.

LEPIDUS Worthily spoken, Maecenas.

ENOBARBUS Or, if you borrow one another's love for the instant, you may, when you hear no more words of Pompey, return it again: you shall have time to wrangle in when you have nothing else to do.

ANTONY
Thou art a soldier only. Speak no more.

ENOBARBUS That truth should be silent I had almost forgot.

ANTONY
You wrong this presence; therefore speak no more.

ENOBARBUS Go to, then; your considerate stone.

CAESAR
I do not much dislike the matter, but
The manner of his speech; for't cannot be
We shall remain in friendship, our conditions
So diff'ring in their acts. Yet if I knew
What hoop should hold us staunch, from edge to edge
O'th'world I would pursue it.

AGRIPPA Give me leave, Caesar.

CAESAR
Speak, Agrippa.

AGRIPPA
Thou hast a sister by the mother's side,
Admired Octavia. Great Mark Antony
Is now a widower.

CAESAR Say not so, Agrippa.
If Cleopatra heard you, your reproof
Were well deserved of rashness.

ANTONY
I am not married, Caesar. Let me hear
Agrippa further speak.

AGRIPPA
To hold you in perpetual amity,
To make you brothers, and to knit your hearts
With an unslipping knot, take Antony
Octavia to his wife; whose beauty claims
No worse a husband than the best of men;
Whose virtue and whose general graces speak

That which none else can utter. By this marriage
All little jealousies, which now seem great,
And all great fears, which now import their dangers,
Would then be nothing. Truths would be tales,
Where now half-tales be truths. Her love to both
Would each to other, and all loves to both,
Draw after her. Pardon what I have spoke,
For 'tis a studied, not a present thought,
By duty ruminated.

ANTONY
Will Caesar speak?

CAESAR
Not till he hears how Antony is touched
With what is spoke already.

ANTONY
What power is in Agrippa,
If I would say 'Agrippa, be it so',
To make this good?

CAESAR
The power of Caesar, and
His power unto Octavia.

ANTONY
May I never
To this good purpose, that so fairly shows,
Dream of impediment! Let me have thy hand.
Further this act of grace, and from this hour
The heart of brothers govern in our loves
And sway our great designs.

CAESAR
There's my hand.
A sister I bequeath you whom no brother
Did ever love so dearly. Let her live
To join our kingdoms and our hearts; and never
Fly off our loves again.

LEPIDUS
Happily, amen.

ANTONY
I did not think to draw my sword 'gainst Pompey,
For he hath laid strange courtesies and great
Of late upon me. I must thank him only,

Lest my remembrance suffer ill report;
At heel of that, defy him.

LEPIDUS Time calls upon's.
Of us must Pompey presently be sought,
Or else he seeks out us.

ANTONY Where lies he?

CAESAR
About the Mount Misena.

ANTONY What is his strength?

CAESAR
By land, great and increasing; but by sea
He is an absolute master.

ANTONY So is the fame.
Would we had spoke together! Haste we for it.
Yet, ere we put ourselves in arms, dispatch we
The business we have talked of.

CAESAR With most gladness;
And do invite you to my sister's view,
Whither straight I'll lead you.

ANTONY Let us, Lepidus,
Not lack your company.

LEPIDUS Noble Antony,
Not sickness should detain me.

*Flourish. Exeunt all but Enobarbus, Agrippa, and Maecenas*

MAECENAS Welcome from Egypt, sir.

ENOBARBUS Half the heart of Caesar, worthy Maecenas.
My honourable friend, Agrippa.

AGRIPPA Good Enobarbus.

MAECENAS We have cause to be glad that matters are so well disgested. You stayed well by't in Egypt.

ENOBARBUS Ay, sir, we did sleep day out of countenance and made the night light with drinking.

MAECENAS Eight wild boars roasted whole at a breakfast,

and but twelve persons there. Is this true?

ENOBARBUS This was but as a fly by an eagle. We had much more monstrous matter of feast, which worthily deserved noting.

MAECENAS She's a most triumphant lady, if report be square to her.

ENOBARBUS When she first met Mark Antony, she pursed up his heart, upon the river of Cydnus.

AGRIPPA There she appeared indeed! Or my reporter devised well for her.

ENOBARBUS
I will tell you.
The barge she sat in, like a burnished throne,
Burned on the water. The poop was beaten gold;
Purple the sails, and so perfumèd that
The winds were lovesick with them. The oars were silver,
Which to the tune of flutes kept stroke and made
The water which they beat to follow faster,
As amorous of their strokes. For her own person,
It beggared all description. She did lie
In her pavilion, cloth-of-gold of tissue,
O'erpicturing that Venus where we see
The fancy outwork nature. On each side her
Stood pretty dimpled boys, like smiling cupids,
With divers-coloured fans, whose wind did seem
To glow the delicate cheeks which they did cool,
And what they undid did.

AGRIPPA O, rare for Antony!

ENOBARBUS
Her gentlewomen, like the Nereides,
So many mermaids, tended her i'th'eyes,
And made their bends adornings. At the helm
A seeming mermaid steers. The silken tackle
Swell with the touches of those flower-soft hands,

That yarely frame the office. From the barge
A strange invisible perfume hits the sense
Of the adjacent wharfs. The city cast
Her people out upon her; and Antony,
Enthroned i'th'market-place, did sit alone,
Whistling to th'air; which, but for vacancy,
Had gone to gaze on Cleopatra too,
And made a gap in nature.

AGRIPPA Rare Egyptian!

ENOBARBUS

Upon her landing, Antony sent to her,
Invited her to supper. She replied
It should be better he became her guest;
Which she entreated. Our courteous Antony,
Whom ne'er the word of 'No' woman heard speak,
Being barbered ten times o'er, goes to the feast,
And, for his ordinary, pays his heart
For what his eyes eat only.

AGRIPPA Royal wench!
She made great Caesar lay his sword to bed.
He ploughed her, and she cropped.

ENOBARBUS I saw her once
Hop forty paces through the public street;
And, having lost her breath, she spoke, and panted,
That she did make defect perfection,
And, breathless, power breathe forth.

MAECENAS

Now Antony must leave her utterly.

ENOBARBUS

Never; he will not.
Age cannot wither her, nor custom stale
Her infinite variety. Other women cloy
The appetites they feed, but she makes hungry
Where most she satisfies; for vilest things

Become themselves in her, that the holy priests
Bless her when she is riggish.

MAECENAS
If beauty, wisdom, modesty, can settle
The heart of Antony, Octavia is
A blessèd lottery to him.

AGRIPPA Let us go.
Good Enobarbus, make yourself my guest
Whilst you abide here.

ENOBARBUS Humbly, sir, I thank you.
*Exeunt*

## II.3

*Enter Antony and Caesar, with Octavia between them*

ANTONY
The world and my great office will sometimes
Divide me from your bosom.

OCTAVIA All which time,
Before the gods my knee shall bow my prayers
To them for you.

ANTONY Good night, sir. My Octavia,
Read not my blemishes in the world's report.
I have not kept my square, but that to come
Shall all be done by th'rule. Good night, dear lady.
Good night, sir.

CAESAR Good night. *Exeunt Caesar and Octavia*

*Enter the Soothsayer*

ANTONY Now, sirrah: you do wish yourself in Egypt?

SOOTHSAYER Would I had never come from thence, nor you thither.

ANTONY If you can, your reason?

SOOTHSAYER I see it in my motion, have it not in my tongue; but yet hie you to Egypt again.

ANTONY

Say to me, whose fortunes shall rise higher,
Caesar's, or mine?

SOOTHSAYER

Caesar's.
Therefore, O Antony, stay not by his side.
Thy daemon – that thy spirit which keeps thee – is
Noble, courageous, high, unmatchable,
Where Caesar's is not. But near him thy angel
Becomes afeard, as being o'erpowered. Therefore
Make space enough between you.

ANTONY

Speak this no more.

SOOTHSAYER

To none but thee; no more but when to thee.
If thou dost play with him at any game,
Thou art sure to lose; and of that natural luck
He beats thee 'gainst the odds. Thy lustre thickens
When he shines by. I say again, thy spirit
Is all afraid to govern thee near him;
But, he away, 'tis noble.

ANTONY

Get thee gone.
Say to Ventidius I would speak with him.
He shall to Parthia.

*Exit Soothsayer*

Be it art or hap,
He hath spoken true. The very dice obey him,
And in our sports my better cunning faints
Under his chance. If we draw lots, he speeds;
His cocks do win the battle still of mine
When it is all to nought, and his quails ever
Beat mine, inhooped, at odds. I will to Egypt;
And though I make this marriage for my peace,
I'th'East my pleasure lies.

*Enter Ventidius*

O, come, Ventidius.
You must to Parthia. Your commission's ready;
Follow me, and receive't. *Exeunt*

II.4 *Enter Lepidus, Maecenas, and Agrippa*

LEPIDUS
Trouble yourselves no further. Pray you, hasten
Your generals after.

AGRIPPA Sir, Mark Antony
Will e'en but kiss Octavia, and we'll follow.

LEPIDUS
Till I shall see you in your soldier's dress,
Which will become you both, farewell.

MAECENAS We shall,
As I conceive the journey, be at th'Mount
Before you, Lepidus.

LEPIDUS Your way is shorter.
My purposes do draw me much about.
You'll win two days upon me.

MAECENAS *and* AGRIPPA Sir, good success.

LEPIDUS
Farewell. *Exeunt*

II.5 *Enter Cleopatra, Charmian, Iras, and Alexas*

CLEOPATRA
Give me some music – music, moody food
Of us that trade in love.

ALL The music, ho!

*Enter Mardian the eunuch*

CLEOPATRA
Let it alone! Let's to billiards. Come, Charmian.

CHARMIAN
My arm is sore; best play with Mardian.

CLEOPATRA
As well a woman with an eunuch played
As with a woman. Come, you'll play with me, sir?

MARDIAN
As well as I can, madam.

CLEOPATRA
And when good will is showed, though't come too short,
The actor may plead pardon. I'll none now.
Give me mine angle. We'll to th'river; there,
My music playing far off, I will betray
Tawny-finned fishes. My bended hook shall pierce
Their slimy jaws; and as I draw them up,
I'll think them every one an Antony,
And say 'Ah, ha! Y'are caught!'

CHARMIAN 'Twas merry when
You wagered on your angling; when your diver
Did hang a salt fish on his hook, which he
With fervency drew up.

CLEOPATRA That time – O times! –
I laughed him out of patience; and that night
I laughed him into patience; and next morn,
Ere the ninth hour, I drunk him to his bed;
Then put my tires and mantles on him, whilst
I wore his sword Philippan.

*Enter a Messenger*

O, from Italy!
Ram thou thy fruitful tidings in mine ears,
That long time have been barren.

MESSENGER Madam, madam –

CLEOPATRA
Antonio's dead! If thou say so, villain,
Thou kill'st thy mistress; but well and free,

If thou so yield him, there is gold and here
My bluest veins to kiss, a hand that kings
Have lipped, and trembled kissing.

MESSENGER
First, madam, he is well.

CLEOPATRA
Why, there's more gold.
But, sirrah, mark, we use
To say the dead are well. Bring it to that,
The gold I give thee will I melt and pour
Down thy ill-uttering throat.

MESSENGER
Good madam, hear me.

CLEOPATRA
Well, go to, I will.
But there's no goodness in thy face if Antony
Be free and healthful; so tart a favour
To trumpet such good tidings? If not well,
Thou shouldst come like a Fury crowned with snakes,
Not like a formal man.

MESSENGER
Will't please you hear me?

CLEOPATRA
I have a mind to strike thee ere thou speak'st.
Yet, if thou say Antony lives, is well,
Or friends with Caesar, or not captive to him,
I'll set thee in a shower of gold, and hail
Rich pearls upon thee.

MESSENGER
Madam, he's well.

CLEOPATRA
Well said.

MESSENGER
And friends with Caesar.

CLEOPATRA
Th'art an honest man.

MESSENGER
Caesar and he are greater friends than ever.

CLEOPATRA
Make thee a fortune from me.

MESSENGER But yet, madam –

CLEOPATRA
I do not like 'But yet'; it does allay
The good precedence. Fie upon 'But yet'!
'But yet' is as a gaoler to bring forth
Some monstrous malefactor. Prithee, friend,
Pour out the pack of matter to mine ear,
The good and bad together. He's friends with Caesar,
In state of health, thou sayst, and, thou sayst, free.

MESSENGER
Free, madam! No; I made no such report.
He's bound unto Octavia.

CLEOPATRA For what good turn?

MESSENGER
For the best turn i'th'bed.

CLEOPATRA I am pale, Charmian.

MESSENGER
Madam, he's married to Octavia.

CLEOPATRA
The most infectious pestilence upon thee!
*She strikes him down*

MESSENGER
Good madam, patience.

CLEOPATRA What say you?
*She strikes him*
Hence,
Horrible villain, or I'll spurn thine eyes
Like balls before me! I'll unhair thy head!
*She hales him up and down*
Thou shalt be whipped with wire and stewed in brine,
Smarting in lingering pickle!

MESSENGER Gracious madam,
I that do bring the news made not the match.

CLEOPATRA
Say 'tis not so, a province I will give thee,
And make thy fortunes proud. The blow thou hadst
Shall make thy peace for moving me to rage,
And I will boot thee with what gift beside
Thy modesty can beg.

MESSENGER He's married, madam.

CLEOPATRA
Rogue, thou hast lived too long.
*She draws a knife*

MESSENGER Nay, then I'll run.
What mean you, madam? I have made no fault. *Exit*

CHARMIAN
Good madam, keep yourself within yourself.
The man is innocent.

CLEOPATRA
Some innocents 'scape not the thunderbolt.
Melt Egypt into Nile, and kindly creatures
Turn all to serpents! Call the slave again.
Though I am mad, I will not bite him. Call!

CHARMIAN
He is afeard to come.

CLEOPATRA I will not hurt him.
*Exit Charmian*
These hands do lack nobility, that they strike
A meaner than myself; since I myself
Have given myself the cause.
*Enter Charmian and the Messenger*
Come hither, sir.
Though it be honest, it is never good
To bring bad news. Give to a gracious message
An host of tongues, but let ill tidings tell
Themselves when they be felt.

MESSENGER I have done my duty.

CLEOPATRA
Is he married?
I cannot hate thee worser than I do
If thou again say 'Yes.'
MESSENGER He's married, madam.
CLEOPATRA
The gods confound thee! Dost thou hold there still?
MESSENGER
Should I lie, madam?
CLEOPATRA O, I would thou didst,
So half my Egypt were submerged and made
A cistern for scaled snakes! Go get thee hence.
Hadst thou Narcissus in thy face, to me
Thou wouldst appear most ugly. He is married?
MESSENGER
I crave your highness' pardon.
CLEOPATRA He is married?
MESSENGER
Take no offence that I would not offend you;
To punish me for what you make me do
Seems much unequal. He's married to Octavia.
CLEOPATRA
O, that his fault should make a knave of thee,
That art not what th'art sure of! Get thee hence.
The merchandise which thou hast brought from Rome
Are all too dear for me. Lie they upon thy hand,
And be undone by 'em. *Exit Messenger*
CHARMIAN Good your highness, patience.
CLEOPATRA
In praising Antony I have dispraised Caesar.
CHARMIAN
Many times, madam.
CLEOPATRA I am paid for't now.
Lead me from hence;

I faint. O, Iras, Charmian! 'Tis no matter.
Go to the fellow, good Alexas; bid him
Report the feature of Octavia, her years,
Her inclination. Let him not leave out
The colour of her hair. Bring me word quickly.

*Exit Alexas*

Let him for ever go – let him not, Charmian.
Though he be painted one way like a Gorgon,
The other way's a Mars. (*To Mardian*) Bid you Alexas
Bring me word how tall she is. – Pity me, Charmian,
But do not speak to me. Lead me to my chamber.

*Exeunt*

## II.6

*Flourish. Enter Pompey and Menas at one door, with drum and trumpet; at another, Caesar, Lepidus, Antony, Enobarbus, Maecenas, Agrippa, with Soldiers marching*

POMPEY

Your hostages I have; so have you mine;
And we shall talk before we fight.

CAESAR Most meet

That first we come to words; and therefore have we
Our written purposes before us sent;
Which if thou hast considered, let us know
If 'twill tie up thy discontented sword
And carry back to Sicily much tall youth
That else must perish here.

POMPEY To you all three,

The senators alone of this great world,
Chief factors for the gods: I do not know
Wherefore my father should revengers want,
Having a son and friends, since Julius Caesar,

Who at Philippi the good Brutus ghosted,
There saw you labouring for him. What was't
That moved pale Cassius to conspire? And what
Made the all-honoured, honest, Roman Brutus,
With the armed rest, courtiers of beauteous freedom,
To drench the Capitol, but that they would
Have one man but a man? And that is it
Hath made me rig my navy, at whose burden
The angered ocean foams; with which I meant
To scourge th'ingratitude that despiteful Rome
Cast on my noble father.

CAESAR Take your time.

ANTONY
Thou canst not fear us, Pompey, with thy sails.
We'll speak with thee at sea. At land thou know'st
How much we do o'ercount thee.

POMPEY At land indeed
Thou dost o'ercount me of my father's house;
But since the cuckoo builds not for himself,
Remain in't as thou mayst.

LEPIDUS Be pleased to tell us –
For this is from the present – how you take
The offers we have sent you.

CAESAR There's the point.

ANTONY
Which do not be entreated to, but weigh
What it is worth embraced.

CAESAR And what may follow,
To try a larger fortune.

POMPEY You have made me offer
Of Sicily, Sardinia; and I must
Rid all the sea of pirates; then, to send
Measures of wheat to Rome; this 'greed upon,

To part with unhacked edges and bear back
Our targes undinted.

ALL THE TRIUMVIRS That's our offer.

POMPEY Know, then,
I came before you here a man prepared
To take this offer. But Mark Antony
Put me to some impatience. Though I lose
The praise of it by telling, you must know,
When Caesar and your brother were at blows,
Your mother came to Sicily and did find
Her welcome friendly.

ANTONY I have heard it, Pompey,
And am well studied for a liberal thanks,
Which I do owe you.

POMPEY Let me have your hand.
I did not think, sir, to have met you here.

ANTONY
The beds i'th'East are soft; and thanks to you,
That called me timelier than my purpose hither;
For I have gained by't.

CAESAR (*to Pompey*) Since I saw you last
There is a change upon you.

POMPEY Well, I know not
What counts harsh Fortune casts upon my face,
But in my bosom shall she never come
To make my heart her vassal.

LEPIDUS Well met here.

POMPEY
I hope so, Lepidus. Thus we are agreed.
I crave our composition may be written,
And sealed between us.

CAESAR That's the next to do.

POMPEY
We'll feast each other ere we part, and let's

Draw lots who shall begin.

ANTONY
That will I, Pompey.

POMPEY
No, Antony, take the lot.
But, first or last, your fine Egyptian cookery
Shall have the fame. I have heard that Julius Caesar
Grew fat with feasting there.

ANTONY
You have heard much.

POMPEY
I have fair meanings, sir.

ANTONY
And fair words to them.

POMPEY
Then so much have I heard.
And I have heard Apollodorus carried –

ENOBARBUS
No more of that: he did so.

POMPEY
What, I pray you?

ENOBARBUS
A certain queen to Caesar in a mattress.

POMPEY
I know thee now. How far'st thou, soldier?

ENOBARBUS
Well;
And well am like to do, for I perceive
Four feasts are toward.

POMPEY
Let me shake thy hand.
I never hated thee; I have seen thee fight
When I have envied thy behaviour.

ENOBARBUS
Sir,
I never loved you much; but I ha'praised ye
When you have well deserved ten times as much
As I have said you did.

POMPEY
Enjoy thy plainness;
It nothing ill becomes thee.
Aboard my galley I invite you all.

Will you lead, lords?

ALL Show's the way, sir.

POMPEY Come.

*Exeunt all but Enobarbus and Menas*

MENAS (*aside*) Thy father, Pompey, would ne'er have made this treaty. – You and I have known, sir.

ENOBARBUS At sea, I think.

MENAS We have, sir.

ENOBARBUS You have done well by water.

MENAS And you by land.

ENOBARBUS I will praise any man that will praise me; though it cannot be denied what I have done by land.

MENAS Nor what I have done by water.

ENOBARBUS Yes, something you can deny for your own safety: you have been a great thief by sea.

MENAS And you by land.

ENOBARBUS There I deny my land service. But give me your hand, Menas. If our eyes had authority, here they might take two thieves kissing.

MENAS All men's faces are true, whatsome'er their hands are.

ENOBARBUS But there is never a fair woman has a true face.

MENAS No slander; they steal hearts.

ENOBARBUS We came hither to fight with you.

MENAS For my part, I am sorry it is turned to a drinking. Pompey doth this day laugh away his fortune.

ENOBARBUS If he do, sure he cannot weep't back again.

MENAS Y'have said, sir. We looked not for Mark Antony here. Pray you, is he married to Cleopatra?

ENOBARBUS Caesar's sister is called Octavia.

MENAS True, sir; she was the wife of Caius Marcellus.

ENOBARBUS But she is now the wife of Marcus Antonius.

MENAS Pray ye, sir?

ENOBARBUS 'Tis true.

MENAS Then is Caesar and he for ever knit together.

ENOBARBUS If I were bound to divine of this unity, I would not prophesy so.

MENAS I think the policy of that purpose made more in the marriage than the love of the parties.

ENOBARBUS I think so too. But you shall find the band that seems to tie their friendship together will be the very strangler of their amity. Octavia is of a holy, cold, and still conversation.

MENAS Who would not have his wife so?

ENOBARBUS Not he that himself is not so; which is Mark Antony. He will to his Egyptian dish again. Then shall the sighs of Octavia blow the fire up in Caesar, and, as I said before, that which is the strength of their amity shall prove the immediate author of their variance. Antony will use his affection where it is. He married but his occasion here.

MENAS And thus it may be. Come, sir, will you aboard? I have a health for you.

ENOBARBUS I shall take it, sir. We have used our throats in Egypt.

MENAS Come, let's away. *Exeunt*

II.7

*Music plays. Enter two or three Servants, with a banquet*

FIRST SERVANT Here they'll be, man. Some o'their plants are ill-rooted already; the least wind i'th'world will blow them down.

SECOND SERVANT Lepidus is high-coloured.

FIRST SERVANT They have made him drink alms drink.

SECOND SERVANT As they pinch one another by the disposition, he cries out 'No more'; reconciles them to his entreaty, and himself to th'drink.

FIRST SERVANT But it raises the greater war between him and his discretion.

SECOND SERVANT Why, this it is to have a name in great men's fellowship. I had as lief have a reed that will do me no service as a partisan I could not heave.

FIRST SERVANT To be called into a huge sphere, and not to be seen to move in't, are the holes where eyes should be, which pitifully disaster the cheeks.

*A sennet sounded. Enter Caesar, Antony, Pompey, Lepidus, Agrippa, Maecenas, Enobarbus, Menas, with other Captains, and a Boy*

ANTONY (*to Lepidus*)
Thus do they, sir: they take the flow o'th'Nile
By certain scales i'th'pyramid. They know
By th'height, the lowness, or the mean if dearth
Or foison follow. The higher Nilus swells,
The more it promises; as it ebbs, the seedsman
Upon the slime and ooze scatters his grain,
And shortly comes to harvest.

LEPIDUS Y'have strange serpents there.

ANTONY Ay, Lepidus.

LEPIDUS Your serpent of Egypt is bred now of your mud by the operation of your sun; so is your crocodile.

ANTONY They are so.

POMPEY Sit – and some wine! A health to Lepidus!

LEPIDUS I am not so well as I should be, but I'll ne'er out.

ENOBARBUS Not till you have slept; I fear me you'll be in till then.

LEPIDUS Nay, certainly, I have heard the Ptolemies'

pyramises are very goodly things; without contradiction I have heard that.

MENAS (*aside to Pompey*)
Pompey, a word.

POMPEY (*aside to Menas*) Say in mine ear; what is't?

MENAS (*aside to Pompey*)
Forsake thy seat, I do beseech thee, captain,
And hear me speak a word.

POMPEY (*aside to Menas*) Forbear me till anon.
(*Aloud*) This wine for Lepidus!

LEPIDUS What manner o'thing is your crocodile?

ANTONY It is shaped, sir, like itself, and it is as broad as it has breadth. It is just so high as it is, and moves with it own organs. It lives by that which nourisheth it, and the elements once out of it, it transmigrates.

LEPIDUS What colour is it of?

ANTONY Of it own colour too.

LEPIDUS 'Tis a strange serpent.

ANTONY 'Tis so; and the tears of it are wet.

CAESAR Will this description satisfy him?

ANTONY With the health that Pompey gives him; else he is a very epicure.

*Menas whispers to Pompey*

POMPEY (*aside to Menas*)
Go hang, sir, hang! Tell me of that? Away!
Do as I bid you. – Where's this cup I called for?

MENAS (*aside to Pompey*)
If for the sake of merit thou wilt hear me,
Rise from thy stool.

POMPEY (*aside to Menas*) I think th'art mad. The matter?

*He rises and they walk aside*

MENAS
I have ever held my cap off to thy fortunes.

POMPEY

Thou hast served me with much faith. What's else to say? –
Be jolly, lords.

ANTONY These quicksands, Lepidus,
Keep off them, for you sink.

MENAS

Wilt thou be lord of all the world?

POMPEY What sayst thou?

MENAS

Wilt thou be lord of the whole world? That's twice.

POMPEY

How should that be?

MENAS But entertain it,
And though thou think me poor, I am the man
Will give thee all the world.

POMPEY Hast thou drunk well?

MENAS

No, Pompey, I have kept me from the cup.
Thou art, if thou dar'st be, the earthly Jove;
Whate'er the ocean pales, or sky inclips,
Is thine, if thou wilt ha't.

POMPEY Show me which way.

MENAS

These three world-sharers, these competitors,
Are in thy vessel. Let me cut the cable;
And when we are put off, fall to their throats.
All there is thine.

POMPEY Ah, this thou shouldst have done,
And not have spoke on't. In me 'tis villainy;
In thee't had been good service. Thou must know
'Tis not my profit that does lead mine honour;
Mine honour, it. Repent that e'er thy tongue
Hath so betrayed thine act. Being done unknown,

I should have found it afterwards well done,
But must condemn it now. Desist, and drink.

MENAS (*aside*)
For this I'll never follow thy palled fortunes more.
Who seeks, and will not take when once 'tis offered,
Shall never find it more.

POMPEY This health to Lepidus!

ANTONY
Bear him ashore. – I'll pledge it for him, Pompey.

ENOBARBUS
Here's to thee, Menas!

MENAS Enobarbus, welcome.

POMPEY
Fill till the cup be hid.

ENOBARBUS (*pointing to the Servant who is carrying off Lepidus*)
There's a strong fellow, Menas.

MENAS
Why?

ENOBARBUS
'A bears the third part of the world, man; seest not?

MENAS
The third part then is drunk. Would it were all,
That it might go on wheels!

ENOBARBUS
Drink thou; increase the reels.

MENAS
Come.

POMPEY
This is not yet an Alexandrian feast.

ANTONY
It ripens towards it. Strike the vessels, ho!
Here's to Caesar!

CAESAR I could well forbear't.

It's monstrous labour when I wash my brain
And it grows fouler.

ANTONY Be a child o'th'time.

CAESAR
Possess it, I'll make answer.
But I had rather fast from all, four days,
Than drink so much in one.

ENOBARBUS (*to Antony*) Ha, my brave emperor!
Shall we dance now the Egyptian bacchanals
And celebrate our drink?

POMPEY Let's ha't, good soldier.

ANTONY
Come, let's all take hands
Till that the conquering wine hath steeped our sense
In soft and delicate Lethe.

ENOBARBUS All take hands.
Make battery to our ears with the loud music;
The while I'll place you; then the boy shall sing.
The holding every man shall beat as loud
As his strong sides can volley.

*Music plays. Enobarbus places them hand in hand*

BOY (*sings*)
Come, thou monarch of the vine,
Plumpy Bacchus with pink eyne!
In thy fats our cares be drowned;
With thy grapes our hairs be crowned.
Cup us till the world go round,
Cup us till the world go round!

CAESAR
What would you more? Pompey, good night. (*To Antony*) Good brother,
Let me request you off. Our graver business
Frowns at this levity. Gentle lords, let's part.
You see we have burnt our cheeks. Strong Enobarb

Is weaker than the wine, and mine own tongue
Spleets what it speaks. The wild disguise hath almost
Anticked us all. What needs more words? Good night.
Good Antony, your hand.

POMPEY I'll try you on the shore.

ANTONY
And shall, sir. Give's your hand.

POMPEY O, Antony,
You have my father's house. But what, we are friends!
Come down into the boat.

*Exeunt all but Enobarbus and Menas*

ENOBARBUS Take heed you fall not.
Menas, I'll not on shore.

MENAS No, to my cabin.
These drums! These trumpets, flutes! What!
Let Neptune hear we bid a loud farewell
To these great fellows. Sound and be hanged, sound out!

*Sound a flourish, with drums*

ENOBARBUS Hoo, says 'a. There's my cap.

*He throws his cap in the air*

MENAS Hoa! Noble captain, come. *Exeunt*

*

III.1

*Enter Ventidius, as it were in triumph, with Silius and other Officers and Soldiers. Before Ventidius is borne the dead body of Pacorus*

VENTIDIUS
Now, darting Parthia, art thou struck; and now
Pleased Fortune does of Marcus Crassus' death
Make me revenger. Bear the King's son's body
Before our army. Thy Pacorus, Orodes,
Pays this for Marcus Crassus.

SILIUS Noble Ventidius,
Whilst yet with Parthian blood thy sword is warm,
The fugitive Parthians follow. Spur through Media,
Mesopotamia, and the shelters whither
The routed fly. So thy grand captain, Antony,
Shall set thee on triumphant chariots, and
Put garlands on thy head.

VENTIDIUS O Silius, Silius,
I have done enough. A lower place, note well,
May make too great an act. For learn this, Silius:
Better to leave undone than by our deed
Acquire too high a fame when him we serve's away.
Caesar and Antony have ever won
More in their officer than person. Sossius,
One of my place in Syria, his lieutenant,
For quick accumulation of renown,
Which he achieved by th'minute, lost his favour.
Who does i'th'wars more than his captain can
Becomes his captain's captain; and ambition,
The soldier's virtue, rather makes choice of loss
Than gain which darkens him.
I could do more to do Antonius good,
But 'twould offend him, and in his offence
Should my performance perish.

SILIUS Thou hast, Ventidius, that
Without the which a soldier and his sword
Grants scarce distinction. Thou wilt write to Antony?

VENTIDIUS
I'll humbly signify what in his name,
That magical word of war, we have effected;
How, with his banners and his well-paid ranks,
The ne'er-yet-beaten horse of Parthia
We have jaded out o'th'field.

SILIUS Where is he now?

VENTIDIUS

He purposeth to Athens; whither, with what haste
The weight we must convey with's will permit,
We shall appear before him. – On, there. Pass along.

*Exeunt*

## III.2

*Enter Agrippa at one door, Enobarbus at another*

AGRIPPA

What, are the brothers parted?

ENOBARBUS

They have dispatched with Pompey; he is gone.
The other three are sealing. Octavia weeps
To part from Rome; Caesar is sad, and Lepidus
Since Pompey's feast, as Menas says, is troubled
With the green-sickness.

AGRIPPA

'Tis a noble Lepidus.

ENOBARBUS

A very fine one. O, how he loves Caesar!

AGRIPPA

Nay, but how dearly he adores Mark Antony!

ENOBARBUS

Caesar? Why, he's the Jupiter of men.

AGRIPPA

What's Antony? The god of Jupiter.

ENOBARBUS

Spake you of Caesar? How! The nonpareil!

AGRIPPA

O Antony! O thou Arabian bird!

ENOBARBUS

Would you praise Caesar, say 'Caesar' – go no further.

AGRIPPA

Indeed, he plied them both with excellent praises.

ENOBARBUS

But he loves Caesar best, yet he loves Antony –
Hoo! Hearts, tongues, figures, scribes, bards, poets, cannot
Think, speak, cast, write, sing, number – hoo! –
His love to Antony. But as for Caesar,
Kneel down, kneel down, and wonder.

AGRIPPA Both he loves.

ENOBARBUS

They are his shards, and he their beetle. So –
(*Trumpet within*)
This is to horse. Adieu, noble Agrippa.

AGRIPPA

Good fortune, worthy soldier, and farewell!

*Enter Caesar, Antony, Lepidus, and Octavia*

ANTONY

No further, sir.

CAESAR

You take from me a great part of myself;
Use me well in't. Sister, prove such a wife
As my thoughts make thee, and as my farthest band
Shall pass on thy approof. Most noble Antony,
Let not the piece of virtue which is set
Betwixt us as the cement of our love,
To keep it builded, be the ram to batter
The fortress of it; for better might we
Have loved without this mean, if on both parts
This be not cherished.

ANTONY Make me not offended
In your distrust.

CAESAR I have said.

ANTONY You shall not find,
Though you be therein curious, the least cause
For what you seem to fear. So, the gods keep you,

And make the hearts of Romans serve your ends!
We will here part.

CAESAR
Farewell, my dearest sister, fare thee well.
The elements be kind to thee, and make
Thy spirits all of comfort. Fare thee well.

OCTAVIA (*weeping*)
My noble brother!

ANTONY
The April's in her eyes; it is love's spring,
And these the showers to bring it on. Be cheerful.

OCTAVIA
Sir, look well to my husband's house; and –

CAESAR What,
Octavia?

OCTAVIA I'll tell you in your ear.

ANTONY
Her tongue will not obey her heart, nor can
Her heart inform her tongue – the swan's-down feather
That stands upon the swell at the full of tide,
And neither way inclines.

ENOBARBUS (*aside to Agrippa*) Will Caesar weep?

AGRIPPA (*aside to Enobarbus*)
He has a cloud in's face.

ENOBARBUS (*aside to Agrippa*)
He were the worse for that, were he a horse;
So is he, being a man.

AGRIPPA (*aside to Enobarbus*) Why, Enobarbus,
When Antony found Julius Caesar dead,
He cried almost to roaring; and he wept
When at Philippi he found Brutus slain.

ENOBARBUS (*aside to Agrippa*)
That year indeed he was troubled with a rheum.
What willingly he did confound he wailed,

Believe't, till I wept too.

CAESAR No, sweet Octavia,
You shall hear from me still; the time shall not
Outgo my thinking on you.

ANTONY Come, sir, come,
I'll wrestle with you in my strength of love.
Look, here I have you; thus I let you go,
And give you to the gods.

CAESAR Adieu; be happy!

LEPIDUS (*to Octavia*)
Let all the number of the stars give light
To thy fair way!

CAESAR Farewell, farewell!

*He kisses Octavia*

ANTONY Farewell!

*Trumpets sound. Exeunt*

## III.3

*Enter Cleopatra, Charmian, Iras, and Alexas*

CLEOPATRA
Where is the fellow?

ALEXAS Half afeard to come.

CLEOPATRA
Go to, go to.

*Enter the Messenger as before*

Come hither, sir.

ALEXAS Good majesty,
Herod of Jewry dare not look upon you
But when you are well pleased.

CLEOPATRA That Herod's head
I'll have; but how, when Antony is gone,
Through whom I might command it? – Come thou
near.

MESSENGER
Most gracious majesty!

CLEOPATRA Didst thou behold Octavia?

MESSENGER
Ay, dread queen.

CLEOPATRA Where?

MESSENGER Madam, in Rome.
I looked her in the face, and saw her led
Between her brother and Mark Antony.

CLEOPATRA
Is she as tall as me?

MESSENGER She is not, madam.

CLEOPATRA
Didst hear her speak? Is she shrill-tongued or low?

MESSENGER
Madam, I heard her speak; she is low-voiced.

CLEOPATRA
That's not so good. He cannot like her long.

CHARMIAN
Like her? O Isis! 'Tis impossible.

CLEOPATRA
I think so, Charmian. Dull of tongue, and dwarfish.
What majesty is in her gait? Remember,
If e'er thou look'st on majesty.

MESSENGER She creeps;
Her motion and her station are as one.
She shows a body rather than a life,
A statue than a breather.

CLEOPATRA Is this certain?

MESSENGER
Or I have no observance.

CHARMIAN Three in Egypt
Cannot make better note.

CLEOPATRA He's very knowing,
I do perceive't. There's nothing in her yet.
The fellow has good judgement.
CHARMIAN Excellent.
CLEOPATRA
Guess at her years, I prithee.
MESSENGER Madam,
She was a widow –
CLEOPATRA Widow? Charmian, hark.
MESSENGER
And I do think she's thirty.
CLEOPATRA
Bear'st thou her face in mind? Is't long or round?
MESSENGER
Round, even to faultiness.
CLEOPATRA
For the most part, too, they are foolish that are so.
Her hair, what colour?
MESSENGER Brown, madam; and her forehead
As low as she would wish it.
CLEOPATRA There's gold for thee.
Thou must not take my former sharpness ill.
I will employ thee back again. I find thee
Most fit for business. Go, make thee ready.
Our letters are prepared. *Exit Messenger*
CHARMIAN A proper man.
CLEOPATRA
Indeed he is so: I repent me much
That so I harried him. Why, methinks, by him,
This creature's no such thing.
CHARMIAN Nothing, madam.
CLEOPATRA
The man hath seen some majesty, and should know.

CHARMIAN
Hath he seen majesty? Isis else defend,
And serving you so long!

CLEOPATRA
I have one thing more to ask him yet, good Charmian.
But 'tis no matter; thou shalt bring him to me
Where I will write. All may be well enough.

CHARMIAN
I warrant you, madam. *Exeunt*

## III.4

*Enter Antony and Octavia*

ANTONY
Nay, nay, Octavia, not only that;
That were excusable, that and thousands more
Of semblable import – but he hath waged
New wars 'gainst Pompey; made his will, and read it
To public ear;
Spoke scantly of me; when perforce he could not
But pay me terms of honour, cold and sickly
He vented them, most narrow measure lent me;
When the best hint was given him, he not took't,
Or did it from his teeth.

OCTAVIA O, my good lord,
Believe not all; or, if you must believe,
Stomach not all. A more unhappy lady,
If this division chance, ne'er stood between,
Praying for both parts.
The good gods will mock me presently
When I shall pray 'O, bless my lord and husband!';
Undo that prayer by crying out as loud
'O, bless my brother!' Husband win, win brother,
Prays, and destroys the prayer; no midway
'Twixt these extremes at all.

ANTONY Gentle Octavia,
Let your best love draw to that point which seeks
Best to preserve it. If I lose mine honour,
I lose myself; better I were not yours
Than yours so branchless. But, as you requested,
Yourself shall go between's. The meantime, lady,
I'll raise the preparation of a war
Shall stain your brother. Make your soonest haste;
So your desires are yours.

OCTAVIA Thanks to my lord.
The Jove of power make me, most weak, most weak,
Your reconciler! Wars 'twixt you twain would be
As if the world should cleave, and that slain men
Should solder up the rift.

ANTONY
When it appears to you where this begins,
Turn your displeasure that way, for our faults
Can never be so equal that your love
Can equally move with them. Provide your going;
Choose your own company, and command what cost
Your heart has mind to. *Exeunt*

## III.5

*Enter Enobarbus and Eros*

ENOBARBUS How now, friend Eros?

EROS There's strange news come, sir.

ENOBARBUS What, man?

EROS Caesar and Lepidus have made wars upon Pompey.

ENOBARBUS This is old. What is the success?

EROS Caesar, having made use of him in the wars 'gainst Pompey, presently denied him rivality, would not let him partake in the glory of the action; and, not resting here, accuses him of letters he had formerly wrote to Pompey; upon his own appeal, seizes him; so the poor third is up, till death enlarge his confine.

ENOBARBUS

Then, world, thou hast a pair of chaps, no more;
And throw between them all the food thou hast,
They'll grind the one the other. Where's Antony?

EROS

He's walking in the garden – thus, and spurns
The rush that lies before him; cries 'Fool Lepidus!'
And threats the throat of that his officer
That murdered Pompey.

ENOBARBUS Our great navy's rigged.

EROS

For Italy and Caesar. More, Domitius:
My lord desires you presently. My news
I might have told hereafter.

ENOBARBUS 'Twill be naught;
But let it be. Bring me to Antony.

EROS Come, sir. *Exeunt*

## III.6

*Enter Agrippa, Maecenas, and Caesar*

CAESAR

Contemning Rome, he has done all this and more
In Alexandria. Here's the manner of't:
I'th'market-place on a tribunal silvered,
Cleopatra and himself in chairs of gold
Were publicly enthroned; at the feet sat
Caesarion, whom they call my father's son,
And all the unlawful issue that their lust
Since then hath made between them. Unto her
He gave the stablishment of Egypt; made her
Of lower Syria, Cyprus, Lydia,
Absolute queen.

MAECENAS This in the public eye?

CAESAR

I'th'common showplace, where they exercise.
His sons he there proclaimed the kings of kings;
Great Media, Parthia, and Armenia
He gave to Alexander; to Ptolemy he assigned
Syria, Cilicia, and Phoenicia. She
In th'habiliments of the goddess Isis
That day appeared, and oft before gave audience,
As 'tis reported, so.

MAECENAS Let Rome be thus informed.

AGRIPPA

Who, queasy with his insolence already,
Will their good thoughts call from him.

CAESAR

The people knows it, and have now received
His accusations.

AGRIPPA Who does he accuse?

CAESAR

Caesar; and that, having in Sicily
Sextus Pompeius spoiled, we had not rated him
His part o'th'isle. Then does he say he lent me
Some shipping, unrestored. Lastly, he frets
That Lepidus of the triumvirate
Should be deposed; and, being, that we detain
All his revenue.

AGRIPPA Sir, this should be answered.

CAESAR

'Tis done already, and the messenger gone.
I have told him Lepidus was grown too cruel,
That he his high authority abused,
And did deserve his change. For what I have conquered,
I grant him part; but then in his Armenia,
And other of his conquered kingdoms, I
Demand the like.

MAECENAS He'll never yield to that.

CAESAR
Nor must not then be yielded to in this.
*Enter Octavia with her train*

OCTAVIA
Hail, Caesar and my lord! Hail, most dear Caesar!

CAESAR
That ever I should call thee castaway!

OCTAVIA
You have not called me so, nor have you cause.

CAESAR
Why have you stol'n upon us thus? You come not
Like Caesar's sister. The wife of Antony
Should have an army for an usher, and
The neighs of horse to tell of her approach
Long ere she did appear. The trees by th'way
Should have borne men, and expectation fainted,
Longing for what it had not. Nay, the dust
Should have ascended to the roof of heaven,
Raised by your populous troops. But you are come
A market maid to Rome, and have prevented
The ostentation of our love; which, left unshown,
Is often left unloved. We should have met you
By sea and land, supplying every stage
With an augmented greeting.

OCTAVIA Good my lord,
To come thus was I not constrained, but did it
On my free will. My lord, Mark Antony,
Hearing that you prepared for war, acquainted
My grievèd ear withal; whereon I begged
His pardon for return.

CAESAR Which soon he granted,
Being an obstruct 'tween his lust and him.

OCTAVIA
Do not say so, my lord.
CAESAR I have eyes upon him,
And his affairs come to me on the wind.
Where is he now?
OCTAVIA My lord, in Athens.
CAESAR
No, my most wrongèd sister; Cleopatra
Hath nodded him to her. He hath given his empire
Up to a whore; who now are levying
The kings o'th'earth for war. He hath assembled
Bocchus, the King of Libya; Archelaus,
Of Cappadocia; Philadelphos, King
Of Paphlagonia; the Thracian king, Adallas;
King Mauchus of Arabia; King of Pont;
Herod of Jewry; Mithridates, King
Of Comagene; Polemon and Amyntas,
The Kings of Mede and Lycaonia;
With a more larger list of sceptres.
OCTAVIA Ay me most wretched,
That have my heart parted betwixt two friends
That does afflict each other!
CAESAR Welcome hither.
Your letters did withhold our breaking forth,
Till we perceived both how you were wrong led
And we in negligent danger. Cheer your heart;
Be you not troubled with the time, which drives
O'er your content these strong necessities;
But let determined things to destiny
Hold unbewailed their way. Welcome to Rome;
Nothing more dear to me. You are abused
Beyond the mark of thought, and the high gods,
To do you justice, makes his ministers

Of us and those that love you. Best of comfort,
And ever welcome to us.

AGRIPPA Welcome, lady.

MAECENAS
Welcome, dear madam.
Each heart in Rome does love and pity you.
Only th'adulterous Antony, most large
In his abominations, turns you off
And gives his potent regiment to a trull
That noises it against us.

OCTAVIA Is it so, sir?

CAESAR
Most certain. Sister, welcome. Pray you
Be ever known to patience. My dear'st sister! *Exeunt*

III.7

*Enter Cleopatra and Enobarbus*

CLEOPATRA
I will be even with thee, doubt it not.

ENOBARBUS
But why, why, why?

CLEOPATRA
Thou hast forspoke my being in these wars,
And sayst it is not fit.

ENOBARBUS Well, is it, is it?

CLEOPATRA
Is't not denounced against us? Why should not we
Be there in person?

ENOBARBUS (*aside*) Well, I could reply:
If we should serve with horse and mares together,
The horse were merely lost; the mares would bear
A soldier and his horse.

CLEOPATRA What is't you say?

ENOBARBUS
Your presence needs must puzzle Antony,
Take from his heart, take from his brain, from's time,
What should not then be spared. He is already
Traduced for levity; and 'tis said in Rome
That Photinus, an eunuch, and your maids
Manage this war.

CLEOPATRA Sink Rome, and their tongues rot
That speak against us! A charge we bear i'th'war,
And as the president of my kingdom will
Appear there for a man. Speak not against it;
I will not stay behind.

*Enter Antony and Canidius*

ENOBARBUS Nay, I have done.
Here comes the Emperor.

ANTONY Is it not strange, Canidius,
That from Tarentum and Brundisium
He could so quickly cut the Ionian sea
And take in Toryne? – You have heard on't, sweet?

CLEOPATRA
Celerity is never more admired
Than by the negligent.

ANTONY A good rebuke,
Which might have well becomed the best of men
To taunt at slackness. Canidius, we
Will fight with him by sea.

CLEOPATRA By sea; what else?

CANIDIUS
Why will my lord do so?

ANTONY For that he dares us to't.

ENOBARBUS
So hath my lord dared him to single fight.

CANIDIUS
Ay, and to wage this battle at Pharsalia,

Where Caesar fought with Pompey. But these offers,
Which serve not for his vantage, he shakes off;
And so should you.

ENOBARBUS Your ships are not well manned.
Your mariners are muleters, reapers, people
Engrossed by swift impress. In Caesar's fleet
Are those that often have 'gainst Pompey fought;
Their ships are yare; yours, heavy. No disgrace
Shall fall you for refusing him at sea,
Being prepared for land.

ANTONY By sea, by sea.

ENOBARBUS
Most worthy sir, you therein throw away
The absolute soldiership you have by land,
Distract your army, which doth most consist
Of war-marked footmen, leave unexecuted
Your own renownèd knowledge, quite forgo
The way which promises assurance, and
Give up yourself merely to chance and hazard
From firm security.

ANTONY I'll fight at sea.

CLEOPATRA
I have sixty sails, Caesar none better.

ANTONY
Our overplus of shipping will we burn,
And with the rest full-manned, from th'head of Actium
Beat th'approaching Caesar. But if we fail,
We then can do't at land.

*Enter a Messenger*

Thy business?

MESSENGER
The news is true, my lord; he is descried.
Caesar has taken Toryne.

ANTONY

Can he be there in person? 'Tis impossible;
Strange that his power should be. Canidius,
Our nineteen legions thou shalt hold by land
And our twelve thousand horse. We'll to our ship.
Away, my Thetis!

*Enter a Soldier*

How now, worthy soldier?

SOLDIER

O noble Emperor, do not fight by sea.
Trust not to rotten planks. Do you misdoubt
This sword and these my wounds? Let th'Egyptians
And the Phoenicians go a-ducking; we
Have used to conquer standing on the earth
And fighting foot to foot.

ANTONY Well, well; away!

*Exeunt Antony, Cleopatra, and Enobarbus*

SOLDIER

By Hercules, I think I am i'th'right.

CANIDIUS

Soldier, thou art; but his whole action grows
Not in the power on't. So our leader's led,
And we are women's men.

SOLDIER You keep by land
The legions and the horse whole, do you not?

CANIDIUS

Marcus Octavius, Marcus Justeius,
Publicola, and Caelius are for sea;
But we keep whole by land. This speed of Caesar's
Carries beyond belief.

SOLDIER While he was yet in Rome,
His power went out in such distractions as
Beguiled all spies.

CANIDIUS Who's his lieutenant, hear you?

SOLDIER
They say one Taurus.

CANIDIUS
Well I know the man.

*Enter a Messenger*

MESSENGER
The Emperor calls Canidius.

CANIDIUS
With news the time's with labour and throes forth
Each minute some. *Exeunt*

III.8

*Enter Caesar and Taurus, with their army, marching*

CAESAR
Taurus!

TAURUS
My lord?

CAESAR
Strike not by land; keep whole; provoke not battle
Till we have done at sea. Do not exceed
The prescript of this scroll. Our fortune lies
Upon this jump. *Exeunt*

III.9

*Enter Antony and Enobarbus*

ANTONY
Set we our squadrons on yond side o'th'hill
In eye of Caesar's battle; from which place
We may the number of the ships behold,
And so proceed accordingly. *Exeunt*

III.10

*Canidius marcheth with his land army one way over the stage, and Taurus, the lieutenant of Caesar, with his army, the other way. After their going in is heard the noise of a sea fight*

*Alarum. Enter Enobarbus*

ENOBARBUS

Naught, naught, all naught! I can behold no longer.
Th'*Antoniad*, the Egyptian admiral,
With all their sixty, fly and turn the rudder.
To see't mine eyes are blasted.

*Enter Scarus*

SCARUS Gods and goddesses,
All the whole synod of them!

ENOBARBUS What's thy passion?

SCARUS

The greater cantle of the world is lost
With very ignorance. We have kissed away
Kingdoms and provinces.

ENOBARBUS How appears the fight?

SCARUS

On our side like the tokened pestilence,
Where death is sure. Yon ribaudred nag of Egypt –
Whom leprosy o'ertake! – i'th'midst o'th'fight,
When vantage like a pair of twins appeared,
Both as the same, or rather ours the elder,
The breese upon her, like a cow in June,
Hoists sails and flies.

ENOBARBUS That I beheld.
Mine eyes did sicken at the sight, and could not
Endure a further view.

SCARUS She once being loofed,
The noble ruin of her magic, Antony,
Claps on his sea wing and, like a doting mallard,
Leaving the fight in height, flies after her.

I never saw an action of such shame.
Experience, manhood, honour, ne'er before
Did violate so itself.

ENOBARBUS Alack, alack!

*Enter Canidius*

CANIDIUS
Our fortune on the sea is out of breath,
And sinks most lamentably. Had our general
Been what he knew himself, it had gone well.
O, he has given example for our flight
Most grossly by his own.

ENOBARBUS
Ay, are you thereabouts? Why then, good night indeed.

CANIDIUS
Toward Peloponnesus are they fled.

SCARUS
'Tis easy to't; and there I will attend
What further comes.

CANIDIUS To Caesar will I render
My legions and my horse. Six kings already
Show me the way of yielding.

ENOBARBUS I'll yet follow
The wounded chance of Antony, though my reason
Sits in the wind against me. *Exeunt*

III.11

*Enter Antony with Attendants*

ANTONY
Hark! The land bids me tread no more upon't;
It is ashamed to bear me. Friends, come hither.
I am so lated in the world that I
Have lost my way for ever. I have a ship
Laden with gold; take that; divide it. Fly,
And make your peace with Caesar.

ALL Fly? Not we.

ANTONY
I have fled myself, and have instructed cowards
To run and show their shoulders. Friends, be gone.
I have myself resolved upon a course
Which has no need of you. Be gone.
My treasure's in the harbour. Take it. O,
I followed that I blush to look upon.
My very hairs do mutiny, for the white
Reprove the brown for rashness, and they them
For fear and doting. Friends, be gone; you shall
Have letters from me to some friends that will
Sweep your way for you. Pray you, look not sad,
Nor make replies of loathness; take the hint
Which my despair proclaims. Let that be left
Which leaves itself. To the seaside straightway!
I will possess you of that ship and treasure.
Leave me, I pray, a little. Pray you now,
Nay, do so; for indeed I have lost command.
Therefore I pray you. I'll see you by and by.

*Exeunt Attendants. Antony sits down*

*Enter Cleopatra, led by Charmian, Iras, and Eros*

EROS
Nay, gentle madam, to him, comfort him.

IRAS Do, most dear queen.

CHARMIAN Do; why, what else?

CLEOPATRA Let me sit down. O, Juno!

ANTONY No, no, no, no, no.

EROS See you here, sir?

ANTONY O, fie, fie, fie!

CHARMIAN Madam!

IRAS Madam, O, good empress!

EROS Sir, sir!

ANTONY
Yes, my lord, yes. He at Philippi kept
His sword e'en like a dancer, while I struck
The lean and wrinkled Cassius; and 'twas I
That the mad Brutus ended. He alone
Dealt on lieutenantry, and no practice had
In the brave squares of war. Yet now – no matter.

CLEOPATRA Ah, stand by.

EROS The Queen, my lord, the Queen.

IRAS
Go to him, madam, speak to him;
He's unqualitied with very shame.

CLEOPATRA Well then, sustain me. O!

EROS
Most noble sir, arise. The Queen approaches.
Her head's declined, and death will seize her but
Your comfort makes the rescue.

ANTONY
I have offended reputation,
A most unnoble swerving.

EROS Sir, the Queen.

ANTONY
O, whither hast thou led me, Egypt? See
How I convey my shame out of thine eyes
By looking back what I have left behind
'Stroyed in dishonour.

CLEOPATRA O my lord, my lord,
Forgive my fearful sails! I little thought
You would have followed.

ANTONY Egypt, thou knew'st too well
My heart was to thy rudder tied by th'strings,
And thou shouldst tow me after. O'er my spirit
Thy full supremacy thou knew'st, and that

Thy beck might from the bidding of the gods
Command me.

CLEOPATRA O, my pardon!

ANTONY Now I must
To the young man send humble treaties, dodge
And palter in the shifts of lowness, who
With half the bulk o'th'world played as I pleased,
Making and marring fortunes. You did know
How much you were my conqueror, and that
My sword, made weak by my affection, would
Obey it on all cause.

CLEOPATRA Pardon, pardon!

ANTONY
Fall not a tear, I say; one of them rates
All that is won and lost. Give me a kiss.
Even this repays me. – We sent our schoolmaster;
Is 'a come back? – Love, I am full of lead.
Some wine, within there, and our viands! Fortune knows
We scorn her most when most she offers blows.

*Exeunt*

III.12

*Enter Caesar, Agrippa, Dolabella, and Thidias, with others*

CAESAR
Let him appear that's come from Antony.
Know you him?

DOLABELLA Caesar, 'tis his schoolmaster:
An argument that he is plucked, when hither
He sends so poor a pinion of his wing,
Which had superfluous kings for messengers
Not many moons gone by.

*Enter Ambassador from Antony*

CAESAR Approach and speak.

AMBASSADOR

Such as I am, I come from Antony.
I was of late as petty to his ends
As is the morn-dew on the myrtle leaf
To his grand sea.

CAESAR Be't so. Declare thine office.

AMBASSADOR

Lord of his fortunes he salutes thee, and
Requires to live in Egypt; which not granted,
He lessons his requests, and to thee sues
To let him breathe between the heavens and earth,
A private man in Athens. This for him.
Next, Cleopatra does confess thy greatness,
Submits her to thy might, and of thee craves
The circle of the Ptolemies for her heirs,
Now hazarded to thy grace.

CAESAR For Antony,
I have no ears to his request. The Queen
Of audience nor desire shall fail, so she
From Egypt drive her all-disgracèd friend
Or take his life there. This if she perform,
She shall not sue unheard. So to them both.

AMBASSADOR

Fortune pursue thee!

CAESAR Bring him through the bands.

*Exit Ambassador*

(*To Thidias*) To try thy eloquence now 'tis time. Dispatch.
From Antony win Cleopatra. Promise,
And in our name, what she requires; add more,
From thine invention, offers. Women are not
In their best fortunes strong, but want will perjure
The ne'er-touched vestal. Try thy cunning, Thidias.
Make thine own edict for thy pains, which we
Will answer as a law.

THIDIAS Caesar, I go.

CAESAR
Observe how Antony becomes his flaw,
And what thou think'st his very action speaks
In every power that moves.

THIDIAS Caesar, I shall. *Exeunt*

## III.13

*Enter Cleopatra, Enobarbus, Charmian, and Iras*

CLEOPATRA
What shall we do, Enobarbus?

ENOBARBUS Think, and die.

CLEOPATRA
Is Antony or we in fault for this?

ENOBARBUS
Antony only, that would make his will
Lord of his reason. What though you fled
From that great face of war, whose several ranges
Frighted each other? Why should he follow?
The itch of his affection should not then
Have nicked his captainship, at such a point,
When half to half the world opposed, he being
The merèd question. 'Twas a shame no less
Than was his loss, to course your flying flags
And leave his navy gazing.

CLEOPATRA Prithee, peace.

*Enter the Ambassador, with Antony*

ANTONY
Is that his answer?

AMBASSADOR
Ay, my lord.

ANTONY
The Queen shall then have courtesy, so she
Will yield us up.

AMBASSADOR He says so.

ANTONY Let her know't. –
To the boy Caesar send this grizzled head,
And he will fill thy wishes to the brim
With principalities.

CLEOPATRA That head, my lord?

ANTONY (*to Ambassador*)
To him again! Tell him he wears the rose
Of youth upon him; from which the world should note
Something particular. His coin, ships, legions,
May be a coward's, whose ministers would prevail
Under the service of a child as soon
As i'th'command of Caesar. I dare him therefore
To lay his gay comparisons apart,
And answer me declined, sword against sword,
Ourselves alone. I'll write it. Follow me.

*Exeunt Antony and Ambassador*

ENOBARBUS (*aside*)
Yes, like enough, high-battled Caesar will
Unstate his happiness and be staged to th'show
Against a sworder! I see men's judgements are
A parcel of their fortunes, and things outward
Do draw the inward quality after them
To suffer all alike. That he should dream,
Knowing all measures, the full Caesar will
Answer his emptiness! Caesar, thou hast subdued
His judgement too.

*Enter a Servant*

SERVANT A messenger from Caesar.

CLEOPATRA
What, no more ceremony? See, my women,
Against the blown rose may they stop their nose
That kneeled unto the buds. Admit him, sir.

*Exit Servant*

ENOBARBUS (*aside*)
Mine honesty and I begin to square.
The loyalty well held to fools does make
Our faith mere folly. Yet he that can endure
To follow with allegiance a fallen lord
Does conquer him that did his master conquer
And earns a place i'th'story.

*Enter Thidias*

CLEOPATRA Caesar's will?

THIDIAS
Hear it apart.

CLEOPATRA None but friends; say boldly.

THIDIAS
So, haply, are they friends to Antony.

ENOBARBUS
He needs as many, sir, as Caesar has,
Or needs not us. If Caesar please, our master
Will leap to be his friend; for us, you know,
Whose he is we are, and that is Caesar's.

THIDIAS So.
Thus then, thou most renowned: Caesar entreats
Not to consider in what case thou stand'st
Further than he is Caesar.

CLEOPATRA Go on; right royal.

THIDIAS
He knows that you embraced not Antony
As you did love, but as you feared him.

CLEOPATRA O!

THIDIAS
The scars upon your honour therefore he
Does pity, as constrainèd blemishes,
Not as deserved.

CLEOPATRA He is a god, and knows

What is most right. Mine honour was not yielded,
But conquered merely.

ENOBARBUS (*aside*) To be sure of that,
I will ask Antony. Sir, sir, thou art so leaky
That we must leave thee to thy sinking, for
Thy dearest quit thee. *Exit*

THIDIAS Shall I say to Caesar
What you require of him? For he partly begs
To be desired to give. It much would please him
That of his fortunes you should make a staff
To lean upon. But it would warm his spirits
To hear from me you had left Antony,
And put yourself under his shroud,
The universal landlord.

CLEOPATRA What's your name?

THIDIAS
My name is Thidias.

CLEOPATRA Most kind messenger,
Say to great Caesar this: in deputation
I kiss his conquering hand. Tell him I am prompt
To lay my crown at's feet, and there to kneel,
Till from his all-obeying breath I hear
The doom of Egypt.

THIDIAS 'Tis your noblest course.
Wisdom and fortune combating together,
If that the former dare but what it can,
No chance may shake it. Give me grace to lay
My duty on your hand.

*She gives him her hand*

CLEOPATRA Your Caesar's father oft,
When he hath mused of taking kingdoms in,
Bestowed his lips on that unworthy place,
As it rained kisses.

*Enter Antony and Enobarbus*

ANTONY Favours, by Jove that thunders!
What art thou, fellow?

THIDIAS One that but performs
The bidding of the fullest man, and worthiest
To have command obeyed.

ENOBARBUS (*aside*) You will be whipped.

ANTONY
Approach there! – Ah, you kite! Now, gods and devils!
Authority melts from me. Of late, when I cried 'Ho!',
Like boys unto a muss, kings would start forth
And cry 'Your will?' Have you no ears? I am
Antony yet.

*Enter Servants*

Take hence this Jack and whip him.

ENOBARBUS (*aside*)
'Tis better playing with a lion's whelp
Than with an old one dying.

ANTONY Moon and stars!
Whip him! Were't twenty of the greatest tributaries
That do acknowledge Caesar, should I find them
So saucy with the hand of she here – what's her name
Since she was Cleopatra? Whip him, fellows,
Till like a boy you see him cringe his face
And whine aloud for mercy. Take him hence.

THIDIAS
Mark Antony –

ANTONY Tug him away. Being whipped,
Bring him again. The Jack of Caesar's shall
Bear us an errand to him. *Exeunt Servants with Thidias*
You were half blasted ere I knew you. Ha!
Have I my pillow left unpressed in Rome,
Forborne the getting of a lawful race,
And by a gem of women, to be abused

By one that looks on feeders?

CLEOPATRA
Good my lord –

ANTONY
You have been a boggler ever.
But when we in our viciousness grow hard –
O, misery on't! – the wise gods seel our eyes,
In our own filth drop our clear judgements, make us
Adore our errors, laugh at's while we strut
To our confusion.

CLEOPATRA
O, is't come to this?

ANTONY
I found you as a morsel cold upon
Dead Caesar's trencher. Nay, you were a fragment
Of Gnaeus Pompey's, besides what hotter hours,
Unregistered in vulgar fame, you have
Luxuriously picked out. For I am sure,
Though you can guess what temperance should be,
You know not what it is.

CLEOPATRA
Wherefore is this?

ANTONY
To let a fellow that will take rewards
And say 'God quit you!' be familiar with
My playfellow, your hand, this kingly seal
And plighter of high hearts! O that I were
Upon the hill of Basan to outroar
The hornèd herd! For I have savage cause,
And to proclaim it civilly were like
A haltered neck which does the hangman thank
For being yare about him.

*Enter a Servant with Thidias*

Is he whipped?

SERVANT
Soundly, my lord.

ANTONY
Cried he? And begged 'a pardon?

SERVANT
He did ask favour.

ANTONY
If that thy father live, let him repent
Thou wast not made his daughter; and be thou sorry
To follow Caesar in his triumph, since
Thou hast been whipped for following him. Henceforth
The white hand of a lady fever thee;
Shake thou to look on't. Get thee back to Caesar.
Tell him thy entertainment. Look thou say
He makes me angry with him; for he seems
Proud and disdainful, harping on what I am,
Not what he knew I was. He makes me angry,
And at this time most easy 'tis to do't,
When my good stars that were my former guides
Have empty left their orbs and shot their fires
Into th'abysm of hell. If he mislike
My speech and what is done, tell him he has
Hipparchus, my enfranchèd bondman, whom
He may at pleasure whip, or hang, or torture,
As he shall like, to quit me. Urge it thou.
Hence with thy stripes, be gone! *Exit Thidias*

CLEOPATRA
Have you done yet?

ANTONY Alack, our terrene moon
Is now eclipsed, and it portends alone
The fall of Antony.

CLEOPATRA I must stay his time.

ANTONY
To flatter Caesar, would you mingle eyes
With one that ties his points?

CLEOPATRA Not know me yet?

ANTONY
Cold-hearted toward me?

CLEOPATRA Ah, dear, if I be so,
From my cold heart let heaven engender hail,
And poison it in the source, and the first stone
Drop in my neck: as it determines, so
Dissolve my life! The next Caesarion smite,
Till by degrees the memory of my womb,
Together with my brave Egyptians all,
By the discandying of this pelleted storm,
Lie graveless, till the flies and gnats of Nile
Have buried them for prey!

ANTONY I am satisfied.
Caesar sits down in Alexandria, where
I will oppose his fate. Our force by land
Hath nobly held; our severed navy too
Have knit again, and fleet, threatening most sea-like.
Where hast thou been, my heart? Dost thou hear, lady?
If from the field I shall return once more
To kiss these lips, I will appear in blood.
I and my sword will earn our chronicle.
There's hope in't yet.

CLEOPATRA That's my brave lord!

ANTONY
I will be treble-sinewed, hearted, breathed,
And fight maliciously. For when mine hours
Were nice and lucky, men did ransom lives
Of me for jests; but now I'll set my teeth
And send to darkness all that stop me. Come,
Let's have one other gaudy night. Call to me
All my sad captains. Fill our bowls once more.
Let's mock the midnight bell.

CLEOPATRA It is my birthday.
I had thought t'have held it poor. But since my lord
Is Antony again, I will be Cleopatra.

ANTONY

We will yet do well.

CLEOPATRA

Call all his noble captains to my lord.

ANTONY

Do so, we'll speak to them; and tonight I'll force
The wine peep through their scars. Come on, my queen,
There's sap in't yet! The next time I do fight,
I'll make death love me, for I will contend
Even with his pestilent scythe.

*Exeunt all but Enobarbus*

ENOBARBUS

Now he'll outstare the lightning. To be furious
Is to be frighted out of fear, and in that mood
The dove will peck the estridge; and I see still
A diminution in our captain's brain
Restores his heart. When valour preys on reason,
It eats the sword it fights with. I will seek
Some way to leave him. *Exit*

*

IV.1 *Enter Caesar, Agrippa, and Maecenas, with their army, Caesar reading a letter*

CAESAR

He calls me boy, and chides as he had power
To beat me out of Egypt. My messenger
He hath whipped with rods; dares me to personal combat,
Caesar to Antony. Let the old ruffian know
I have many other ways to die; meantime
Laugh at his challenge.

MAECENAS

Caesar must think,
When one so great begins to rage, he's hunted

Even to falling. Give him no breath, but now
Make boot of his distraction. Never anger
Made good guard for itself.

CAESAR Let our best heads
Know that tomorrow the last of many battles
We mean to fight. Within our files there are,
Of those that served Mark Antony but late,
Enough to fetch him in. See it done,
And feast the army; we have store to do't,
And they have earned the waste. Poor Antony!

*Exeunt*

IV.2

*Enter Antony, Cleopatra, Enobarbus, Charmian, Iras, Alexas, with others*

ANTONY
He will not fight with me, Domitius?

ENOBARBUS No.

ANTONY
Why should he not?

ENOBARBUS
He thinks, being twenty times of better fortune,
He is twenty men to one.

ANTONY Tomorrow, soldier,
By sea and land I'll fight. Or I will live
Or bathe my dying honour in the blood
Shall make it live again. Woo't thou fight well?

ENOBARBUS
I'll strike, and cry 'Take all.'

ANTONY Well said; come on.
Call forth my household servants. Let's tonight
Be bounteous at our meal.

*Enter three or four Servitors*

Give me thy hand.

Thou hast been rightly honest. So hast thou;
Thou, and thou, and thou. You have served me well,
And kings have been your fellows.

CLEOPATRA (*aside to Enobarbus*) What means this?

ENOBARBUS (*aside to Cleopatra*)
'Tis one of those odd tricks which sorrow shoots
Out of the mind.

ANTONY And thou art honest too.
I wish I could be made so many men,
And all of you clapped up together in
An Antony, that I might do you service
So good as you have done.

ALL THE SERVANTS The gods forbid!

ANTONY
Well, my good fellows, wait on me tonight.
Scant not my cups, and make as much of me
As when mine empire was your fellow too
And suffered my command.

CLEOPATRA (*aside to Enobarbus*) What does he mean?

ENOBARBUS (*aside to Cleopatra*)
To make his followers weep.

ANTONY Tend me tonight.
May be it is the period of your duty.
Haply you shall not see me more; or if,
A mangled shadow. Perchance tomorrow
You'll serve another master. I look on you
As one that takes his leave. Mine honest friends,
I turn you not away, but, like a master
Married to your good service, stay till death.
Tend me tonight two hours, I ask no more,
And the gods yield you for't!

ENOBARBUS What mean you, sir,
To give them this discomfort? Look, they weep,

And I, an ass, am onion-eyed. For shame,
Transform us not to women.

ANTONY Ho, ho, ho!
Now the witch take me if I meant it thus!
Grace grow where those drops fall! My hearty friends,
You take me in too dolorous a sense,
For I spake to you for your comfort, did desire you
To burn this night with torches. Know, my hearts,
I hope well of tomorrow, and will lead you
Where rather I'll expect victorious life
Than death and honour. Let's to supper, come,
And drown consideration. *Exeunt*

*Enter a company of Soldiers* IV.3

FIRST SOLDIER
Brother, good night. Tomorrow is the day.

SECOND SOLDIER
It will determine one way. Fare you well.
Heard you of nothing strange about the streets?

FIRST SOLDIER Nothing. What news?

SECOND SOLDIER Belike 'tis but a rumour. Good night to you.

FIRST SOLDIER Well, sir, good night.

*They meet other Soldiers*

SECOND SOLDIER Soldiers, have careful watch.

THIRD SOLDIER And you. Good night, good night.

*They place themselves in every corner of the stage*

SECOND SOLDIER
Here we. An if tomorrow
Our navy thrive, I have an absolute hope
Our landmen will stand up.

FIRST SOLDIER 'Tis a brave army,

And full of purpose.

*Music of hautboys under the stage*

SECOND SOLDIER Peace! What noise?

FIRST SOLDIER List, list!

SECOND SOLDIER
Hark!

FIRST SOLDIER Music i'th'air.

THIRD SOLDIER Under the earth.

FOURTH SOLDIER
It signs well, does it not?

THIRD SOLDIER No.

FIRST SOLDIER Peace, I say!
What should this mean?

SECOND SOLDIER
'Tis the god Hercules, whom Antony loved,
Now leaves him.

FIRST SOLDIER Walk; let's see if other watchmen
Do hear what we do.

SECOND SOLDIER How now, masters?

ALL (*speaking together*) How now? How now? Do you hear this?

FIRST SOLDIER Ay. Is't not strange?

THIRD SOLDIER Do you hear, masters? Do you hear?

FIRST SOLDIER
Follow the noise so far as we have quarter.
Let's see how it will give off.

ALL Content. 'Tis strange. *Exeunt*

## IV.4

*Enter Antony and Cleopatra, with Charmian and others*

ANTONY
Eros! Mine armour, Eros!

CLEOPATRA Sleep a little.

ANTONY
No, my chuck. Eros! Come, mine armour, Eros!
*Enter Eros with armour*
Come, good fellow, put thine iron on.
If fortune be not ours today, it is
Because we brave her. Come.

CLEOPATRA
Nay, I'll help too.
What's this for?

ANTONY
Ah, let be, let be! Thou art
The armourer of my heart. False, false; this, this.

CLEOPATRA
Sooth, la, I'll help; thus it must be.

ANTONY
Well, well,
We shall thrive now. Seest thou, my good fellow?
Go put on thy defences.

EROS
Briefly, sir.

CLEOPATRA
Is not this buckled well?

ANTONY
Rarely, rarely.
He that unbuckles this, till we do please
To daff't for our repose, shall hear a storm.
Thou fumblest, Eros, and my queen's a squire
More tight at this than thou. Dispatch. O, love,
That thou couldst see my wars today, and knew'st
The royal occupation; thou shouldst see
A workman in't.
*Enter an armed Soldier*
Good morrow to thee. Welcome.
Thou look'st like him that knows a warlike charge.
To business that we love we rise betime
And go to't with delight.

SOLDIER
A thousand, sir,
Early though't be, have on their riveted trim,
And at the port expect you.

*Shout. Trumpets flourish. Enter Captains and Soldiers*

CAPTAIN

The morn is fair. Good morrow, General.

ALL THE SOLDIERS

Good morrow, General.

ANTONY 'Tis well blown, lads.

This morning, like the spirit of a youth
That means to be of note, begins betimes.
So, so. Come, give me that; this way; well said.
Fare thee well, dame. Whate'er becomes of me,
This is a soldier's kiss. Rebukeable
And worthy shameful check it were to stand
On more mechanic compliment. I'll leave thee
Now like a man of steel. You that will fight,
Follow me close; I'll bring you to't. Adieu.

*Exeunt all but Cleopatra and Charmian*

CHARMIAN

Please you retire to your chamber?

CLEOPATRA Lead me.

He goes forth gallantly. That he and Caesar might
Determine this great war in single fight!
Then Antony – but now. Well, on. *Exeunt*

## IV.5

*Trumpets sound. Enter Antony and Eros, a Soldier meeting them*

SOLDIER

The gods make this a happy day to Antony!

ANTONY

Would thou and those thy scars had once prevailed
To make me fight at land!

SOLDIER Hadst thou done so,

The kings that have revolted, and the soldier
That has this morning left thee, would have still

Followed thy heels.

ANTONY Who's gone this morning?

SOLDIER Who?

One ever near thee; call for Enobarbus,
He shall not hear thee, or from Caesar's camp
Say 'I am none of thine.'

ANTONY What sayst thou?

SOLDIER Sir,

He is with Caesar.

EROS Sir, his chests and treasure
He has not with him.

ANTONY Is he gone?

SOLDIER Most certain.

ANTONY

Go, Eros, send his treasure after; do it.
Detain no jot, I charge thee. Write to him –
I will subscribe – gentle adieus and greetings.
Say that I wish he never find more cause
To change a master. O, my fortunes have
Corrupted honest men! Dispatch. Enobarbus!

*Exeunt*

IV.6

*Flourish. Enter Agrippa and Caesar, with Enobarbus, and Dolabella*

CAESAR

Go forth, Agrippa, and begin the fight.
Our will is Antony be took alive;
Make it so known.

AGRIPPA Caesar, I shall. *Exit*

CAESAR

The time of universal peace is near.
Prove this a prosperous day, the three-nooked world
Shall bear the olive freely.

*Enter a Messenger*

MESSENGER Antony
Is come into the field.

CAESAR Go charge Agrippa
Plant those that have revolted in the vant,
That Antony may seem to spend his fury
Upon himself. *Exeunt all but Enobarbus*

ENOBARBUS
Alexas did revolt and went to Jewry on
Affairs of Antony; there did dissuade
Great Herod to incline himself to Caesar
And leave his master Antony. For this pains
Caesar hath hanged him. Canidius and the rest
That fell away have entertainment, but
No honourable trust. I have done ill,
Of which I do accuse myself so sorely
That I will joy no more.

*Enter a Soldier of Caesar's*

SOLDIER Enobarbus, Antony
Hath after thee sent all thy treasure, with
His bounty overplus. The messenger
Came on my guard, and at thy tent is now
Unloading of his mules.

ENOBARBUS I give it you.

SOLDIER
Mock not, Enobarbus.
I tell you true. Best you safed the bringer
Out of the host. I must attend mine office
Or would have done't myself. Your emperor
Continues still a Jove. *Exit*

ENOBARBUS
I am alone the villain of the earth,
And feel I am so most. O Antony,

Thou mine of bounty, how wouldst thou have paid
My better service, when my turpitude
Thou dost so crown with gold! This blows my heart.
If swift thought break it not, a swifter mean
Shall outstrike thought; but thought will do't, I feel.
I fight against thee? No, I will go seek
Some ditch wherein to die; the foul'st best fits
My latter part of life. *Exit*

*Alarum. Drums and trumpets. Enter Agrippa and others* IV.7

AGRIPPA
Retire! We have engaged ourselves too far.
Caesar himself has work, and our oppression
Exceeds what we expected. *Exeunt*

*Alarums. Enter Antony, and Scarus wounded*

SCARUS
O my brave emperor, this is fought indeed!
Had we done so at first, we had droven them home
With clouts about their heads.

ANTONY Thou bleed'st apace.

SCARUS
I had a wound here that was like a T,
But now 'tis made an H.

*Retreat sounded far off*

ANTONY They do retire.

SCARUS
We'll beat 'em into bench-holes. I have yet
Room for six scotches more.

*Enter Eros*

EROS
They are beaten, sir, and our advantage serves
For a fair victory.

SCARUS Let us score their backs
And snatch 'em up, as we take hares, behind.
'Tis sport to maul a runner.

ANTONY I will reward thee
Once for thy sprightly comfort, and tenfold
For thy good valour. Come thee on.

SCARUS I'll halt after.

*Exeunt*

## IV.8

*Alarum. Enter Antony, with Scarus and others, marching*

ANTONY
We have beat him to his camp. Run one before
And let the Queen know of our gests. Tomorrow,
Before the sun shall see's, we'll spill the blood
That has today escaped. I thank you all,
For doughty-handed are you, and have fought
Not as you served the cause, but as't had been
Each man's like mine; you have shown all Hectors.
Enter the city, clip your wives, your friends,
Tell them your feats, whilst they with joyful tears
Wash the congealment from your wounds, and kiss
The honoured gashes whole.

*Enter Cleopatra*

(*To Scarus*) Give me thy hand.
To this great fairy I'll commend thy acts,
Make her thanks bless thee. – O thou day o'th'world,
Chain mine armed neck; leap thou, attire and all,
Through proof of harness to my heart, and there
Ride on the pants triumphing.

CLEOPATRA Lord of lords!
O infinite virtue, com'st thou smiling from
The world's great snare uncaught?

ANTONY My nightingale,
We have beat them to their beds. What, girl! Though grey
Do something mingle with our younger brown, yet ha' we
A brain that nourishes our nerves, and can
Get goal for goal of youth. Behold this man.
Commend unto his lips thy favouring hand. –
Kiss it, my warrior. – He hath fought today
As if a god in hate of mankind had
Destroyed in such a shape.

CLEOPATRA I'll give thee, friend,
An armour all of gold; it was a king's.

ANTONY
He has deserved it, were it carbuncled
Like holy Phoebus' car. Give me thy hand.
Through Alexandria make a jolly march.
Bear our hacked targets like the men that owe them.
Had our great palace the capacity
To camp this host, we all would sup together
And drink carouses to the next day's fate,
Which promises royal peril. Trumpeters,
With brazen din blast you the city's ear;
Make mingle with our rattling tabourines,
That heaven and earth may strike their sounds together,
Applauding our approach. *Trumpets sound. Exeunt*

IV.9

*Enter a Sentry and his company, the Watch. Enobarbus follows*

SENTRY
If we be not relieved within this hour,
We must return to th'court of guard. The night
Is shiny, and they say we shall embattle
By th'second hour i'th'morn.

FIRST WATCH This last day was
A shrewd one to's.

ENOBARBUS O, bear me witness, night –

SECOND WATCH
What man is this?

FIRST WATCH Stand close, and list him.

ENOBARBUS
Be witness to me, O thou blessèd moon,
When men revolted shall upon record
Bear hateful memory, poor Enobarbus did
Before thy face repent!

SENTRY Enobarbus?

SECOND WATCH Peace;
Hark further.

ENOBARBUS
O sovereign mistress of true melancholy,
The poisonous damp of night disponge upon me,
That life, a very rebel to my will,
May hang no longer on me. Throw my heart
Against the flint and hardness of my fault,
Which, being dried with grief, will break to powder,
And finish all foul thoughts. O Antony,
Nobler than my revolt is infamous,
Forgive me in thine own particular,
But let the world rank me in register
A master-leaver and a fugitive.
O Antony! O Antony! *He dies*

FIRST WATCH Let's speak to him.

SENTRY
Let's hear him, for the things he speaks
May concern Caesar.

SECOND WATCH Let's do so. But he sleeps.

SENTRY
Swoons rather, for so bad a prayer as his
Was never yet for sleep.

FIRST WATCH Go we to him.

SECOND WATCH
Awake, sir, awake; speak to us.

FIRST WATCH Hear you, sir?

SENTRY
The hand of death hath raught him.
*Drums afar off*
Hark! The drums
Demurely wake the sleepers. Let us bear him
To th'court of guard; he is of note. Our hour
Is fully out.

SECOND WATCH
Come on then; he may recover yet.
*Exeunt with the body*

IV.10

*Enter Antony and Scarus, with their army*

ANTONY
Their preparation is today by sea;
We please them not by land.

SCARUS For both, my lord.

ANTONY
I would they'd fight i'th'fire or i'th'air;
We'd fight there too. But this it is: our foot
Upon the hills adjoining to the city
Shall stay with us. Order for sea is given;
They have put forth the haven –
Where their appointment we may best discover
And look on their endeavour. *Exeunt*

## IV.11

*Enter Caesar and his army*

CAESAR

But being charged, we will be still by land –
Which, as I take't, we shall, for his best force
Is forth to man his galleys. To the vales,
And hold our best advantage. *Exeunt*

## IV.12

*Alarum afar off, as at a sea fight*
*Enter Antony and Scarus*

ANTONY

Yet they are not joined. Where yond pine does stand
I shall discover all. I'll bring thee word
Straight how 'tis like to go. *Exit*

SCARUS

Swallows have built
In Cleopatra's sails their nests. The augurers
Say they know not, they cannot tell, look grimly,
And dare not speak their knowledge. Antony
Is valiant, and dejected, and by starts
His fretted fortunes give him hope and fear
Of what he has and has not.

*Enter Antony*

ANTONY

All is lost!
This foul Egyptian hath betrayèd me.
My fleet hath yielded to the foe, and yonder
They cast their caps up and carouse together
Like friends long lost. Triple-turned whore! 'Tis thou
Hast sold me to this novice, and my heart
Makes only wars on thee. Bid them all fly;
For when I am revenged upon my charm,
I have done all. Bid them all fly, begone!
*Exit Scarus*
O sun, thy uprise shall I see no more.
Fortune and Antony part here; even here

Do we shake hands. All come to this? The hearts
That spanieled me at heels, to whom I gave
Their wishes, do discandy, melt their sweets
On blossoming Caesar; and this pine is barked
That overtopped them all. Betrayed I am.
O this false soul of Egypt! This grave charm,
Whose eye becked forth my wars, and called them
home,
Whose bosom was my crownet, my chief end,
Like a right gypsy hath at fast and loose
Beguiled me to the very heart of loss.
What, Eros, Eros!

*Enter Cleopatra*

Ah, thou spell! Avaunt!

CLEOPATRA

Why is my lord enraged against his love?

ANTONY

Vanish, or I shall give thee thy deserving
And blemish Caesar's triumph. Let him take thee
And hoist thee up to the shouting plebeians;
Follow his chariot, like the greatest spot
Of all thy sex; most monster-like be shown
For poor'st diminutives, for doits, and let
Patient Octavia plough thy visage up
With her preparèd nails. *Exit Cleopatra*

'Tis well th'art gone,
If it be well to live; but better 'twere
Thou fell'st into my fury, for one death
Might have prevented many. Eros, ho!
The shirt of Nessus is upon me. Teach me,
Alcides, thou mine ancestor, thy rage.
Let me lodge Lichas on the horns o'th'moon,
And with those hands that grasped the heaviest club
Subdue my worthiest self. The witch shall die.

To the young Roman boy she hath sold me, and I fall
Under this plot; she dies for't. Eros, ho! *Exit*

## IV.13

*Enter Cleopatra, Charmian, Iras, and Mardian*

CLEOPATRA
Help me, my women! O, he's more mad
Than Telamon for his shield; the boar of Thessaly
Was never so embossed.

CHARMIAN
To th'monument!
There lock yourself, and send him word you are dead.
The soul and body rive not more in parting
Than greatness going off.

CLEOPATRA
To th'monument!
Mardian, go tell him I have slain myself;
Say that the last I spoke was 'Antony',
And word it, prithee, piteously. Hence, Mardian,
And bring me how he takes my death to the monument.
*Exeunt*

## IV.14

*Enter Antony and Eros*

ANTONY
Eros, thou yet behold'st me?

EROS
Ay, noble lord.

ANTONY
Sometime we see a cloud that's dragonish,
A vapour sometime like a bear or lion,
A towered citadel, a pendent rock,
A forkèd mountain, or blue promontory
With trees upon't that nod unto the world
And mock our eyes with air. Thou hast seen these signs;
They are black vesper's pageants.

EROS
Ay, my lord.

ANTONY

That which is now a horse, even with a thought
The rack dislimns, and makes it indistinct
As water is in water.

EROS It does, my lord.

ANTONY

My good knave Eros, now thy captain is
Even such a body. Here I am Antony,
Yet cannot hold this visible shape, my knave.
I made these wars for Egypt; and the Queen –
Whose heart I thought I had, for she had mine,
Which, whilst it was mine, had annexed unto't
A million more, now lost – she, Eros, has
Packed cards with Caesar, and false-played my glory
Unto an enemy's triumph.
Nay, weep not, gentle Eros, there is left us
Ourselves to end ourselves.

*Enter Mardian*

O, thy vile lady!
She has robbed me of my sword.

MARDIAN No, Antony;
My mistress loved thee, and her fortunes mingled
With thine entirely.

ANTONY Hence, saucy eunuch, peace!
She hath betrayed me and shall die the death.

MARDIAN

Death of one person can be paid but once,
And that she has discharged. What thou wouldst do
Is done unto thy hand. The last she spake
Was 'Antony! Most noble Antony!'
Then in the midst a tearing groan did break
The name of Antony; it was divided
Between her heart and lips. She rendered life,
Thy name so buried in her.

ANTONY Dead, then?

MARDIAN Dead.

ANTONY

Unarm, Eros. The long day's task is done,
And we must sleep. (*To Mardian*) That thou depart'st hence safe
Does pay thy labour richly. Go. *Exit Mardian*
Off, pluck off!
The sevenfold shield of Ajax cannot keep
The battery from my heart. O, cleave, my sides!
Heart, once be stronger than thy continent,
Crack thy frail case! Apace, Eros, apace!
No more a soldier. Bruisèd pieces, go;
You have been nobly borne. – From me awhile.
*Exit Eros*
I will o'ertake thee, Cleopatra, and
Weep for my pardon. So it must be, for now
All length is torture; since the torch is out,
Lie down, and stray no farther. Now all labour
Mars what it does; yea, very force entangles
Itself with strength. Seal then, and all is done.
Eros! – I come, my queen – Eros! Stay for me.
Where souls do couch on flowers, we'll hand in hand,
And with our sprightly port make the ghosts gaze:
Dido and her Aeneas shall want troops,
And all the haunt be ours. – Come, Eros, Eros!

*Enter Eros*

EROS

What would my lord?

ANTONY Since Cleopatra died,
I have lived in such dishonour that the gods
Detest my baseness. I, that with my sword
Quartered the world, and o'er green Neptune's back
With ships made cities, condemn myself to lack

The courage of a woman; less noble mind
Than she which by her death our Caesar tells
'I am conqueror of myself.' Thou art sworn, Eros,
That, when the exigent should come, which now
Is come indeed, when I should see behind me
Th'inevitable prosecution of
Disgrace and horror, that on my command
Thou then wouldst kill me. Do't; the time is come.
Thou strik'st not me; 'tis Caesar thou defeat'st.
Put colour in thy cheek.

EROS
The gods withhold me!
Shall I do that which all the Parthian darts,
Though enemy, lost aim and could not?

ANTONY
Eros,
Wouldst thou be windowed in great Rome and see
Thy master thus: with pleached arms, bending down
His corrigible neck, his face subdued
To penetrative shame, whilst the wheeled seat
Of fortunate Caesar, drawn before him, branded
His baseness that ensued?

EROS
I would not see't.

ANTONY
Come then; for with a wound I must be cured.
Draw that thy honest sword, which thou hast worn
Most useful for thy country.

EROS
O, sir, pardon me.

ANTONY
When I did make thee free, swor'st thou not then
To do this when I bade thee? Do it at once,
Or thy precedent services are all
But accidents unpurposed. Draw, and come.

EROS
Turn from me then that noble countenance
Wherein the worship of the whole world lies.

ANTONY
Lo thee!
*He turns from him*

EROS
My sword is drawn.

ANTONY Then let it do at once
The thing why thou hast drawn it.

EROS My dear master,
My captain, and my emperor, let me say,
Before I strike this bloody stroke, farewell.

ANTONY
'Tis said, man, and farewell.

EROS
Farewell, great chief. Shall I strike now?

ANTONY Now, Eros.

EROS
Why, there then! Thus I do escape the sorrow
Of Antony's death. *He kills himself*

ANTONY Thrice nobler than myself,
Thou teachest me, O valiant Eros, what
I should, and thou couldst not. My queen and Eros
Have by their brave instruction got upon me
A nobleness in record. But I will be
A bridegroom in my death, and run into't
As to a lover's bed. Come then; and, Eros,
Thy master dies thy scholar. To do thus
I learned of thee.
*He falls on his sword*
How? Not dead? Not dead?
The guard, ho! O, dispatch me!
*Enter Decretas and a company of the Guard*

FIRST GUARD What's the noise?

ANTONY
I have done my work ill, friends. O, make an end

Of what I have begun.

SECOND GUARD The star is fallen.

FIRST GUARD

And time is at his period.

ALL THE GUARDS Alas, and woe!

ANTONY

Let him that loves me strike me dead.

FIRST GUARD Not I.

SECOND GUARD

Nor I.

THIRD GUARD

Nor anyone. *Exeunt Guard*

DECRETAS

Thy death and fortunes bid thy followers fly.
This sword but shown to Caesar, with this tidings,
Shall enter me with him.

*Enter Diomedes*

DIOMEDES

Where's Antony?

DECRETAS There, Diomed, there.

DIOMEDES Lives he?

Wilt thou not answer, man? *Exit Decretas*

ANTONY

Art thou there, Diomed? Draw thy sword, and give me
Sufficing strokes for death.

DIOMEDES Most absolute lord,

My mistress Cleopatra sent me to thee.

ANTONY

When did she send thee?

DIOMEDES Now, my lord.

ANTONY Where is she?

DIOMEDES

Locked in her monument. She had a prophesying fear
Of what hath come to pass; for when she saw –

Which never shall be found – you did suspect
She had disposed with Caesar, and that your rage
Would not be purged, she sent you word she was dead;
But, fearing since how it might work, hath sent
Me to proclaim the truth, and I am come,
I dread, too late.

ANTONY

Too late, good Diomed. Call my guard, I prithee.

DIOMEDES

What ho! The Emperor's guard! The guard, what ho!
Come, your lord calls!

*Enter four or five of the Guard of Antony*

ANTONY

Bear me, good friends, where Cleopatra bides.
'Tis the last service that I shall command you.

FIRST GUARD

Woe, woe are we, sir, you may not live to wear
All your true followers out.

ALL THE GUARDS Most heavy day!

ANTONY

Nay, good my fellows, do not please sharp fate
To grace it with your sorrows. Bid that welcome
Which comes to punish us, and we punish it,
Seeming to bear it lightly. Take me up.
I have led you oft; carry me now, good friends,
And have my thanks for all. *Exeunt, bearing Antony*

IV.15 *Enter Cleopatra and her maids, aloft, with Charmian and Iras*

CLEOPATRA

O, Charmian, I will never go from hence.

CHARMIAN

Be comforted, dear madam.

CLEOPATRA No, I will not.
All strange and terrible events are welcome,
But comforts we despise. Our size of sorrow,
Proportioned to our cause, must be as great
As that which makes it.
*Enter Diomedes below*
How now? Is he dead?

DIOMEDES
His death's upon him, but not dead.
Look out o'th'other side your monument;
His guard have brought him thither.
*Enter, below, the Guard, bearing Antony*

CLEOPATRA O sun,
Burn the great sphere thou mov'st in; darkling stand
The varying shore o'th'world! O Antony,
Antony, Antony! Help, Charmian, help, Iras, help!
Help, friends below! Let's draw him hither.

ANTONY Peace!
Not Caesar's valour hath o'erthrown Antony,
But Antony's hath triumphed on itself.

CLEOPATRA
So it should be, that none but Antony
Should conquer Antony, but woe 'tis so!

ANTONY
I am dying, Egypt, dying; only
I here importune death awhile, until
Of many thousand kisses the poor last
I lay upon thy lips.

CLEOPATRA I dare not, dear;
Dear my lord, pardon. I dare not,
Lest I be taken. Not th'imperious show
Of the full-fortuned Caesar ever shall
Be brooched with me. If knife, drugs, serpents, have
Edge, sting, or operation, I am safe.

Your wife Octavia, with her modest eyes
And still conclusion, shall acquire no honour
Demuring upon me. But come, come, Antony –
Help me, my women – we must draw thee up.
Assist, good friends.

ANTONY O, quick, or I am gone.

CLEOPATRA

Here's sport indeed! How heavy weighs my lord!
Our strength is all gone into heaviness,
That makes the weight. Had I great Juno's power,
The strong-winged Mercury should fetch thee up
And set thee by Jove's side. Yet come a little;
Wishers were ever fools. O, come, come, come.

*They heave Antony aloft to Cleopatra*

And welcome, welcome! Die when thou hast lived;
Quicken with kissing. Had my lips that power,
Thus would I wear them out.

ALL THE GUARDS A heavy sight!

ANTONY

I am dying, Egypt, dying.
Give me some wine, and let me speak a little.

CLEOPATRA

No, let me speak, and let me rail so high
That the false housewife Fortune break her wheel,
Provoked by my offence.

ANTONY One word, sweet queen.
Of Caesar seek your honour, with your safety. O!

CLEOPATRA

They do not go together.

ANTONY Gentle, hear me:
None about Caesar trust but Proculeius.

CLEOPATRA

My resolution and my hands I'll trust,

None about Caesar.

ANTONY

The miserable change now at my end
Lament nor sorrow at, but please your thoughts
In feeding them with those my former fortunes,
Wherein I lived; the greatest prince o'th'world,
The noblest; and do now not basely die,
Not cowardly put off my helmet to
My countryman; a Roman, by a Roman
Valiantly vanquished. Now my spirit is going;
I can no more.

CLEOPATRA Noblest of men, woo't die?
Hast thou no care of me? Shall I abide
In this dull world, which in thy absence is
No better than a sty? O, see, my women,

*Antony dies*

The crown o'th'earth doth melt. My lord!
O, withered is the garland of the war,
The soldier's pole is fall'n; young boys and girls
Are level now with men. The odds is gone,
And there is nothing left remarkable
Beneath the visiting moon.

*She faints*

CHARMIAN O, quietness, lady!

IRAS

She's dead too, our sovereign.

CHARMIAN Lady!

IRAS Madam!

CHARMIAN

O madam, madam, madam!

IRAS

Royal Egypt! Empress!

CHARMIAN Peace, peace, Iras!

CLEOPATRA

No more but e'en a woman, and commanded
By such poor passion as the maid that milks
And does the meanest chares. It were for me
To throw my sceptre at the injurious gods,
To tell them that this world did equal theirs
Till they had stolen our jewel. All's but naught.
Patience is sottish, and impatience does
Become a dog that's mad; then is it sin
To rush into the secret house of death
Ere death dare come to us? How do you, women?
What, what, good cheer! Why, how now, Charmian?
My noble girls! Ah, women, women, look,
Our lamp is spent, it's out. Good sirs, take heart.
We'll bury him; and then, what's brave, what's noble,
Let's do't after the high Roman fashion,
And make death proud to take us. Come, away.
This case of that huge spirit now is cold.
Ah, women, women! Come; we have no friend
But resolution, and the briefest end.

*Exeunt, bearing off Antony's body*

*

V.1 *Enter Caesar, Agrippa, Dolabella, Maecenas, Gallus, Proculeius, with his council of war*

CAESAR

Go to him, Dolabella, bid him yield.
Being so frustrate, tell him, he mocks
The pauses that he makes.

DOLABELLA Caesar, I shall. *Exit*

*Enter Decretas, with the sword of Antony*

CAESAR
Wherefore is that? And what art thou that dar'st
Appear thus to us?
DECRETAS I am called Decretas.
Mark Antony I served, who best was worthy
Best to be served. Whilst he stood up and spoke,
He was my master, and I wore my life
To spend upon his haters. If thou please
To take me to thee, as I was to him
I'll be to Caesar; if thou pleasest not,
I yield thee up my life.
CAESAR What is't thou sayst?
DECRETAS
I say, O Caesar, Antony is dead.
CAESAR
The breaking of so great a thing should make
A greater crack. The round world
Should have shook lions into civil streets
And citizens to their dens. The death of Antony
Is not a single doom; in the name lay
A moiety of the world.
DECRETAS He is dead, Caesar,
Not by a public minister of justice
Nor by a hirèd knife; but that self hand
Which writ his honour in the acts it did
Hath, with the courage which the heart did lend it,
Splitted the heart. This is his sword;
I robbed his wound of it. Behold it stained
With his most noble blood.
CAESAR Look you, sad friends.
The gods rebuke me, but it is tidings
To wash the eyes of kings.
AGRIPPA And strange it is
That nature must compel us to lament

Our most persisted deeds.

MAECENAS His taints and honours
Waged equal with him.

AGRIPPA A rarer spirit never
Did steer humanity. But you gods will give us
Some faults to make us men. Caesar is touched.

MAECENAS
When such a spacious mirror's set before him,
He needs must see himself.

CAESAR O Antony,
I have followed thee to this. But we do launch
Diseases in our bodies. I must perforce
Have shown to thee such a declining day
Or look on thine. We could not stall together
In the whole world. But yet let me lament
With tears as sovereign as the blood of hearts
That thou, my brother, my competitor
In top of all design, my mate in empire,
Friend and companion in the front of war,
The arm of mine own body, and the heart
Where mine his thoughts did kindle – that our stars,
Unreconciliable, should divide
Our equalness to this. Hear me, good friends –
(*Enter an Egyptian*)
But I will tell you at some meeter season.
The business of this man looks out of him;
We'll hear him what he says. Whence are you?

EGYPTIAN
A poor Egyptian yet. The Queen my mistress,
Confined in all she has, her monument,
Of thy intents desires instruction,
That she preparèdly may frame herself
To th'way she's forced to.

CAESAR Bid her have good heart.

She soon shall know of us, by some of ours,
How honourable and how kindly we
Determine for her. For Caesar cannot live
To be ungentle.

EGYPTIAN So the gods preserve thee! *Exit*

CAESAR
Come hither, Proculeius. Go and say
We purpose her no shame. Give her what comforts
The quality of her passion shall require,
Lest in her greatness, by some mortal stroke,
She do defeat us. For her life in Rome
Would be eternal in our triumph. Go,
And with your speediest bring us what she says
And how you find her.

PROCULEIUS Caesar, I shall. *Exit*

CAESAR
Gallus, go you along. *Exit Gallus*
Where's Dolabella,
To second Proculeius?

ALL CAESAR'S ATTENDANTS Dolabella!

CAESAR
Let him alone, for I remember now
How he's employed. He shall in time be ready.
Go with me to my tent, where you shall see
How hardly I was drawn into this war,
How calm and gentle I proceeded still
In all my writings. Go with me, and see
What I can show in this. *Exeunt*

*Enter Cleopatra, Charmian, Iras, and Mardian* V.2

CLEOPATRA
My desolation does begin to make
A better life. 'Tis paltry to be Caesar:

Not being Fortune, he's but Fortune's knave,
A minister of her will. And it is great
To do that thing that ends all other deeds,
Which shackles accidents and bolts up change;
Which sleeps, and never palates more the dung,
The beggar's nurse and Caesar's.

*Enter, to the gates of the monument, Proculeius, Gallus, and Soldiers*

PROCULEIUS

Caesar sends greeting to the Queen of Egypt,
And bids thee study on what fair demands
Thou mean'st to have him grant thee.

CLEOPATRA What's thy name?

PROCULEIUS

My name is Proculeius.

CLEOPATRA Antony
Did tell me of you, bade me trust you, but
I do not greatly care to be deceived,
That have no use for trusting. If your master
Would have a queen his beggar, you must tell him
That majesty, to keep decorum, must
No less beg than a kingdom. If he please
To give me conquered Egypt for my son,
He gives me so much of mine own as I
Will kneel to him with thanks.

PROCULEIUS Be of good cheer;
Y'are fall'n into a princely hand; fear nothing.
Make your full reference freely to my lord,
Who is so full of grace that it flows over
On all that need. Let me report to him
Your sweet dependency, and you shall find
A conqueror that will pray in aid for kindness,
Where he for grace is kneeled to.

CLEOPATRA Pray you, tell him

I am his fortune's vassal, and I send him
The greatness he has got. I hourly learn
A doctrine of obedience, and would gladly
Look him i'th'face.

PROCULEIUS This I'll report, dear lady.
Have comfort, for I know your plight is pitied
Of him that caused it.

*The Soldiers approach Cleopatra from behind*

GALLUS
You see how easily she may be surprised.

*They seize Cleopatra*

Guard her till Caesar come. *Exit Gallus*

IRAS
Royal queen!

CHARMIAN
O Cleopatra! Thou art taken, queen.

CLEOPATRA
Quick, quick, good hands!

*She draws a dagger*

PROCULEIUS Hold, worthy lady, hold!

*He disarms her*

Do not yourself such wrong, who are in this
Relieved, but not betrayed.

CLEOPATRA What, of death too,
That rids our dogs of languish?

PROCULEIUS Cleopatra,
Do not abuse my master's bounty by
Th'undoing of yourself. Let the world see
His nobleness well acted, which your death
Will never let come forth.

CLEOPATRA Where art thou, death?
Come hither, come! Come, come, and take a queen
Worth many babes and beggars!

PROCULEIUS O, temperance, lady!

CLEOPATRA

Sir, I will eat no meat, I'll not drink, sir –
If idle talk will once be necessary –
I'll not sleep neither. This mortal house I'll ruin,
Do Caesar what he can. Know, sir, that I
Will not wait pinioned at your master's court,
Nor once be chastised with the sober eye
Of dull Octavia. Shall they hoist me up
And show me to the shouting varletry
Of censuring Rome? Rather a ditch in Egypt
Be gentle grave unto me! Rather on Nilus' mud
Lay me stark nak'd and let the waterflies
Blow me into abhorring! Rather make
My country's high pyramides my gibbet
And hang me up in chains!

PROCULEIUS You do extend

These thoughts of horror further than you shall
Find cause in Caesar.

*Enter Dolabella*

DOLABELLA Proculeius,

What thou hast done thy master Caesar knows,
And he hath sent for thee. For the Queen,
I'll take her to my guard.

PROCULEIUS So, Dolabella,

It shall content me best. Be gentle to her.
(*To Cleopatra*) To Caesar I will speak what you shall please,
If you'll employ me to him.

CLEOPATRA Say I would die.

*Exeunt Proculeius and Soldiers*

DOLABELLA

Most noble empress, you have heard of me?

CLEOPATRA

I cannot tell.

DOLABELLA Assuredly you know me.

CLEOPATRA
No matter, sir, what I have heard or known.
You laugh when boys or women tell their dreams;
Is't not your trick?

DOLABELLA I understand not, madam.

CLEOPATRA
I dreamt there was an emperor Antony.
O, such another sleep, that I might see
But such another man!

DOLABELLA If it might please ye –

CLEOPATRA
His face was as the heavens, and therein stuck
A sun and moon, which kept their course and lighted
The little O o'th'earth.

DOLABELLA Most sovereign creature –

CLEOPATRA
His legs bestrid the ocean; his reared arm
Crested the world; his voice was propertied
As all the tunèd spheres, and that to friends;
But when he meant to quail and shake the orb,
He was as rattling thunder. For his bounty,
There was no winter in't; an Antony it was
That grew the more by reaping. His delights
Were dolphin-like; they showed his back above
The element they lived in. In his livery
Walked crowns and crownets; realms and islands were
As plates dropped from his pocket.

DOLABELLA Cleopatra –

CLEOPATRA
Think you there was or might be such a man
As this I dreamt of?

DOLABELLA Gentle madam, no.

CLEOPATRA

You lie, up to the hearing of the gods.
But if there be nor ever were one such,
It's past the size of dreaming. Nature wants stuff
To vie strange forms with fancy, yet t'imagine
An Antony were nature's piece 'gainst fancy,
Condemning shadows quite.

DOLABELLA Hear me, good madam.

Your loss is as yourself, great; and you bear it
As answering to the weight. Would I might never
O'ertake pursued success but I do feel,
By the rebound of yours, a grief that smites
My very heart at root.

CLEOPATRA I thank you, sir.

Know you what Caesar means to do with me?

DOLABELLA

I am loath to tell you what I would you knew.

CLEOPATRA

Nay, pray you, sir.

DOLABELLA Though he be honourable –

CLEOPATRA

He'll lead me, then, in triumph?

DOLABELLA

Madam, he will. I know't.

*Flourish. Enter Proculeius, Caesar, Gallus, Maecenas, and others of Caesar's train*

ALL

Make way there! Caesar!

CAESAR

Which is the Queen of Egypt?

DOLABELLA

It is the Emperor, madam.

*Cleopatra kneels*

CAESAR
Arise! You shall not kneel.
I pray you rise; rise, Egypt.
CLEOPATRA Sir, the gods
Will have it thus. My master and my lord
I must obey.
CAESAR Take to you no hard thoughts.
The record of what injuries you did us,
Though written in our flesh, we shall remember
As things but done by chance.
CLEOPATRA Sole sir o'th'world,
I cannot project mine own cause so well
To make it clear, but do confess I have
Been laden with like frailties which before
Have often shamed our sex.
CAESAR Cleopatra, know,
We will extenuate rather than enforce.
If you apply yourself to our intents,
Which towards you are most gentle, you shall find
A benefit in this change; but if you seek
To lay on me a cruelty by taking
Antony's course, you shall bereave yourself
Of my good purposes, and put your children
To that destruction which I'll guard them from
If thereon you rely. I'll take my leave.
CLEOPATRA
And may, through all the world; 'tis yours, and we,
Your scutcheons and your signs of conquest, shall
Hang in what place you please. Here, my good lord.
*She gives him a paper*
CAESAR
You shall advise me in all for Cleopatra.
CLEOPATRA
This is the brief of money, plate, and jewels

I am possessed of. 'Tis exactly valued,
Not petty things admitted. Where's Seleucus?

*Enter Seleucus*

SELEUCUS

Here, madam.

CLEOPATRA

This is my treasurer. Let him speak, my lord,
Upon his peril, that I have reserved
To myself nothing. Speak the truth, Seleucus.

SELEUCUS

Madam,
I had rather seel my lips than to my peril
Speak that which is not.

CLEOPATRA What have I kept back?

SELEUCUS

Enough to purchase what you have made known.

CAESAR

Nay, blush not, Cleopatra. I approve
Your wisdom in the deed.

CLEOPATRA See, Caesar; O behold,
How pomp is followed! Mine will now be yours,
And should we shift estates, yours would be mine.
The ingratitude of this Seleucus does
Even make me wild. O slave, of no more trust
Than love that's hired! What, goest thou back? Thou shalt
Go back, I warrant thee; but I'll catch thine eyes,
Though they had wings. Slave, soulless villain, dog!
O rarely base!

CAESAR Good queen, let us entreat you.

CLEOPATRA

O Caesar, what a wounding shame is this,
That thou vouchsafing here to visit me,
Doing the honour of thy lordliness
To one so meek, that mine own servant should

Parcel the sum of my disgraces by
Addition of his envy. Say, good Caesar,
That I some lady trifles have reserved,
Immoment toys, things of such dignity
As we greet modern friends withal; and say
Some nobler token I have kept apart
For Livia and Octavia, to induce
Their mediation – must I be unfolded
With one that I have bred? The gods! It smites me
Beneath the fall I have. (*To Seleucus*) Prithee go hence,
Or I shall show the cinders of my spirits
Through th'ashes of my chance. Wert thou a man,
Thou wouldst have mercy on me.

CAESAR
Forbear, Seleucus.

*Exit Seleucus*

CLEOPATRA
Be it known that we, the greatest, are misthought
For things that others do; and when we fall,
We answer others' merits in our name,
Are therefore to be pitied.

CAESAR
Cleopatra,
Not what you have reserved nor what acknowledged
Put we i'th'roll of conquest. Still be't yours;
Bestow it at your pleasure, and believe
Caesar's no merchant, to make prize with you
Of things that merchants sold. Therefore be cheered.
Make not your thoughts your prisons. No, dear queen,
For we intend so to dispose you as
Yourself shall give us counsel. Feed and sleep.
Our care and pity is so much upon you
That we remain your friend; and so adieu.

CLEOPATRA
My master, and my lord!

CAESAR
Not so. Adieu.

*Flourish. Exeunt Caesar, Dolabella, Proculeius, Gallus, Maecenas, and Caesar's other Attendants*

CLEOPATRA

He words me, girls, he words me, that I should not
Be noble to myself. But hark thee, Charmian.

*She whispers to Charmian*

IRAS

Finish, good lady; the bright day is done,
And we are for the dark.

CLEOPATRA Hie thee again.
I have spoke already, and it is provided;
Go put it to the haste.

CHARMIAN Madam, I will.

*Enter Dolabella*

DOLABELLA

Where's the Queen?

CHARMIAN Behold, sir. *Exit*

CLEOPATRA Dolabella!

DOLABELLA

Madam, as thereto sworn, by your command,
Which my love makes religion to obey,
I tell you this: Caesar through Syria
Intends his journey, and within three days
You with your children will he send before.
Make your best use of this. I have performed
Your pleasure and my promise.

CLEOPATRA Dolabella,
I shall remain your debtor.

DOLABELLA I, your servant.
Adieu, good queen; I must attend on Caesar.

CLEOPATRA

Farewell, and thanks. *Exit Dolabella*
Now, Iras, what think'st thou?
Thou, an Egyptian puppet, shall be shown

In Rome as well as I. Mechanic slaves
With greasy aprons, rules, and hammers shall
Uplift us to the view. In their thick breaths,
Rank of gross diet, shall we be enclouded,
And forced to drink their vapour.

IRAS
The gods forbid!

CLEOPATRA
Nay, 'tis most certain, Iras. Saucy lictors
Will catch at us like strumpets, and scald rhymers
Ballad us out o'tune. The quick comedians
Extemporally will stage us, and present
Our Alexandrian revels. Antony
Shall be brought drunken forth, and I shall see
Some squeaking Cleopatra boy my greatness
I'th'posture of a whore.

IRAS
O, the good gods!

CLEOPATRA
Nay that's certain.

IRAS
I'll never see't! For I am sure my nails
Are stronger than mine eyes.

CLEOPATRA
Why, that's the way
To fool their preparation, and to conquer
Their most absurd intents.

*Enter Charmian*

Now, Charmian!
Show me, my women, like a queen. Go fetch
My best attires. I am again for Cydnus,
To meet Mark Antony. Sirrah Iras, go.
Now, noble Charmian, we'll dispatch indeed,
And when thou hast done this chare, I'll give thee leave
To play till doomsday. – Bring our crown and all.

*Exit Iras*

*A noise within*

Wherefore's this noise?

*Enter a Guardsman*

GUARDSMAN Here is a rural fellow
That will not be denied your highness' presence.
He brings you figs.

CLEOPATRA
Let him come in. *Exit Guardsman*
What poor an instrument
May do a noble deed! He brings me liberty.
My resolution's placed, and I have nothing
Of woman in me. Now from head to foot
I am marble-constant; now the fleeting moon
No planet is of mine.

*Enter Guardsman and Clown with a basket*

GUARDSMAN This is the man.

CLEOPATRA
Avoid, and leave him. *Exit Guardsman*
Hast thou the pretty worm of Nilus there,
That kills and pains not?

CLOWN Truly I have him; but I would not be the party that should desire you to touch him, for his biting is immortal. Those that do die of it do seldom or never recover.

CLEOPATRA Remember'st thou any that have died on't?

CLOWN Very many, men and women too. I heard of one of them no longer than yesterday; a very honest woman, but something given to lie, as a woman should not do but in the way of honesty; how she died of the biting of it, what pain she felt; truly, she makes a very good report o'th'worm. But he that will believe all that they say shall never be saved by half that they do. But this is most falliable, the worm's an odd worm.

CLEOPATRA Get thee hence, farewell.

CLOWN I wish you all joy of the worm.

*He sets down the basket*

CLEOPATRA Farewell.

CLOWN You must think this, look you, that the worm will do his kind.

CLEOPATRA Ay, ay, farewell.

CLOWN Look you, the worm is not to be trusted but in the keeping of wise people; for indeed there is no goodness in the worm.

CLEOPATRA Take thou no care; it shall be heeded.

CLOWN Very good. Give it nothing, I pray you, for it is not worth the feeding.

CLEOPATRA Will it eat me?

CLOWN You must not think I am so simple but I know the devil himself will not eat a woman. I know that a woman is a dish for the gods, if the devil dress her not. But truly, these same whoreson devils do the gods great harm in their women; for in every ten that they make, the devils mar five.

CLEOPATRA Well, get thee gone, farewell.

CLOWN Yes, forsooth. I wish you joy o'th'worm. *Exit*

*Enter Iras with a robe, crown, sceptre, and other regalia*

CLEOPATRA

Give me my robe; put on my crown; I have
Immortal longings in me. Now no more
The juice of Egypt's grape shall moist this lip.
Yare, yare, good Iras; quick – methinks I hear
Antony call. I see him rouse himself
To praise my noble act. I hear him mock
The luck of Caesar, which the gods give men
To excuse their after wrath. Husband, I come.
Now to that name my courage prove my title!
I am fire and air; my other elements
I give to baser life. So, have you done?

Come then, and take the last warmth of my lips.
Farewell, kind Charmian, Iras, long farewell.
*She kisses them. Iras falls and dies*
Have I the aspic in my lips? Dost fall?
If thou and nature can so gently part,
The stroke of death is as a lover's pinch,
Which hurts, and is desired. Dost thou lie still?
If thus thou vanishest, thou tell'st the world
It is not worth leave-taking.

CHARMIAN
Dissolve, thick cloud, and rain, that I may say
The gods themselves do weep.

CLEOPATRA This proves me base;
If she first meet the curlèd Antony,
He'll make demand of her, and spend that kiss
Which is my heaven to have. (*To an asp*) Come, thou mortal wretch,
With thy sharp teeth this knot intrinsicate
Of life at once untie. Poor venomous fool,
Be angry, and dispatch. O, couldst thou speak,
That I might hear thee call great Caesar ass
Unpolicied!

CHARMIAN O eastern star!

CLEOPATRA Peace, peace!
Dost thou not see my baby at my breast,
That sucks the nurse asleep?

CHARMIAN O, break! O, break!

CLEOPATRA
As sweet as balm, as soft as air, as gentle –
O, Antony! Nay, I will take thee too.
*She applies another asp to her arm*
What should I stay – *She dies*

CHARMIAN
In this vile world? So, fare thee well.

Now boast thee, death, in thy possession lies
A lass unparalleled. Downy windows, close;
And golden Phoebus never be beheld
Of eyes again so royal! Your crown's awry;
I'll mend it, and then play –

*Enter the Guard, rustling in*

FIRST GUARD
Where's the Queen?

CHARMIAN Speak softly, wake her not.

FIRST GUARD
Caesar hath sent –

CHARMIAN Too slow a messenger.

*She applies an asp to herself*

O, come apace, dispatch. I partly feel thee.

FIRST GUARD
Approach, ho! All's not well; Caesar's beguiled.

SECOND GUARD
There's Dolabella sent from Caesar; call him.

FIRST GUARD
What work is here, Charmian? Is this well done?

CHARMIAN
It is well done, and fitting for a princess
Descended of so many royal kings.
Ah, soldier! *Charmian dies*

*Enter Dolabella*

DOLABELLA
How goes it here?

SECOND GUARD All dead.

DOLABELLA Caesar, thy thoughts
Touch their effects in this. Thyself art coming
To see performed the dreaded act which thou
So sought'st to hinder.

*Enter Caesar, and all his train, marching*

ALL A way there, a way for Caesar!

DOLABELLA
O, sir, you are too sure an augurer;
That you did fear is done.

CAESAR Bravest at the last,
She levelled at our purposes and, being royal,
Took her own way. The manner of their deaths?
I do not see them bleed.

DOLABELLA Who was last with them?

FIRST GUARD
A simple countryman, that brought her figs.
This was his basket.

CAESAR Poisoned, then.

FIRST GUARD O, Caesar,
This Charmian lived but now; she stood and spake.
I found her trimming up the diadem
On her dead mistress. Tremblingly she stood,
And on the sudden dropped.

CAESAR O, noble weakness!
If they had swallowed poison, 'twould appear
By external swelling; but she looks like sleep,
As she would catch another Antony
In her strong toil of grace.

DOLABELLA Here, on her breast,
There is a vent of blood, and something blown;
The like is on her arm.

FIRST GUARD
This is an aspic's trail; and these fig leaves
Have slime upon them, such as th'aspic leaves
Upon the caves of Nile.

CAESAR Most probable
That so she died; for her physician tells me
She hath pursued conclusions infinite
Of easy ways to die. Take up her bed,
And bear her women from the monument.

She shall be buried by her Antony.
No grave upon the earth shall clip in it
A pair so famous. High events as these
Strike those that make them; and their story is
No less in pity than his glory which
Brought them to be lamented. Our army shall
In solemn show attend this funeral,
And then to Rome. Come, Dolabella, see
High order in this great solemnity. *Exeunt*

# *An Account of the Text*

The date of the composition of *Antony and Cleopatra* has to be conjectured. A terminal point is provided by the Stationers' Register for 20 May 1608, when the publisher Edward Blount entered two 'books', *Pericles, Prince of Tyre* and *Antony and Cleopatra*. Secondly, in 1607 Samuel Daniel's tragedy *Cleopatra*, which was first published in 1594, appeared in a new edition, 'newly altered', and this edition contains revisions which can be argued to have been influenced by Shakespeare's play as it was performed on the stage (see The Play in Performance). An earlier limit is less easy to fix. Most scholars nowadays assign the play to 1606, its immediate predecessor probably being *Macbeth* (1606).

The only authoritative text of *Antony and Cleopatra* is the one included in the collected edition of Shakespeare's plays, the first Folio (1623). It was probably printed direct from Shakespeare's own manuscript and not from some intermediate source such as a regularized prompt copy. It shows many signs of the author's hand which would probably have been eliminated had a copyist working for the theatre been the writer of the manuscript. These authorial signs may be grouped under three heads: evidence from spelling, evidence from which conjectures may be made about Shakespeare's handwriting and evidence from stage directions.

Textual critics have assembled a good deal of information about Shakespeare's probable spelling habits. They seem to have been rather old-fashioned, even archaic, by the standards of the 1620s. The Folio text shows a number of such individual spellings which suggest the presence of a Shakespearian manuscript, for instance, 'reciding' (for 'residing'), I.3.103; 'triumpherate' (for 'triumvirate'), III.6.28; and 'arrant' (for 'errand'), III.13.104.

Some of the proper names are also of interest, since they can be compared with the originals which Shakespeare found in North's Plutarch, for example, 'Scicion' for North's 'Sicyon', and 'Camidius', 'Camidias' and 'Camindius' for North's 'Canidius'. The spelling 'Scicion', with its unusual initial 'Sc', may be Shakespearian, since in the scene in the anonymous play *Sir Thomas More* which is thought by good judges to be very probably in Shakespeare's handwriting the form 'scilens' (for 'silence') occurs; in the first Quarto of *Henry IV, Part II* 'Scilens' occurs eighteen times for the name of the character 'Silence'; and in *Coriolanus* the form 'Scicinius' several times occurs for North's 'Sicinius'. In the case of 'Camidius' etc., the question arises whether Shakespeare did not deliberately intend a form beginning with 'Cam', since the form 'Canidius' nowhere occurs in the Folio text. Another odd form is 'Thidias' for North's 'Thyreus'. This may be a deliberate change, as J. Dover Wilson suggested, to make for ease of speaking.

Secondly, it can be argued that some of the misprints in the Folio text arose from the peculiarities of Shakespeare's handwriting. An instance is 'foretell' for 'fertile' (I.2.40), where Shakespeare probably wrote 'fertill' in such a way as to make the confusion easily possible.

Thirdly, the stage directions are such as to suggest an authorial imagination rather than a mind more narrowly intent on directives for a stage performance. Some of them leave the particulars vague, for example, '*Enter two or three Seruants, with a Banket*' (II.7.0). In others the wording suggests a mind in the process of conceiving an effect, as in '*Enter the Guard rustling in, and Dolabella*' (V.2.318). Some are of special interest in showing how Shakespeare imagined a stage grouping, for example, '*Enter Anthony, Cæsar, Octauia betweene them*' (II.3.0), or elsewhere possibly the order in which characters entered the stage, for example, '*Enter Agrippa, Mecenas, and Cæsar*' (III.6.0), where the chief character appears last, or '*Enter Proculeius, Cæsar, Gallus, Mecenas, and others of his Traine*' (V.2.110), where Proculeius is placed first because he has supervised the capture of Cleopatra and is now leading his master to her.

The Folio text is least reliable in its punctuation and lineation: in many cases both clearly need correction. It is, finally, noteworthy that (leaving aside '*Actus Primus. Scæna Prima*' at the beginning) the Folio text is entirely without act and scene divisions, and these have been supplied from Peter Alexander's edition of the *Complete Works* (1951).

## COLLATIONS

These lists are selective. Quotations from the first Folio (F) are given in the original spelling, except that 'long s' (ſ) has been replaced by 's'.

### *1*

The following is a list of departures in the present text from that of F, whose reading is given on the right of the square bracket. Only those readings are included which affect meaning; obvious misprints are not listed. Many of the emendations accepted here were first made by eighteenth-century editors of the play. Those first found in seventeenth-century reprints of the Folio (F2 and F3) are indicated.

The Characters in the Play] *not in* F

I.1

39 On] One
50 whose] F2; who

I.2

4 charge] change
40 fertile] foretell
63–4 CHARMIAN Our . . . mend! Alexas – come] *Char.* Our . . . mend. *Alexas.* Come
81 Saw you my lord?] F2; Saue you, my Lord.
114 ho, the news] how the newes
115 FIRST ATTENDANT] 1. *Mes.*
116 SECOND ATTENDANT] 2. *Mes.*
119 MESSENGER] 3. *Mes.*
138 occasion] an occasion
180 leave] loue
185 Hath] F2; Haue
194 hair] heire

196 place is under us, requires] F2; places vnder vs, require

I.3

43 services] Seruicles
80 blood; no more.] blood no more?
82 my] F2; *not in* F

I.4

3 Our] One
8 Vouchsafed] vouchsafe
9 abstract] F2; abstracts
30 chid] chid:
44 deared] fear'd
46 lackeying] lacking
56 wassails] Vassailes
66 browsèd'st] F2; brows'd
75 we] F2; me

I.5

5 time] time:
24 burgonet] F2; Burganet
48 arrogant] Arme-gaunt
50 dumbed] dumbe
he, sad] he sad,
61 man] F2; mans

II.1

16, 18, 38 MENAS] *Mene.*
21 waned] wand
41 warred] F2; wan'd
43–4 greater. . . . all,] greater, . . . all:

II.2

111 soldier only.] Souldier, onely
120–21 staunch, from . . . world] staunch from . . . world:
125 not so,] not, say
126 reproof] proofe
151 hand.] hand
166–7 ANTONY What . . . strength? CAESAR By land, great] *Anth.* What . . . land? *Cæsar.* Great,
199 lovesick with them. The] Loue-sicke. | With them the
209 glow] gloue

II.3

23 afeard] a feare

25 thee; no more but when to thee.] thee no more but: when to thee,

31 away,] alway

II.5

10–11 river; there, | My . . . off,] Riuer there | My . . . off.

12 Tawny-finned] Tawny fine

28 him, there] him. | There

43 is] ’tis

II.6

16 the] F2; *not in* F

39 ALL THE TRIUMVIRS] *Omnes*

53 There is] ther’s

66 meanings] meaning

69 of] F3; *not in* F

II.7

4 high-coloured] F2; high Conlord

90 part then is] part, then he is

98 grows] F2; grow

111 BOY (*sings*)] The Song.

118 you off. Our] you of our

126 father’s] Father

127–8 ENOBARBUS Take heed you fall not. | Menas, I’ll not on shore. MENAS No,] *Eno*. Take heed you fall not *Menas*: Ile not on shore, | No

130 a loud] aloud

III.1

5 SILIUS] *Romaine*

27, 34 SILIUS] *Rom.*

III.2

10 AGRIPPA] *Ant.*

16 figures] Figure

59 wept] weepe

III.4

6–7 of me; when . . . honour,] of me, | When . . . Honour:

8 them, most] then most

9 took’t] look’t

24 yours] F2; your

30 Your] F2; You

38 has] F2; he’s

III.5

12 Then, world, thou hast] Then would thou hadst
chaps,] chaps
14 the one the other] the other

III.6

13 he there] hither
kings of kings] King of Kings
29 and, being, that] And being that,
61 obstruct] abstract

III.7

5 Is't not denounced] If not, denounc'd
14 Photinus, an eunuch,] *Photinus* an Eunuch,
35 muleters] F2; Militers
69 leader's led] Leaders leade
72 CANIDIUS] *Ven.*
78 Well] Well,

III.10

14 June] F2; Inne
27 he] his

III.11

19 that] them
47 seize] F2; cease
58 tow] stowe
59 Thy] The

III.13

55 Caesar] *Cæsars*
56 embraced] embrace
74 this: in deputation] this in disputation,
77 Till from] Tell him, from
90 me. Of late, when] me of late. When
112–13 eyes, | In our own filth] eyes | In our owne filth,
137 whipped for] whipt. For
162 Caesarion smite] Cæsarian smile
165 discandying] discandering
168 sits] sets
198 preys on] prayes in

IV.1

3 combat,] Combat.

IV.2

19 ALL THE SERVANTS] *Omnes*

38 fall! My hearty friends,] fall (my hearty Friends)

IV.3

9 THIRD SOLDIER] 1

IV.4

5 too] too, *Anthony*

6–8 for? ANTONY Ah . . . this. CLEOPATRA Sooth, la,] For? for? Ah . . . this, | Sooth-law

13 daff't] daft

24 CAPTAIN] *Alex.*

25 ALL THE SOLDIERS] *All*

IV.5

1, 3, 6 SOLDIER] *Eros*

17 Dispatch. Enobarbus!] Dispatch *Enobarbus.*

IV.6

36 do't, I feel.] doo't. I feele

IV.8

2 gests] guests

18 My] F2; Mine

23 favouring] sauouring

IV.12

4 augurers] Auguries

21 spanieled] pannelled

37 doits] Dolts

IV.14

4 towered] toward

10 dislimns] dislimes

19 Caesar] *Cæsars*

104 ho!] how?

107, 134 ALL THE GUARDS] *All*

111 DECRETAS] *Dercetus*

IV.15

25–6 me. If . . . operation,] me, if . . . operation.

40 ALL THE GUARDS] *All*

72 e'en] in

82 what,] what

V.1

28, 31 AGRIPPA] *Dol.*, *Dola.*

59 live] leaue
70 ALL CAESAR'S ATTENDANTS] *All*

V.2

35 GALLUS] *Pro.*
81 little O o'th'earth] little o'th'earth
104 smites] suites
216 Ballad] F2; Ballads
o'tune] a Tune
223 my] F2; mine
313 vile] wilde
317 awry] away

## 2 Rejected Emendations

Below are listed instances where the present text either preserves readings of F (modernized according to the principles of this edition) that have often, with some plausibility, been emended, or introduces an emendation different from the one usually accepted. Emendations found in some modern editions of the play are given after the square brackets, separated by semi-colons where there are more than one.

I.1

47 now] new

I.2

71 the] thy
111 winds] minds
124 doth] do
131 How] Ho

I.3

11 I wish] iwis
20 What says . . . woman – you may go?] (F: What sayes . . . woman you may goe?); What, says . . . woman you may go?; What says . . . woman? You may go.
100 laurel] laurelled

I.4

21 smells] smell
47 motion.] motion. *Enter a second Messenger*
49 Makes] Make

84 knew] know

I.5

48 arrogant] (F: Arme-gaunt); arm-girt; terma-gaunt; war-gaunt; rampaunt

II.1

39 greet] gree

II.2

7 Antonio's] Antonius'

48 theme] then

57 you have] you have not

64 graceful] grateful

75–6 you | When, rioting . . . Alexandria, you] (F: you, when rioting . . . Alexandria you); you | When rioting . . . Alexandria; you

II.3

7–8 lady. | Good] lady. OCTAVIA Good

II.5

24 Ram] Rain

26 Antonio's] Antonius

103 That art not] That sayst but; That art but

II.6

16 honest, Roman] honest Roman,

II.7

109 beat] bear

122 Spleets] Splits

III.2

49 at the full] at full

III.3

18 look'st] looked'st

III.6

22 knows] know

39 lord] lords

78 does] do

80 wrong led] wronged

88 makes] make

his] them

III.7

80 with labour] in labour

III.11

44 He's] He is

III.12

13 lessons] lessens

28–9 add more, | From thine invention, offers] and more | From thine invention offer

31 Thidias] Thyreus (*also at* III.13.73 *and in prefixes and directions*)

III.13

26 comparisons] caparisons

103 The] This

IV.2

12 Thou] And thou

IV.5

17 Dispatch. Enobarbus!] (F: Dispatch *Enobarbus*.); Dispatch my Eros; Eros, dispatch

IV.6

9 vant] van

13 dissuade] persuade

IV.12

0 *See the Commentary*

IV.13

10 death to the monument.] death. To the monument!

IV.14

35 Unarm] Unarm me

IV.15

22 dare not] dare not descend; dare not open

38 when] where

54 lived; the] (F: liued. The); lived the

86 do't] do it

V.1

5 Decretas] Dercetas; Dercetus (*also in prefixes and directions here and in* IV.14)

26 Look you, sad friends.] (F: Looke you sad Friends,); Look you sad, friends?

27 tidings] a tidings

31 Waged] Weighed

36 launch] lance

52 Egyptian yet. The] Egyptian, yet the

V.2

7 dung] dug
66 sent for] sent me for
81 little O o'th'earth] (F: little o'th'earth); little O the earth
87 Antony it was] autumn 'twas
96 nor] or
146 seel] seal
197 Where's] Where is
226 absurd] obscene
257 falliable] fallible
324 here, Charmian? Is] here? Charmian, is
351 caves] canes

### *3 Stage Directions*

The stage directions in this edition are based on those in F, although they have sometimes been modified and others have been added where necessary to clarify the action. The more interesting F stage directions that have been altered are given below in their original form on the right of the square bracket. Also listed are the more significant additional stage directions; asides and indications of the person addressed are not included.

I.1

10 *Charmian and Iras*] *not in* F

I.2

0 *Enter Charmian, Iras, and Alexas*] *Enter Enobarbus, Lamprius, a Southsayer, Rannius, Lucillius, Charmian, Iras, Mardian the Eunuch, and Alexas*
6 *Enter a Soothsayer*] *not in* F
11 *Enter Enobarbus*] *not in* F
87 *and Attendants*] *not in* F
88 *Exeunt all . . . Attendants*] *Exeunt*
113 F *has 'Enter another Messenger'*
122 *He gives him the letter*] *not in* F
*Exit Messenger*] *not in* F

I.3

60 (*he gives her the letter*)] *not in* F

I.5

34 *Enter Alexas*] *Enter Alexas from Cæsar*

II.2

32 *They sit*] *not in* F

II.5

81 *Exit Charmian*] *not in* F

84 *Enter Charmian and the Messenger*] *Enter the Messenger againe*

II.6

0 *Pompey and Menas at . . . Agrippa, with*] *Pompey, at . . . Agrippa, Menas with*

II.7

16 *and a Boy*] *not in* F

39 F *has* '*Whispers in's Eare*' *after* anon

52 *Menas whispers to Pompey*] *not in* F

56 *He rises and they walk aside*] *not in* F

87 *pointing to . . . Lepidus*] *not in* F

127 *Exeunt all but Enobarbus and Menas*] *not in* F

132 *He throws his cap in the air*] *not in* F

III.1

0 *Enter Ventidius, . . . Pacorus*] *Enter Ventidius as it were in triumph, the dead body of Pacorus borne before him*

III.2

20 (*Trumpet within*)] *not in* F

42 (*weeping*)] *not in* F

III.8

0 *and Taurus, with their army*] *with his Army*

III.10

0 *with his army*] *not in* F

*Enobarbus*] *Enobarbus and Scarus*

III.11

24 *Exeunt Attendants. Antony sits down*] *Sits downe*

*Iras*] *not in* F

III.12

0 *and Thidias*] *not in* F

III.13

82 *She gives him her hand*] *not in* F

93 *Servants*] *a Seruant.*

IV.1

0 *their army*] *his Army*

IV.3

13 *hautboys*] *the Hoboyes is*

IV.4

0 *Charmian and*] *not in* F

2 *with armour*] *not in* F

IV.5

0 *a Soldier meeting them*] *not in* F

IV.7

0 *and others*] *not in* F

8 *Retreat sounded far off*] *Far off* (*after* heads *in line* 6)

IV.8

0 *Enter Antony, with Scarus and others, marching*] *Enter Anthony againe in a March. Scarrus, with others*

39 *Trumpets sound*] *not in* F

IV.9

0 *the Watch*] *not in* F

23 *He dies*] *not in* F

33 *with the body*] *not in* F

IV.14

87 *He turns from him*] *not in* F

103 *He falls on his sword*] *not in* F

104 *Enter Decretas and a company of the Guard*] *Enter a Guard*

115 *Exit Decretas*] *not in* F

IV.15

6 *below*] *not in* F

9 *Enter, below, the Guard, bearing Antony*] *Enter Anthony, and the Guard*

62 *Antony dies*] *not in* F

68 *She faints*] *not in* F

V.1

0 *Maecenas, Gallus, Proculeius*] *Menas*

V.2

8 *Enter, to the . . . and Soldiers*] *Enter Proculeius*

34 *The Soldiers approach Cleopatra from behind*] *not in* F

35 *They seize Cleopatra*] *not in* F

36 *Exit Gallus*] *not in* F

39 *She draws a dagger*] *not in* F
*He disarms her*] *not in* F
70 *Exeunt Proculeius and Soldiers*] *Exit Proculeius*
136 *She gives him a paper*] *not in* F
140 *Enter Seleucus*] *not in* F
190 *Dolabella . . . Attendants*] *and his Traine*
192 *She whispers to Charmian*] *not in* F
232 *Exit Iras*] *not in* F
241 *with a basket*] *not in* F
259 *He sets down the basket*] *not in* F
278 *Enter Iras . . . regalia*] *not in* F
291 *She kisses . . . dies*] *not in* F
311 *She applies another asp to her arm*] *not in* F
318 *in*] *in, and Dolabella*
320 *She applies an asp to herself*] *not in* F

# *Commentary*

F refers to the first Folio of Shakespeare's plays (1623); see An Account of the Text. Biblical quotations are from the Bishops' Bible (1568, etc.), the version most likely to have been read by Shakespeare. Quotations from North's Plutarch are from *Shakespeare's Plutarch*, ed. T. J. B. Spencer (1964).

## HISTORICAL NOTE

Shakespeare probably assumes a general knowledge of the historical events which form the subject of the play. The action covers the ten years preceding the deaths of Antony and Cleopatra in 30 BC. The earliest event dramatized is Antony's departure from Alexandria (40 BC). The treaty of Misenum between the second triumvirate (Antony, Octavius and Lepidus) and Sextus Pompeius belonged to 39 BC, the defeat of the Parthians by Ventidius to 38 BC, the deposition of Lepidus to 36 BC, the Roman Senate's declaration of war on Cleopatra to 32 BC and the battle of Actium to 31 BC. A few other events which took place before the play opens are occasionally alluded to; these include the battle of Pharsalus between Julius Caesar and Pompey the Great (48 BC), the assassination of Julius Caesar (44 BC) and the battle of Philippi in which Brutus and Cassius were defeated by Antony and Octavius (42 BC). (The last two were dramatized by Shakespeare in *Julius Caesar*, to which *Antony and Cleopatra* is something of a sequel.)

## I.1

The first appearance of Antony and Cleopatra forms a tableau: Antony rejects Empire for Love. The 'presenters' of the tableau are the disapproving pair Demetrius and Philo, through whose eyes we are invited to view Antony's degeneration. The mutual antipathy of Roman and Egyptian values is at once established.

1 *our general's*: Antony's.

2 *O'erflows the measure*: Exceeds the limit. But the expression suggests abundance as well as a culpable prodigality.

3 *files and musters*: Ordered formations.

4 *plated*: Armoured.

5 *office*: Service.

6 *tawny front*: Dark face.

*captain's*: Captain-like (*captain* meaning 'military commander').

8 *reneges all temper*: Renounces all self-control.

*reneges*: Pronounced as two syllables, with a hard 'g'.

10 *gypsy's*: Since gypsies were thought to be Egyptian in origin, qualities popularly associated with them such as lasciviousness and duplicity could be given to Cleopatra. In the next scene her maids are given another gypsy-like trait – an interest in fortune-telling.

*Flourish*: Fanfare of trumpets.

*train*: Body of attendants, retinue.

12 *The triple pillar of the world*: One of the triumvirs, who between them ruled the Roman empire.

13 *fool*: Dupe.

15 *There's beggary in the love that can be reckoned*: The love that can be computed or assessed is less than infinite, and therefore contemptible (beggarly).

16 *bourn*: Limit.

18 *Grates me! The sum*: It irks me (but) tell it in brief.

20 *Fulvia*: Antony's wife.

21 *the scarce-bearded Caesar*: That is, Octavius. Octavius was Julius Caesar's great-nephew; Caesar made him his adopted son and his heir. At the time of the opening

of the play Octavius was aged twenty-three; Antony was nearly twenty years older.

23 *Take in*: Conquer.

*enfranchise*: Liberate.

24 *How*: What?

25 *Perchance*: She refers back to her earlier words, *Fulvia perchance is angry* (20).

*like*: Likely.

26 *dismission*: Discharge from service.

28 *Where's Fulvia's process . . . Both*: Cleopatra makes, or pretends to make, a slip of the tongue – she meant *Caesar*, but says *Fulvia* by mistake, and then adds that *Both* might have their reasons for wanting Antony in Rome.

*process*: Legal summons (to appear in court).

31 *homager*: Vassal.

*else so*: Or else.

33 *arch*: A triumphal arch is probably imagined. In pageants and civic festivities a triumphal arch was conventionally used to represent a city or realm. (See G. R. Kernodle, *From Art to Theatre* (1944), p. 90.) Shakespeare extends it to signify an empire.

34 *ranged*: (1) Ordered; (2) spacious.

*Here is my space*: My wide-stretching empire is here (in Cleopatra).

36–40 *The nobleness . . . peerless*: These lines dramatize Plutarch's account of the way of life adopted by Antony and Cleopatra after their first meeting: 'For they made an order between them which they called *Amimetobion* (as much to say, "no life comparable and matchable with it"), one feasting each other by turns, and in cost exceeding all measure and reason.' After the words *to do thus* (37) the lovers may embrace; or perhaps these words refer more generally to their present style of life.

37 *such a mutual pair*: A pair so perfectly matched.

38–9 *in which I bind . . . weet*: Antony uses the style of a public proclamation.

39 *weet*: Know.

42–3 *Antony* | *Will be himself*: Antony will be the fool he is (while Cleopatra will *seem the fool I am not*).

43 *stirred*: Roused, excited.

45 *confound*: Waste.

*conference*: Conversation.

46–7 *There's not a minute . . . pleasure now*: The suggestion is that every moment is capable of containing a wealth of present pleasure. The word *now* is stressed. Some editors unnecessarily emend to 'new'.

49–51 *Whom everything . . . admired*: Cf. Cleopatra's tribute to Antony at I.5.59–61 and Enobarbus' to Cleopatra at II.2.240–45.

52–4 *and all alone . . . qualities of people*: Plutarch writes:

> And sometime also when he would go up and down the city disguised like a slave in the night, and would peer into poor men's windows and their shops, and scold and brawl with them within the house, Cleopatra would be also in a chamber-maid's array, and amble up and down the streets with him, so that oftentimes Antonius bare away both mocks and blows.

56 *with*: By.

58 *great property*: Peculiar greatness.

59 *still*: Always.

60 *approves the common liar*: Proves that what the malicious gossips say is true. The suggestion of paradox (what the *liar* says is true) is one of many such in the play.

62 *Of*: For.

I.2

This and the next scene establish the atmosphere of Cleopatra's Egypt, one of sex-talk, idleness and languor out of which Antony has to extricate himself. His reception of the news from Rome and his decision to leave Egypt mark the first move in the action of the play. Plutarch writes:

> Now Antonius delighting in these fond and childish pastimes, very ill news were brought him from two places. The first

from Rome: that his brother Lucius and Fulvia his wife fell out first between themselves, and afterwards fell to open war with Caesar, and had brought all to nought, that they were both driven to fly out of Italy. The second news, as bad as the first: that Labienus conquered all Asia with the army of the Parthians, from the river of Euphrates and from Syria unto the countries of Lydia and Ionia. Then began Antonius with much ado a little to rouse himself, as if he had been wakened out of a deep sleep and, as a man may say, coming out of a great drunkenness.

4–5 *charge his horns with garlands*: Be a contented cuckold. He will load (*charge*) his (emblematic) cuckold's *horns* with the bridegroom's floral chaplet. Alexas has apparently been referring to the man (*this husband*) whom Charmian is destined to marry.

10–11 *In Nature's . . . can read*: The Soothsayer speaks in dignified blank verse.

12 *banquet*: A light refreshment of fruit and wine.

16 *make*: Cause (to happen).

18 *fairer*: More fortunate. In the following lines Charmian takes it to mean 'more plump', 'in better condition', while Iras takes it as 'more beautiful'. The solemn utterances of the Soothsayer serve momentarily to throw our minds forward to the end of the play, since everything he so ambiguously prophesies seems to come true. By saying that Charmian will be *far fairer* than she is, he may mean simply that she is going to die (the dead being, according to this point of view, more fortunate than the living). Similarly Charmian's reference to *figs* (33) will remind anyone who knows Cleopatra's story of the way she met her death.

25 *liver*: When someone was in love, his liver was thought to be inflamed.

27 *Good now*: Come on!

29–30 *Herod of Jewry*: Who martyred the Holy Innocents in his attempt to kill the infant Christ; Charmian is being extravagantly ambitious in hoping for his homage.

30 *Find me*: Discover (in my palm).

33 *figs*: A phallic allusion; figs were thought to look like the male sexual organs, and were also used as an aphrodisiac.

34 *proved*: Experienced.

36 *belike*: Probably.

36–7 *shall have no names*: Will be bastards.

41 *I forgive thee for a witch*: You are no prophet (and so can be acquitted of the charge of being a *witch*).

42 *privy to*: Cognizant of.

47 *be drunk*: To go drunk.

49–50 *E'en . . . famine*: The overflowing of the Nile was of course the cause of Egypt's fertility, not of famine.

51 *wild*: Wanton.

53 *oily palm*: A moist or *oily* palm was thought a sign of a sensual nature.

53–4 *fruitful prognostication*: Sign that she will have children.

55 *workyday*: Commonplace, everyday.

56 *Your fortunes are alike*: There is one difference in their fortunes: Iras dies before Cleopatra, Charmian after her. The Soothsayer may have forgotten that he has just told Charmian *You shall outlive the lady whom you serve* (32).

58 *I have said*: I have no more to say.

62 *husband's nose*: A phallic allusion.

63 *Our worser thoughts heavens mend*: Charmian pretends to be piously shocked.

65 *go*: This seems to mean 'enjoy sexual intercourse'.
*Isis*: Egyptian goddess of the moon and of fertility.

71 *hear that prayer of the people*: Another mock-pietism. Charmian and Iras offer up prayers like priestesses. Iras now goes on to intone gravely, like a preacher.
*the people*: The Egyptians, the worshippers of Isis. Some editors emend to 'thy people'.

73 *loose-wived*: With an unfaithful wife.
*foul*: Ugly.

74 *keep decorum*: Do the appropriate thing.

78–9 *they would make themselves whores but they'd do't*: Even if they had to make themselves whores they would do it.

80 *Not he; the Queen*: The mistake suggests Antony's loss of his former public identity; see also Introduction, p. xxiv.

84 *A Roman thought*: A thought of Rome (and so a sober reflection). Plutarch writes (immediately after the sentence quoted above in the note to I.1.52–4): 'Now, though most men misliked this manner, yet the Alexandrians were commonly glad of this jollity and liked it well, saying very gallantly and wisely that Antonius showed them a comical face, to wit, a merry countenance; and the Romans a tragical face, to say, a grim look.'

89 *field*: Battlefield.

92 *the time's state*: The needs of the moment.

94 *better issue*: Greater success.

96 *The nature of bad news infects the teller*: Bad news makes the teller seem vicious or even criminal, and so liable to harsh treatment.

97–100 *When it concerns ... he flattered*: Cf. II.5, where Cleopatra receives bad news in a way very different from Antony here.

100 *as*: As if.

100–101 *Labienus ... Parthian force*: Parthia occupied much the same territory as modern Iraq and Iran. During the years of the triumvirate the Parthians were exceptionally troublesome to the Romans; Antony himself was to fail in his campaign against them. Labienus was a Roman general who had defected to the Parthians after the defeat of Brutus and Cassius at Philippi.

102 *Extended*: Seized upon (a legal metaphor).

*Euphrates*: Accented on the first syllable.

106 *home*: Plainly.

106 *mince not the general tongue*: Don't soften what everyone is saying.

108 *Rail thou in Fulvia's phrase*: Scold me in Fulvia's manner.

110–12 *then we bring forth . . . earing*: When enlivening winds fail to aerate our soil, we produce nothing fruitful; a dose of home-truths is as good for us as ploughing (*earing*) is to the earth. Many editors unnecessarily emend F's *windes* to 'minds'.

112 *Is*: In Elizabethan English it was not considered grammatically incorrect for a plural subject to govern a singular verb.

116 *stays upon your will*: Is waiting for your orders.

122 *Forbear me*: Leave me.

126 *By revolution lowering*: Moving around and down, as if on a wheel.

128 *could*: Would like to.

129 *enchanting*: Holding in her power as if under a spell.

131 *idleness*: As well as its obvious sense, the word probably has the further connotation of 'lasciviousness'. Cf. I.3.92.

138 *die*: Here, as often in amatory contexts, *die* refers to the sexual act, as well as having its obvious sense. Enobarbus mockingly insists on the idea five times in this single speech.

142–3 *upon far poorer moment*: For a much slighter cause.

143 *mettle*: Vigour, ardour. Enobarbus' phrase makes a satirical paradox: 'she finds something life-giving in "dying"'.

145 *celerity*: Rapidity.

152 *Jove*: Jupiter; one of his duties was arranging the weather.

154 *you had*: You would have.

155 *piece of work*: Masterpiece.

156 *discredited your travel*: Lost you your reputation as a traveller (since a traveller was expected to see everything worthy of note on his route).

164–6 *it shows . . . new*: It shows man that the gods are the world's tailors (that is, makers of people, since 'the tailor makes the man'); and there is this comfort to be had – that when old clothes (or old wives) are worn out, there are always means (or men) to replace them. Enobarbus' notion of the tailor-shop is of course bawdy: *members* alludes to the male sexual role, *cut* and *case* (167–8) to the female. The primary sense of *cut* is 'blow', 'misfortune'. For another bawdy use of 'tailor', with an implied reference to his needle, cf. *The Tempest*, II.2.52: 'Yet a tailor might scratch her where'er she did itch.'

169 *smock*: A woman's undergarment; often used, as here, to mean 'woman'.

170–71 *the tears . . . sorrow*: An onion would bring to your eyes the only tears this sorrow deserves.

176 *abode*: Staying.

177 *light*: Indecent.

*our*: This is the first of several uses in this speech of the royal plural – a means of quickly establishing an unanswerably authoritative tone.

178 *break*: Impart.

179 *expedience*: Hasty departure.

180 *part*: Depart.

181 *touches*: Reasons, motives.

183 *many our contriving friends*: The many friends who work for my interests.

184 *Sextus Pompeius*: Younger son of Pompey the Great; see the note to I.3.49.

186 *Our slippery people*: *Our* may be a royal plural, or it may have a larger, quasi-proverbial reference: 'We all know that the people always behave like this . . .'

188 *throw*: Bestow the title of.

191 *blood and life*: Spirit and energy.

191–2 *stands up | For the main soldier*: Presents himself as the world's leading soldier. But *main* may also mean 'sea'; he has just been said to command *The empire of the sea* (186).

192–3 *whose quality . . . danger*: Who, if he continues as he has begun, may endanger the stability of the Roman world.

192 *quality*: Capacity for effective action.

193 *sides*: Frame.

194 *the courser's hair*: A horse's hair was popularly supposed to turn into a snake when placed in water.

195–7 *Say . . . hence*: This slightly indirect way of saying 'give the army orders to move' expresses Antony's position of absolute command (not he but his *pleasure* requires the move).

I.3

1 *I did not see him since*: I have not seen him recently.

3 *I did not send you*: Don't tell him I sent you.
*sad*: In a serious mood.

10 *Thou teachest like a fool*: *the way to lose him*: This ten-line dialogue between mistress and maid is matched by that in IV.13, where, as a result of Charmian's advice, Cleopatra does in fact lose Antony.

11 *Tempt*: Try, test.
*I wish*: Some editors plausibly emend to 'iwis', meaning 'certainly', 'trust me'.

14 *breathing*: Utterance, words. Antony begins in a tactfully courteous style.

16–17 *the sides of nature* | *Will not sustain*: The human frame cannot endure.

20–21 *What says . . . come*: The two lines are probably based on a line in the verse epistle sent by Dido to Aeneas in Ovid's *Heroides* (vii.139), which Shakespeare is likely to have read at school: '"Sed iubet ire deus." vellem, vetuisset adire . . .' ('"But your god orders you to go." I wish he had forbidden you to come'). The entire situation, as developed by Shakespeare, recalls that of Dido and Aeneas, though of course with differences (see also the note to IV.14.53).

26 *planted*: Prepared, placed ready to grow.

28 *Though you . . . gods*: Cleopatra alludes hyperbolically to the notion that when Jupiter, king of the gods, swore an oath, the whole of Olympus shuddered to its foundations.

30 *mouth-made*: Formed on the tongue, not in the heart.

31 *break themselves in swearing*: Are broken the moment they are spoken.

32 *colour*: Pretext.

33 *sued staying*: Begged to stay.

35–7 *Eternity . . . heaven*: These words are in indirect speech:

they are what Antony in the past assured Cleopatra. He is now tartly reminded of his own lyric phrases. 'According to you,' she tells him, 'eternity was in my lips and eyes . . .' But see the Introduction, p. lxiv.

36 *our brows' bent*: The curve of my eyebrows.

*none our parts so*: None of my qualities, however.

37 *a race of heaven*: Of heavenly origin or stock.

41 *Egypt*: Here, as elsewhere in the play, this means Cleopatra herself, as well as her country.

44 *in use with you*: In your possession.

45 *Shines o'er*: Is everywhere bright (with the flashing of the *swords*).

*civil swords*: Swords of civil war.

47–8 *Equality . . . faction*: When the management of a house is shared between two, squabbles will arise over insignificant points.

48–9 *the hated . . . to love*: Those who have been hated attract love when they acquire power.

49 *The condemned Pompey*: Sextus Pompeius (see also I.2.184–93) was a serious threat to peace and had accordingly been *condemned* (proscribed, declared an outlaw) by the Senate. His fleet commanded the western Mediterranean; he himself was in possession of Sicily.

53–4 *quietness . . . change*: A long peace has produced discontents within the state; civic health must be restored through purging – getting rid of impurities through the bloodletting of violence.

54 *My more particular*: My own more personal reason.

55 *safe my going*: Remove any trace of danger from my going.

57–8 *Though age . . . childishness*: I may be fool enough to love you, but at least I'm not such a child as to do so on the grounds that you may one day be free of your wife. (For the moment Cleopatra does not believe him.)

60 *at thy sovereign leisure*: In your own royal good time (an instance of Antony's polite formality).

61 *garboils*: Trouble, disturbance.

*best*: Best item of news.

63 *sacred vials*: The Romans were thought to place bottles

of tears in the tombs of their loved ones.

64–5 *see . . . be*: The neat rhyme suggests something of the artificiality of Cleopatra's behaviour here.

68–9 *the fire | That quickens Nilus' slime*: The sun that fertilizes the rich earth of the Nile valley.

71 *affects*: Are inclined, are prompted to choose by your feelings.

*Cut my lace*: Cleopatra, tightly laced in a bodice, gasps for breath.

73 *So Antony loves*: If Antony loves. Cleopatra may also mean that her health is as precarious as he is changeable.

74 *give true evidence*: Bear true witness.

*stands*: Will endure.

81 *this is meetly*: You are doing quite well.

82 *target*: Small shield. 'Sword and target' was presumably a common collocation which Cleopatra ironically recalls.

*mends*: Improves.

84–5 *How this . . . chafe*: How admirably this heroic descendant of Hercules assumes the part of an angry man; *carriage* has the sense of 'demeanour', even 'bodily deportment'.

84 *Herculean*: Plutarch writes of Antony:

> He had a goodly thick beard, a broad forehead, crook-nosed; and there appeared such a manly look in his countenance as is commonly seen in Hercules' pictures, stamped or graven in metal. Now it had been a speech of old time that the family of the Antonii were descended from one Anton, the son of Hercules, whereof the family took name. This opinion did Antonius seek to confirm in all his doings, not only resembling him in the likeness of his body, as we have said before, but also in the wearing of his garments.

90–91 *my oblivion . . . forgotten*: (1) My memory, like Antony, has deserted me, so that I have forgotten what I wanted to say; (2) my mind – being entirely absorbed in the idea of Antony – is left a blank.

91–2 *But that your royalty | Holds idleness your subject*: If it were not clear that you are in perfect control of these follies, as a queen is of her subjects. For *idleness*, cf. the note to I.2.131.

94 *bear*: As in childbirth, so linking with *labour* (93).

96 *becomings*: (1) Graces; (2) changes, transformations.

97 *Eye*: Look.

100 *laurel*: A laurel wreath was an emblem of victory.

I.4

Caesar's first appearance establishes him as a man of cool temperance and efficiency. Yet if Antony is an instance of excess (one who *O'erflows the measure*, I.1.2), Caesar seems conversely to suffer from deficiency, something less than the true golden mean.

3 *competitor*: Partner, colleague. But inescapably the word also suggests rivalry and a potential hostility.

6 *the queen of Ptolemy*: Cleopatra had married her brother Ptolemy at the command of Julius Caesar; she was reported to have poisoned him.

8 *there*: In the letter.

9 *abstract*: Epitome, compendium.

11 *enow*: Enough.

12–13 *His faults . . . blackness*: It is in keeping with the play's tendency to paradox that Lepidus should speak of Antony's faults as stars.

14 *purchased*: Acquired.

18 *mirth*: Joke.

19 *keep the turn of tippling*: Take turns in drinking toasts.

20 *stand the buffet*: Endure the blows. See the note to I.1.52–4.

22 *As*: Although.

*composure*: Character.

24 *foils*: Blemishes.

24–5 *do bear | So great weight in his lightness*: Carry so heavy a burden as a result of his irresponsibility.

26 *vacancy*: Free time (with a pejorative implication).

27–8 *Full surfeits . . . for't*: Let stomach disorders and syphilis call him to an account.

28 *confound*: Waste.

29–30 *speaks as loud | As his own state and ours*: Counts as much as his and our public position (that is, as triumvirs).

30–33 *'tis to be chid . . . judgement*: Should be reprimanded as we would rebuke boys who, old enough to know better, surrender what they have learned of life to secure immediate pleasure.

39 *discontents*: Discontented people.

40 *Give him*: Say he is.

41 *from the primal state*: Since the first commonwealth that ever was.

42 *he which is was wished until he were*: The man who is now in power was supported only until he secured power.

43–4 *the ebbed man . . . lacked*: The man whose tide is low (who has lost power), unappreciated till he has ceased to deserve it, wins favour by being absent.

44 *Comes*: Becomes.

*deared*: Loved.

*common body*: Common people.

45 *vagabond flag*: Drifting reed.

46 *lackeying*: F reads *lacking*. Most editors accept the emendation *lackeying*, meaning 'following every aimless movement as a lackey does his master'. This emendation can be supported by line 967 of *The Rape of Lucrece*, where Time is addressed as 'Thou ceaseless lackey to Eternity'. On the other hand, *lacking* is not impossible; the phrase would then mean 'without the firmly directed movements of the tide'.

48–54 *Menecrates . . . seen*: Plutarch writes: 'Sextus Pompeius at that time kept in Sicilia, and so made many an inroad into Italy with a great number of pinnaces and other pirates' ships, of the which were captains two notable pirates, Menas and Menecrates, who so scoured all the sea thereabouts that none durst peep out with a sail.'

48 *famous*: Notorious.

49 *ear*: Plough.

52 *Lack blood*: Turn pale (with fear).

*flush*: Lusty.

54–5 *Pompey's name . . . resisted*: Pompey's mere name causes more trouble than would be caused if he actually made war on you.

56 *wassails*: Carousals, drunken revelling. F's reading is *Vassailes*, that is, 'vassals', meaning 'low-born servants or followers'. This is possible, but the emendation *wassails* seems preferable.

56–71 *When thou once . . . not*: The war referred to in these lines is the war of Mutina (Modena), 43 BC, in which Antony was defeated by the army of the Roman Senate. Plutarch writes:

> Cicero . . . being at that time the chiefest man of authority and estimation in the city, he stirred up all men against Antonius; so that in the end he made the Senate pronounce him an enemy to his country . . .; and moreover sent Hircius and Pansa, then Consuls, to drive Antonius out of Italy. These two Consuls together with Caesar, who also had an army, went against Antonius that besieged the city of Modena, and there overthrew him in battle. But both the Consuls were slain there.
>
> Antonius, flying upon this overthrow, fell into great misery all at once; but the chiefest want of all other, and that pinched him most, was famine . . . it was a wonderful example to the soldiers to see Antonius, that was brought up in all fineness and superfluity, so easily to drink puddle water and to eat wild fruits and roots. And moreover it is reported that, even as they passed the Alps, they did eat the barks of trees and such beasts as never man tasted of their flesh before.

57 *Modena*: Accented on the second syllable.

59 *whom*: That is, famine.

60–61 *patience more . . . suffer*: More fortitude than savages could show in suffering.

62 *stale*: Urine.

*gilded*: With glittering scum on the surface.

63 *cough at*: And so refuse.

63 *deign*: Not refuse.

66 *browsèd'st*: Fed upon (used of animals).

71 *lanked*: Grew thinner.

74 *i'th'field*: In military array.

78 *Both what ... I can be able*: What forces both by sea and by land I can muster.

79 *front*: Confront.

82 *stirs*: Events, happenings.

84 *knew it for my bond*: Understood it to be my duty (or 'my commitment').

## I.5

Antony's offstage journey between Egypt and Rome continues, while Cleopatra, having nothing else to do in his absence, mentally accompanies him. As in the previous and in the following scenes, the arrival of a messenger with news provides a focusing point.

4 *mandragora*: Mandrake (a powerful narcotic).

11 *unseminared*: Emasculated.

12 *affections*: Passions.

16 *honest*: Chaste.

18 *What Venus did with Mars*: The goddess of love and the god of war once had an adulterous love affair. In the present play Venus is of course associated with Cleopatra and Mars with Antony.

22 *wot'st*: Knowest.

23 *demi-Atlas*: In classical mythology the Titan Atlas supported the heavens. Cleopatra seems to be speaking without reference to the triumvirate, although at I.1.12 Antony is said to be *The triple pillar of the world*, in virtue of being a triumvir.

23–4 *the arm | And burgonet of men*: He is pre-eminent both in attack – *arm* – and in defence – *burgonet*. The *burgonet* was an exceptionally efficient helmet of Burgundian origin; it was so fitted to the gorget or neck-piece that the head could be turned without exposing the neck.

27–9 *Think on me ... time*: Cleopatra sees herself as dark-skinned (that is, sunburnt) from the pinches of her lover *Phoebus* (the sun). The intonation of the sentence is elusive: *wrinkled deep in time* may be humorously meant.

29–34 *Broad-fronted Caesar ... life*: Plutarch writes of Cleopatra, just before her first meeting with Antony, that,

> guessing by the former access and credit she had with Julius Caesar and Cneius [Gnaeus] Pompey, the son of Pompey the Great, only for her beauty, she began to have good hope that she might more easily win Antonius. For Caesar and Pompey knew her when she was but a young thing, and knew not then what the world meant. But now she went to Antonius at the age when a woman's beauty is at the prime, and she also of best judgement.

29 *Broad-fronted Caesar*: 'Front' can mean 'forehead' or 'face'. Julius Caesar had 'a rather broad face', according to Suetonius (in *The Lives of the Twelve Caesars*); or the phrase may refer to his receding hair, also mentioned by Suetonius.

31 *morsel*: Tasty mouthful. Sexual experience is several times in the play described in terms of eating; cf. II.1.12, 23–7, 33; II.2.229–31, 241–3; II.6.63–5, 124; III.13.116–20.

*great Pompey*: Gnaeus Pompey (elder son of Pompey the Great). Shakespeare may be deliberately confusing the two Pompeys so as to enhance the status of Cleopatra's former lovers. Plutarch clearly distinguishes them (see the passage quoted in the note to 29–34).

33 *aspect*: Gaze (accented on the second syllable).

36–7 *that great medicine ... thee*: An alchemical metaphor: in their experiments the alchemists sought the elixir of life – the *great medicine* – by means of which they hoped to transform base metals to gold and to prolong life indefinitely. The metaphor is important and revealing, since the play is as a whole much concerned with the transformation of 'base' human materials into exalted ones; Cleopatra herself is the clearest example of this.

37 *tinct*: 'Tincture' was another term for the elixir of life.

41 *orient*: Lustrous (originally applied to pearls from the East, which were more brilliant than those found nearer home).

42–50 *Good friend. . . . by him*: Alexas' report forms a vignette of Antony in heroic posture. Though still a lover, he has recovered his warrior's toughness. The action of mounting his horse is perhaps emblematic: the image of a rider in control of his horse is not uncommon in classical antiquity as well as in Shakespeare's period, and could signify a rational man in control of his passions. Cf. Plutarch's reference to '"the horse of the mind", as Plato termeth it, that is so hard of rein (I mean the unreined lust of concuspience)', which destroyed Antony's character.

43 *firm*: Resolute.

45 *piece*: Augment.

48 *arrogant*: F reads *Arme-gaunt*, and many attempts have been made to gloss this, such as 'battle-worn', 'lean from much warlike service'. The word occurs nowhere else and, if genuine, is probably a Shakespearian coinage. The emendation adopted here makes good sense and can be plausibly explained as being what the printer mistakenly read as 'Arme-gaunt' (for 'Arrogaunt', a common spelling of the word).

50 *beastly dumbed*: (1) Obliterated or negated in an animal-like way; (2) reduced to an animal-like inarticulateness.

52 *nor . . . nor*: Neither . . . nor.

53 *well-divided disposition*: Well-balanced temperament.

54 *'tis the man*: That's just what he's like.

*but*: Just, only.

59–61 *Be'st thou . . . else*: Cf. with this tribute Antony's to Cleopatra at I.1.49–51 and Enobarbus' at II.2.240–45.

60 *violence*: The word suggests an exuberant commitment to whatever mood he happens to be in.

61 *posts*: Messengers.

62 *several*: Separate.

63 *Who's*: Anyone who is.

65 *Shall die a beggar*: Since bad luck will dog him throughout his life for being born on such a day.

67 *brave*: Excellent, fine.

68 *emphasis*: Emphatic expression.

71 *paragon*: Compare, match (so as to imply equality).

73–5 *My salad days . . . then*: Cf. the passage from Plutarch quoted in the note to 29–34.

74 *green*: Immature.

77 *several*: Separate, different.

78 *Or I'll unpeople Egypt*: Even if I have to send every one of my subjects out of Egypt as messengers to Antony.

II.1

Sextus Pompeius, one of the seekers after power in the unstable world of Rome, affords a new viewpoint on Antony. Offstage, Antony concludes his journey to Rome.

1 *shall*: Surely will.

3 *what they do delay they not deny*: A delay in answering prayers is not a refusal.

4–5 *Whiles . . . sue for*: Even while we are begging something from the gods, it is ceasing to exist.

10 *crescent*: Waxing like the moon.
*auguring*: Prophesying.

12 *sits at dinner*: Possibly a sexual allusion; see the note to I.5.31.

13 *without doors*: Out of doors (the only wars Antony will make are the wars of love).

17 *in the field*: In military array.

20 *Looking for*: Waiting for.
*charms*: Spells, enchantments.

21 *Salt*: Lascivious.
*waned*: Faded (like the waning moon).

23 *Tie up . . . in a field of feasts*: This seems to mean 'tie (him) up like an animal in a rich pasture'.

25 *Sharpen*: Subjunctive: 'May Epicurean cooks sharpen . . .'
*cloyless*: That will never satiate.

26 *prorogue*: Suspend the operation of.

27 *Lethe'd*: Oblivious, all-forgetting. Lethe was a river in the classical Hades; those who drank from it forgot their past. Pompey's words are interrupted by the arrival of the messenger – a way of bringing out the fact that he is out-of-date in his appraisal of Antony's situation.

30–31 *'tis | A space for farther travel*: There has been time to travel even further than he has.

35 *rear*: Raise.

36 *opinion*: Opinion of ourselves.

38 *hope*: Expect.

39 *well greet together*: Meet each other like friends.

40 *did trespasses to*: Committed offences against.

42 *moved*: Prompted, encouraged.

45 *'Twere pregnant they should square between*: They would probably quarrel among.

46 *entertainèd*: Received.

48 *cement their divisions*: Firmly bring them together. *cement*: Accented on the first syllable.

50–51 *It only stands | Our lives upon*: But it is a matter of life and death for us.

II.2

This, the longest and weightiest scene so far, shows Antony back in Rome and the triumvirate in action. But the understanding reached by Antony and Caesar is precarious. As soon as the subordinates are left alone together, Enobarbus powerfully evokes Cleopatra's personal magnetism.

4 *like himself*: In a way suitable to one so great. *move*: Angers.

5 *look over Caesar's head*: Treat Caesar as a man of small stature.

8 *I would not shave't today*: That is, I would dare him to pluck it. To pluck another man's beard was to give him a grave insult.

9 *stomaching*: Resentments, squabbles.

15 *compose*: Reach agreement.

19 *leaner*: Slighter.

20–21 *debate . . . loud*: Violently argue over.

23 *The rather for I earnestly beseech*: The more readily for the fact that I am making a special request.

25 *Nor curstness grow to th'matter*: And keep ill humour out of it.

27 *thus*: Antony either refers to the moderation of Lepidus' speech or possibly embraces Caesar. The former seems more likely.

34 *being*: Being so.

35 *or . . . or*: Either . . . or.

36 *say*: Call.

38 *derogately*: Disparagingly.

43 *practise on my state*: Plot against my well-being.

44 *question*: Business.

45 *catch at*: Gather, infer.

48 *theme for you*: A debate on your behalf.

*were the word*: Prompted the declaration.

50 *Did urge me*: Used my name as a pretext.

51 *true reports*: Reliable sources.

54 *stomach*: Wish.

55 *Having alike your cause*: Since I was involved for the same reason as yourself.

56–7 *If you'll patch . . . with*: If you insist on making a quarrel for inadequate reasons, though in fact you have much better reasons.

56 *patch*: Make up out of odd remnants.

59 *patched up*: Caesar picks up Antony's word *patch* and throws it back.

60–68 *Not so . . . wife*: The style of this and Antony's next speech seems deliberately tortuous, evasive and graceless. Shakespeare no doubt meant it to express the double-talk of politicians.

61–2 *I know . . . thought*: I am sure you must have known.

64 *graceful*: Favourable.

*attend*: Regard.

65 *fronted*: Opposed.

66 *I would you had her spirit in such another*: I wish you had a wife like her.

67 *snaffle*: Bridle-bit.

68 *pace*: Train (used of horses).

71 *garboils*: Tumults.

72 *not wanted*: Did not lack.

75 *But*: Only.

78 *missive out of audience*: Messenger out of your presence.

79 *fell upon me, ere admitted, then*: Burst in on me there and then, before he had been given permission to enter.

80–81 *did want | Of*: Was not up to.

82 *told him of myself*: Explained why I was not quite myself.

84 *Be nothing of*: Have nothing to do with.

86 *article*: Terms.

87 *Soft*: Go gently (since the matter is so delicate).

94–5 *bound . . . knowledge*: Kept me from all knowledge of myself.

98 *Work without it*: This may mean 'operate without a due sense of my dignity (*greatness*)', or possibly *it* refers to *honesty* (96).

102 *noble*: Nobly.

104 *griefs*: Grievances.

104–6 *to forget . . . atone you*: To forget them completely would be a (wise) acknowledgement of the fact that the present emergency requires you to stand together.

106 *atone*: Reconcile.

114 *this presence*: The present dignified company.

115 *your considerate stone*: Enobarbus will be as mute as a stone, but nevertheless will have his thoughts (be *considerate*).

118 *conditions*: Dispositions.

120 *staunch*: Firm.

123 *by the mother's side*: Plutarch calls Octavia 'the eldest sister of Caesar – not by one mother'; in fact she was a full younger sister of Caesar.

126–7 *reproof . . . rashness*: Reproof for rashness would be well deserved.

132 *take Antony*: Let Antony take.

133 *to*: As.

137 *jealousies*: Suspicions.

138 *import*: Carry with them (with a further suggestion that the *dangers* are of importance).

139–40 *Truths would . . . truths*: Inconvenient (or unwelcome) true things would be dismissed as fables, whereas now malicious half-truths are readily believed.

143 *present*: Sudden.

145–6 *touched | With*: Affected by.

150 *so fairly shows*: Looks so promisingly.

152 *of grace*: Gracious.

157–8 *never . . . again*: May our love for each other never again desert us.

160 *strange*: Exceptional.

161 *thank him only*: Just thank him.

162 *my remembrance suffer ill report*: I am said to be ungrateful.

*remembrance*: Memory.

163 *At heel of that*: As soon as that is done.

164 *presently*: At once.

166 *Mount Misena*: Mount Misenum, a port in southern Italy.

168 *fame*: Report.

172 *do*: I do.

*view*: Presence (where Antony can see her, and she him).

177 *Half the heart*: The beloved friend.

181 *disgested*: Digested (that is, arranged).

*stayed well by't*: Stood up to it well (a military expression, meaning 'stand firm', here used ironically of the soft living in Egypt).

182 *did sleep day out of countenance*: Put the day out of countenance by sleeping through it (so turning it into night).

184–5 *Eight wild boars . . . there*: Attested by Plutarch, though it was for supper, not breakfast.

186 *by*: Compared with.

190 *square*: True, fair.

192 *pursed up*: Took possession of.

194 *devised*: Invented.

196–231 *The barge ... only*: The whole description follows Plutarch closely:

Therefore when she was sent unto by divers letters, both from Antonius himself and also from his friends, she made so light of it and mocked Antonius so much that she disdained to set forward otherwise but to take her barge in the river of Cydnus, the poop whereof was of gold, the sails of purple, and the oars of silver, which kept stroke in rowing after the sound of the music of flutes, howboys, citherns, viols, and such other instruments as they played upon in the barge. And now for the person of herself: she was laid under a pavilion of cloth-of-gold of tissue, apparelled and attired like the goddess Venus commonly drawn in picture; and hard by her, on either hand of her, pretty fair boys apparelled as painters do set forth god Cupid, with little fans in their hands, with the which they fanned wind upon her. Her ladies and gentlewomen also, the fairest of them were apparelled like the nymphs Nereides (which are the mermaids of the waters) and like the Graces, some steering the helm, others tending the tackle and ropes of the barge, out of the which there came a wonderful passing sweet savour of perfumes, that perfumed the wharf's side, pestered with innumerable multitudes of people. Some of them followed the barge all alongst the river's side; others also ran out of the city to see her coming in; so that in the end there ran such multitudes of people one after another to see her that Antonius was left post-alone in the market-place in his imperial seat to give audience. And there went a rumour in the people's mouths that the goddess Venus was come to play with the god Bacchus, for the general good of all Asia.

When Cleopatra landed, Antonius sent to invite her to supper to him. But she sent him word again, he should do better rather to come and sup with her. Antonius therefore, to show himself courteous unto her at her arrival, was contented to obey her, and went to supper to her; where he found such passing sumptuous fare, that no tongue can express it.

202 *As*: As if.

204 *cloth-of-gold of tissue*: An especially rich fabric containing gold thread.

205–6 *O'erpicturing . . . nature*: Surpassing those pictures of Venus in which we see the imagination transcending what is possible in nature.

208 *divers-coloured*: Many-coloured (or perhaps iridescent).

209 *glow*: Make flush.

210 *what they undid did*: Although meant to cool, they seemed to warm.

211 *Nereides*: Sea-nymphs (pronounced with four syllables).

212 *So*: Like so.

212–13 *tended her . . . adornings*: Stood and moved about in front of her, seeing to it that their postures and movements were pleasing to look at.

214 *tackle*: Rigging, cordage. But in view of the next line (*Swell*), presumably sails are also included.

216 *yarely frame the office*: Nimbly perform their tasks.

218 *wharfs*: Banks.

218–19 *cast . . . out*: Expelled.

219 *upon her*: On her account, because of her.

221 *but for vacancy*: But for the fact that nature abhors a vacuum.

230 *ordinary*: Meal in a public eating-house or inn. The commonplace word is humorously chosen.

231 *Royal wench*: The phrase has the effect of an oxymoron: *wench* would normally be applied only to a woman or girl of low birth.

233 *cropped*: Bore a child. Cleopatra's son by Julius Caesar was called Caesarion.

236 *That*: So that.

237 *breathless, power breathe forth*: F has *breathlesse powre breath forth*. This might be read as 'breathless, pour breath forth', since F's spelling of 'power' is normal for 'pour' in Shakespeare's period. The point would then simply turn on the contrast between having no breath and pouring it forth. But the more usual reading, adopted here, is preferable. F's *breath* is a

well-attested spelling for *breathe*; Cleopatra not only pants for breath – which anyone might do – but emanates *power* as she does so. Cf. III.3.20–21, where Octavia is described as a *body rather than a life, | A statue than a breather*.

244 *Become themselves*: Are made becoming, justify themselves.

245 *riggish*: Wanton.

248 *lottery*: Prize.

II.3

6 *kept my square*: Kept to the straight line. A golden set-square was an emblem of temperance.
*that*: That which is.

9–31 *Soothsayer . . . gone*: Plutarch writes:

> With Antonius there was a soothsayer or astronomer of Egypt, that could cast a figure and judge of men's nativities, to tell them what should happen to them. He, either to please Cleopatra or else for that he found it so by his art, told Antonius plainly that his fortune, which of itself was excellent good and very great, was altogether blemished and obscured by Caesar's fortune; and therefore he counselled him utterly to leave his company and to get him as far from him as he could.
>
> 'For thy Demon,' said he, '(that is to say, the good angel and spirit that keepeth thee) is afraid of his, and, being courageous and high when he is alone, becometh fearful and timorous when he cometh near unto the other.'

14 *motion*: Inward prompting.

20 *daemon*: Guardian angel.
*that thy spirit*: That spirit of thine.

22 *Where*: Whereas.

25 *no more but*: Only.

27 *of*: By, through.

28 *lustre*: Light, glory.
*thickens*: Dims.

33 *art or hap*: Skill or mere luck.

34–9 *The very dice . . . odds*: Based on Plutarch: 'For it is said that as often as they two drew cuts for pastime who should have anything, or whether they played at dice, Antonius alway lost. Oftentimes when they were disposed to see cock-fight, or quails that were taught to fight one with another, Caesar's cocks or quails did ever overcome.'

35 *cunning*: Skill.

36 *chance*: Luck.

*speeds*: Wins.

37 *still*: Always.

38 *it is all to nought*: The odds are all to nothing (in my favour).

39 *inhooped*: Confined within a hoop or a circle (in order to make them fight).

II.4

This short scene reminds us of the main direction of the action – the coming meeting at Mount Misenum – and once more evokes the distances involved in the movements of its personages.

2 *Your generals after*: After your generals.

3 *e'en but*: Just, only.

6 *conceive*: Understand, see.

8 *My purposes do draw me much about*: I have to go a long way round.

9 *good success*: (We wish you) favourable outcome.

II.5

During this part of the play Cleopatra has nothing to do but wait for Antony's return. In this scene and its sequel (III.3) Shakespeare invents an episode which relates her to the main action. He adapts to Cleopatra's dealings with the Messenger Plutarch's account of her ill-treatment of her treasurer Seleucus, which occurred shortly before her death (see V.2.141–75). Plutarch writes: 'Cleopatra was in such a rage with him that she flew upon him, and took him by the hair of the head, and boxed him well-favouredly.'

1 *moody*: Melancholy.

3 *billiards*: In George Chapman's comedy *The Blind Beggar of Alexandria* (1598) the ladies also play billiards.

8–9 *when good will . . . pardon*: Spoken as a good-humoured parody of a sententious maxim, with an indecent quibble on the words *come too short*.

10 *angle*: Fishing-tackle.

11 *betray*: Deceive (into being caught).

15–18 *'Twas merry . . . up*: Based on Plutarch:

> On a time he went to angle for fish; and when he could take none he was as angry as could be, because Cleopatra stood by. Wherefore he secretly commanded the fishermen that when he cast in his line they should straight dive under the water and put a fish on his hook which they had taken before; and so snatched up his angling rod and brought up fish twice or thrice. Cleopatra found it straight; yet she seemed not to see it, but wondered at his excellent fishing. But when she was alone by herself among her own people, she told them how it was and bade them the next morning to be on the water to see the fishing. A number of people came to the haven and got into the fisher-boats to see this fishing. Antonius then threw in his line; and Cleopatra straight commanded one of her men to dive under water before Antonius' men and to put some old salt fish upon his bait, like unto those that are brought out of the country of Pont. When he had hung the fish on his hook, Antonius, thinking he had taken a fish indeed, snatched up his line presently. Then they all fell a-laughing.

17 *salt*: Dried.

18 *With fervency*: Excitedly.

21 *the ninth hour*: 9 a.m.

22 *tires*: Apparel (or possibly 'head-dresses').

23 *sword Philippan*: Named after the battle of Philippi, where Antony defeated Brutus and Cassius.

28 *yield*: Grant, allow. Cleopatra treats the Messenger as if he himself were responsible for Antony's present condition.

33 *the dead are well*: A common euphemism, meaning that the dead are incapable of suffering further harm. *Bring it to*: If you take it to mean.

34–5 *The gold . . . throat*: This was actually done to the Roman millionaire Crassus (see the note to III.1.2).

38 *so tart a favour*: So sour an expression.

40 *Fury*: In classical mythology the Furies were avenging goddesses, with snakes twined in their hair; they were associated with madness or frenzy.

41 *formal*: Sane, normal.

50–51 *allay | The good precedence*: Spoil what had begun so promisingly.

54 *Pour out the pack*: Empty your load (like a pedlar's *pack*).

58 *For what good turn*: Cleopatra assumes that Antony must be indebted to Octavia, since the Messenger says he is *bound unto* her.

59 *the best turn i'th'bed*: In the sexual sense.

63 *spurn*: Kick.

64 *hales*: Drags.

71 *boot*: Compensate.

72 *Thy modesty*: This seems to mean 'someone as humble and deferential as yourself'.

75 *keep yourself within yourself*: Control yourself.

78 *kindly*: Friendly, well-disposed.

82–4 *These hands . . . cause*: I act ignobly in striking a person lower in estate than myself, since the person who ought to be punished is myself, the true culprit.

92 *confound*: Destroy.

94 *So*: Even if.

96 *Narcissus*: In Greek mythology, a beautiful youth who fell in love with his own reflection.

99 *Take no offence that I would not offend you*: Don't take offence that I am unwilling to offend you (by giving an answer that is unwelcome).

101 *unequal*: Unjust.

103 *That art not what th'art sure of*: Who are not as bad as the message of whose truth you are so certain.

105–6 *Lie they upon thy hand, | And be undone*: May you be unable to sell them and may you be ruined.

112 *feature*: Physical appearance.

113 *inclination*: Character.

115 *him*: Antony.

116–17 *Though he be . . . Mars*: The implied comparison is with a 'perspective' picture, a form of trick painting fashionable in Shakespeare's time. It showed two quite different images according to the viewpoint of the spectator.

116 *Gorgon*: One of three mythical female personages, with snakes for hair, whose look had the power to turn others to stone; hence, a hideous monster.

## II.6

This and the next scene bring the business concerning Pompey to a conclusion. The triumvirate is seen in action for the last time: when Pompey is disposed of, there is nothing to prevent it from breaking up. Even now, the temporary concord is uneasy and strained.

0 *one door . . . another*: The entry doors at each side of the Elizabethan playhouse stage.

2 *meet*: Fit.

7 *tall*: Brave, gallant.

10 *factors*: Agents.

10–23 *I do not . . . father*: Sextus Pompeius appeals to the events of recent Roman history, some of which had formed the subject of Shakespeare's previous Roman tragedy, *Julius Caesar*, including Antony and Octavius, avenging Caesar's assassination, defeating Brutus and Cassius at Philippi. Sextus Pompeius now argues that, since Julius Caesar found avengers in them, Pompey should also find an avenger in his son.

11 *want*: Lack.

13 *ghosted*: Haunted.

17 *courtiers*: Wooers, questers.

18 *drench*: In blood.

19 *but a man*: Only a man (not a king).

20 *rig*: Equip.

22 *despiteful*: Cruel, malicious.

23 *Take your time*: That is, don't get carried away by your anger.

24 *fear*: Frighten.

25 *speak with*: Encounter.

26 *o'ercount*: Outnumber.

27 *o'ercount me of my father's house*: Pompey bitterly puns on Antony's word. The allusion is explained by Plutarch: 'when Pompey's house was put to open sale, Antonius bought it. But when they asked him money for it, he made it very strange and was offended with them . . .'

28–9 *since the cuckoo . . . mayst*: Since cuckoos always use the nests of other birds, keep it while you can.

30 *from the present*: Beside the point.

32–3 *weigh | What it is worth embraced*: Think carefully how much you will gain if you accept it.

33–4 *what may . . . fortune*: That is, how disastrous it may be for you if you pursue your ambitions (into war against us).

38 *unhacked edges*: Unused swords.

39 *targes*: Shields (pronounced with a hard 'g').

43 *praise of*: Credit for.

47 *studied*: Prepared by having given thought.

51 *timelier*: Earlier (but also perhaps 'more opportunely').

54 *What counts harsh Fortune casts upon my face*: Fortune has used Pompey as a tavern-board, working out exactly what everything has cost and what he must pay.
*counts*: Sums.
*casts*: Calculates.

58 *composition*: Agreement.

62 *take the lot*: Accept the result of the lottery.

66 *I have . . . to them*: Pompey's tactless remark has just earned a warning reproof from Antony (*You have heard much*) and he hastily tries to placate him: *I have fair meanings* ('My intentions are above-board'). Antony accepts the implied apology by making him a trivial compliment, which turns on a different meaning of 'fair': *And fair words to them* ('Your words are as finely chosen as your intentions are proper'). For the rest of the dialogue (68–79), Antony apparently moves out of earshot, leaving Pompey free to pursue his offensive topic.

70 *A certain queen . . . mattress*: The incident (familiar to

modern audiences from George Bernard Shaw's *Caesar and Cleopatra*) is described in Plutarch's *Life of Julius Caesar*. When Caesar was in Alexandria, he 'secretly sent for Cleopatra, which was in the country, to come unto him'. Plutarch goes on:

> She, only taking Apollodorus Sicilian of all her friends, took a little boat, and went away with him in it in the night, and came and landed hard by the foot of the castle. Then, having no other mean to come into the court without being known, she laid herself down upon a mattress or flock-bed which Apollodorus her friend tied and bound up together like a bundle with a great leather thong, and so took her up on his back, and brought her thus hampered in this fardel unto Caesar, in at the castle gate.

73 *toward*: In the immediate future (accented on the first syllable).

78 *Enjoy*: Continue to practise.
*plainness*: Blunt frankness.

79 *It nothing ill becomes thee*: It is in no way unbecoming to you.

83 *known*: Met.

94 *land service*: Military (as opposed to naval) service. There may have been an association between 'land-service' and the idea of thieving: see *Henry IV, Part II*, I.2.127–36.

95 *authority*: Legal powers (to arrest).

96 *take*: Into custody.
*two thieves kissing*: Their hands clasping.

97 *true*: (1) Honest; (2) without cosmetics.

111 *Pray ye*: I beg your pardon?

114 *bound to divine*: Required to predict the outcome.

116 *policy*: Politics, statecraft.
*made*: Mattered.

121 *still*: Quiet, silent.
*conversation*: Way of life.

128 *use his affection*: Satisfy his appetite.

129 *occasion*: Political opportunity, convenience.

132 *used*: Exercised, made good use of (for drinking).

II.7

0 *banquet*: See the note to I.2.12.

2 *plants*: Wordplay: the second meaning is 'feet' or 'soles of the feet'.

5 *alms drink*: This may mean 'drink taken as a work of charity', that is, to increase conviviality and to heal differences between friends. Another suggestion is 'leavings', since *alms drink* was ordinarily drink left over for alms people.

6–7 *pinch one another by the disposition*: Get on one another's nerves.

7 *No more*: No more bickering!

7–8 *reconciles . . . drink*: Gets them to yield to his plea (for amity) and at the same time consents to take a drink with them.

12 *had as lief*: Would just as soon.

13 *partisan I could not heave*: Long-handled spear too heavy for me to lift.

14 *sphere*: See the note to IV.15.10.

15 *move*: (1) Revolve; (2) exert influence.

16 *disaster*: Ruin (an astrological term, used of a star's malignant influence).

*sennet*: Trumpet notes signalling the entry of an important person.

17 *take*: Measure.

18 *scales i'*: Measuring marks on.

19 *dearth*: Famine.

20 *foison*: Plenty.

23 *shortly*: It shortly.

26–7 *Your serpent . . . sun*: This alludes to the belief, still common in the sixteenth century, that certain forms of organic life (for example, snakes and insects) could be created from inorganic matter. The colloquial use of *your* for 'the' suggests a complacent knowingness: Lepidus, now drunk, is showing off.

30 *I am not so well*: Lepidus takes the reference to *health* (29) literally.

30–31 *I'll ne'er out*: I won't be stand-offish, I'm with you.

33 *in*: (1) In drink; (2) indoors.

35 *pyramises*: Probably a drunken plural form.

39 *Forbear me till anon*: Leave me alone till a little later.

44 *it own*: Its own. The older form of 'its'; it probably has a slightly childish effect here, as elsewhere in Shakespeare.

45 *the elements once out of it*: When it decomposes (in death).

*transmigrates*: Decomposes and so passes into other forms of life.

52 *epicure*: The Epicureans did not believe in an afterlife.

55 *merit*: My good service.

57–80 *I have . . . drink*: Plutarch writes:

> Now in the midst of the feast, when they fell to be merry with Antonius' love unto Cleopatra, Menas the pirate came to Pompey and, whispering in his ear, said unto him:
>
> 'Shall I cut the gables of the anchors, and make thee lord not only of Sicilia and Sardinia, but of the whole Empire of Rome besides?'
>
> Pompey, having paused awhile upon it, at length answered him:
>
> 'Thou shouldst have done it and never have told it me; but now we must content us with that we have. As for myself, I was never taught to break my faith nor to be counted a traitor.'

57 *held my cap off*: Been respectful to.

63 *But entertain it*: Just grant the possibility.

65 *Will*: Who will.

*Hast thou drunk well*: Have you been drinking a lot?

68 *pales*: Encloses.

*inclips*: Embraces.

70 *competitors*: Partners (but see the note to I.4.3).

78 *Being done unknown*: If you had done it without my knowledge.

81 *palled*: Decayed, weakened.

89 *'A*: He (a colloquialism).

91 *go on wheels*: (1) Go smoothly; (2) whirl dizzily.

92 *reels*: (1) Fun; (2) reeling movements.

95 *Strike the vessels*: This may mean 'Broach the casks'.

Other suggestions are ‘Fill the cups full’ and even ‘Beat the kettledrums’. An injunction to drink seems the most likely.

97–8 *It’s monstrous ... fouler*: The more he rinses his brain with wine, the more hopelessly clogged it becomes.

99 *Possess it, I’ll make answer*: Be master of the time, I say.

102 *bacchanals*: A dance in honour of Bacchus, god of wine and revelry.

106 *Lethe*: Forgetfulness. See the note to II.1.27.

107 *Make battery to*: Assault, smite.

108 *place you*: Put you in the right positions.

*the boy*: A boy is provided at this point simply to sing the song.

109 *The holding every man shall beat*: Every man shall stamp in time to the refrain (*holding*). Editors usually emend F’s *beate* to ‘bear’ on the analogy of the common phrase ‘bear the burden’ (meaning ‘sing the refrain’). But Shakespeare probably envisages a very lively drunken ring-dance with a great deal of rhythmic stamping. Horace’s Cleopatra ode (I.37) opens with a reference to wine-heated dancers beating the earth with their feet: ‘Nunc est bibendum, nunc pede libero pulsanda tellus ...’ (‘Now is the time to drink and to beat the earth with unrestrained foot’). Shakespeare may well have recalled this poem; see the headnote to V.2.

111–16 *Come, thou monarch ... round*: According to Richmond Noble (*Shakespeare’s Use of Song* (1923)) and F. W. Sternfeld (*Music in Shakespearean Tragedy* (1963)), this bacchanalian song is modelled on the famous ninth-century Whit Sunday hymn, of which the following is the first stanza:

Veni Creator Spiritus
Mentes tuorum visita:
Imple superna gratia
Quae tu creasti pectora ...

(‘Come, thou Creative Spirit, visit the souls of thy

people; fill with thy heavenly grace the hearts which thou hast created'). The opening word 'Veni' may have suggested the trochaic metre of *Come, thou monarch*. The song in Thomas Heywood's Roman tragedy *The Rape of Lucrece* (1603–8), 'O thou Delphian God, inspire', has a comparable rhythm. On the other hand, the resemblance to 'Veni Creator Spiritus' may be fortuitous. A more likely influence is Anacreon, the Greek lyric poet, whose drinking songs were much imitated in the Renaissance, often in trochaic metre. No contemporary music for 'Come, thou monarch' survives.

112 *pink*: Half-shut.

*eyne*: The old plural of 'eyes'.

113 *fats*: Vats.

115 *Cup us*: Ply us with drink, intoxicate us.

118 *request you off*: Ask you to come ashore with me.

122 *Spleets*: Splits. The *Oxford English Dictionary* recognizes this as a distinct word. It seems, in the context, more ludicrously expressive than 'splits', to which it is usually emended.

*wild disguise*: Transformation effected by drunkenness.

123 *Anticked us*: Reduced us to fools ('antics').

124 *try you*: Test your capacity (to hold liquor).

126 *my father's house*: See the note to II.6.27.

III.1

This scene, set in Syria, on the frontiers of the Roman empire, follows on the previous scene without pause and implies an ironical comment on it. For a few moments we see the task of government through the eyes of subordinates.

0 *as it were in triumph*: The phrase does not refer literally to the Roman 'triumph', which was a victory procession into Rome. It means 'in an exultant manner'. Historically, Ventidius was granted a 'triumph' by the Roman Senate, as Plutarch remarks (see the following note).

1–5 *Now, darting . . . Marcus Crassus*: Antony had sent

Ventidius into Asia to keep the Parthians at bay (see II.3.42). Plutarch writes:

> Ventidius once again overcame Pacorus (Orodes' son, King of Parthia) in a battle fought in the country of Cyrrestica, he being come again with a great army to invade Syria; at which battle was slain a great number of the Parthians, and among them Pacorus the King's own son slain. This noble exploit, as famous as ever any was, was a full revenge to the Romans of the shame and loss they had received before by the death of Marcus Crassus ... Howbeit Ventidius durst not undertake to follow them any farther, fearing lest he should have gotten Antonius' displeasure by it ... Ventidius was the only man that ever triumphed of the Parthians until this present day; a mean man born, and of no noble house nor family, who only came to that he attained unto through Antonius' friendship, the which delivered him happy occasion to achieve to great matters. And yet, to say truly, he did so well quit himself in all his enterprises, that he confirmed that which was spoken of Antonius and Caesar: to wit, that they were alway more fortunate when they made war by their lieutenants than by themselves.

1 *darting*: The Parthian horsemen used to advance flinging their darts, and then rapidly retreat shooting flights of arrows behind them.

2 *Marcus Crassus*: A man of enormous wealth, he was one of the first triumvirate along with Pompey the Great and Julius Caesar. He was defeated by the Parthians in 53 BC. Orodes, father of Pacorus, put Crassus to death by pouring molten gold down his throat – as a punishment fitted to one who had thirsted for gold all his life.

7 *The ... Parthians follow*: That is, follow the ... Parthians.

9 *grand captain*: Great commander.

10 *triumphant*: Triumphal.

12 *lower place*: Man of subordinate rank.

18 *place*: Rank.

18 *his*: Antony's.

20 *by th'minute*: Continually.

24 *darkens him*: Eclipses him (that is, checks his advancement, so bringing loss rather than gain).

27 *perish*: Be worthless.

27–9 *that ... distinction*: That quality (discretion) without which a soldier and his sword can scarcely allow any distinction to be made between them.

33 *The ne'er-yet-beaten horse of Parthia*: The Parthians were brilliant mounted soldiers.

34 *jaded*: Driven like worn-out nags ('jades').

III.2

The triumvirate appears for the last time.

1 *brothers*: Brothers-in-law (Antony and Caesar). The word is probably used with irony.

*parted*: Departed.

3 *sealing*: Finishing their arrangements.

6 *green-sickness*: Form of anaemia supposed to affect lovelorn girls; Lepidus presumably has a hangover, which is mockingly attributed to his love for Antony and Caesar.

7 *A very fine one*: The Latin word '*lepidus*' means 'fine', 'elegant'. The following satire on Lepidus' 'love' for the other two triumvirs brings out obliquely the lack of sympathy with one another shown by all three.

11 *nonpareil*: Incomparable.

12 *Arabian bird*: Phoenix (the mythical immortal bird, of which only one was supposed to exist at a time).

16 *figures*: Figures of speech.

17 *cast*: Count, calculate.

*number*: Versify (put into 'numbers', that is, verse).

20 *his shards, and he their beetle*: The dung patches (*shards*) between which the *beetle* Lepidus crawls to and fro. Enobarbus contemptuously rounds off the satirical flight.

21 *to horse*: The signal for departure.

23 *No further*: You (or 'we') must go no further (that is, we must separate here).

26–7 *As my thoughts ... approof*: As I think you will be, and as I would stake anything you will prove to be.

26 *band*: Commercial term meaning 'bond', 'promissory note'.

28 *piece*: Paragon.

29 *cement*: Principle of union (accented on the first syllable).

32 *mean*: Means, intermediary.

34 *In*: By.

35 *curious*: Exceptionally touchy and particular.

48–9 *the swan's-down feather ... tide*: She is like the swan's-down feather that floats in still water just before the tide turns. This delicately caught moment of silent immobility and indecisiveness on Octavia's part suggests that we are at or near the mid-point of the play.

52 *were he a horse*: A *cloud* (51) on a horse's face – that is, the absence of a white star – impaired its value.

57 *rheum*: Running at the eyes.

58 *confound*: Destroy.

60 *still*: Constantly.

60–61 *the time ... you*: The passage of time will not outdistance my thoughts of you (that is, I shall think of you constantly).

63–4 *Look ... gods*: Antony embraces Caesar as an act of formal leave-taking.

III.3

2 *as before*: This means either that it is the same Messenger as in II.5 or that he is in the same ruffled condition as Cleopatra had left him in at the end of II.5.

3 *Herod of Jewry*: A proverbially fierce tyrant; see also the note to I.2.29–30.

14 *That's not so good*: This seems to treat Octavia's being *low-voiced* (13) as a fault in her; Shakespeare may have intended to show Cleopatra's bad taste. But some editors take the phrase to mean 'That is less favourable news'; the following *He cannot like her long* would then be an abrupt change of mood to optimism.

18 *creeps*: Shuffles.

19 *Her motion and her station are as one*: She has so little vitality that it makes no difference whether she moves or stands still.

20 *shows*: Looks like.

22 *observance*: Powers of observation.

22–3 *Three . . . note*: Few in Egypt have better powers of observation. *Three* is used vaguely here to mean a small or trifling number.

28–9 *thirty . . . her face*: Cleopatra changes the subject; she was herself thirty-eight.

33 *As low as she would wish it*: A colloquialism, used to express petty malice: 'low, and serve her right too!'

35 *employ thee back again*: Send you back (to Rome) again as my messenger.

37 *proper*: Good.

39 *harried*: Maltreated.
*by him*: According to him.

40 *no such thing*: Nothing remarkable.

42 *Isis else defend*: Isis forbid anything else! (that is, I should jolly well think so!).

43 *serving*: The implied subject is *he* (42).

47 *I warrant you*: I'll be bound.

III.4

This and the following two scenes show the hostility between Antony and Caesar coming into the open. With the disposal of Lepidus, the Roman world is left with two 'competitors' for mastery. War suddenly seems imminent.

3 *semblable*: Similar.

4–5 *made his will, and read it | To public ear*: In Plutarch it is Antony's will which Caesar, having obtained possession of it from the custody of the vestal virgins, reads to the Senate and so arouses feeling against Antony. Possibly the text is corrupt at this point.

6 *scantly*: Grudgingly.

8 *most narrow measure lent me*: Did me small justice.

9 *hint*: Opportunity.

10 *from his teeth*: With obvious lack of conviction.

12 *Stomach*: Resent.

12–20 *A more unhappy . . . all*: Plutarch writes that Octavia, meeting with Caesar, Maecenas and Agrippa, appealed to them not to suffer her, that was the happiest woman of the world, to become now the most wretched and unfortunatest creature of all other.

'For now,' said she, 'every man's eyes do gaze on me, that am the sister of one of the Emperors and wife of the other. And if the worst counsel take place (which the gods forbid!) and that they grow to wars, for yourselves it is uncertain to which of them two the gods have assigned the victory or overthrow. But for me, on which side soever victory fall, my state can be but most miserable still.'

13 *between*: Between the two.

15 *presently*: At once.

24 *branchless*: Maimed.

27 *stain*: Eclipse.

34 *our faults*: The faults of Antony and Caesar.

III.5

5 *success*: Outcome.

6–11 *Caesar . . . confine*: In his *Life of Octavius* Plutarch says that Lepidus betrayed Octavius Caesar in the war against Sextus Pompeius. Lepidus' soldiers deserted him for Octavius, who then deposed Lepidus from his position as triumvir but spared his life and allowed him to reside as a state prisoner in Italy. Shakespeare's account, which omits Lepidus' treachery and places Octavius in an unfavourable light, may have been intended to balance the disclosure made shortly afterwards (18) that Antony was responsible for Pompey's death.

7 *presently*: After a short time.
*rivality*: Equal partnership.

10 *appeal*: (Caesar's) accusation.

11 *up*: Shut up, imprisoned.

12 *chaps*: Jaws.

13–14 *throw . . . the other*: Feed them with everything in the world, the jaws will still grind each other down.

15 *spurns*: Kicks. Eros imitates Antony (*thus*).

17–18 *And threats . . . Pompey*: In the *Life of Octavius* Plutarch writes that Antony's lieutenant Titius put Pompey to death in the isle of Samos 'by Antony's commandment'. For this deed, says Plutarch, Antony incurred the hatred of the people of Rome. He regrets the murder presumably because Pompey might have made a useful ally against Octavius.

17 *threats the throat*: Threatens the life.

*that his officer*: The officer of his.

21 *naught*: Something bad.

III.6

1–19 *Contemning Rome . . . so*: Plutarch writes of the growing hostility against Antony felt by the Roman people:

> But yet the greatest cause of their malice unto him was for the division of lands he made amongst his children in the city of Alexandria. And, to confess a troth, it was too arrogant and insolent a part, and done (as a man would say) in derision and contempt of the Romans. For he assembled all the people in the showplace where young men do exercise themselves; and there upon a high tribunal silvered he set two chairs of gold, the one for himself and the other for Cleopatra, and lower chairs for his children. Then he openly published before the assembly that, first of all, he did establish Cleopatra Queen of Egypt, of Cyprus, of Lydia, and of the lower Syria, and, at that time also, Caesarion King of the same realms. (This Caesarion was supposed to be the son of Julius Caesar, who had left Cleopatra great with child.) Secondly he called the sons he had by her 'the Kings of Kings': and gave Alexander for his portion, Armenia, Media, and Parthia (when he had conquered the country); and unto Ptolemy for his portion, Phoenicia, Syria, and Cilicia. And therewithal he brought out Alexander in a long gown after the fashion of the Medes, with a high copped-tank hat on his head, narrow in the top, as the Kings of the Medes and Armenians do use to wear them; and Ptolemy apparelled in a cloak after the Macedonian manner, with slippers on his feet, and a broad hat with a royal band or diadem – such was the apparel and old attire of the ancient kings and successors of Alexander the Great. So, after his sons had done their humble duties and kissed their father and mother, presently

a company of Armenian soldiers set there of purpose, compassed the one about, and a like company of the Macedonians the other. Now, for Cleopatra, she did not only wear at that time, but at all other times else when she came abroad, the apparel of the goddess Isis, and so gave audience unto all her subjects as a new Isis.

1 *Contemning*: Despising.
3 *tribunal*: Raised platform, dais.
6 *my father's*: Julius Caesar had adopted Octavius.
9 *stablishment*: Confirmed possession.
12 *showplace*: Place for public shows or spectacles, theatre.
19 *so*: In those *habiliments* (17).
20 *queasy*: Disgusted.
24–30 *Caesar . . . revenue*: Closely based on Plutarch:

Octavius Caesar reporting all these things unto the Senate and oftentimes accusing him to the whole people and assembly in Rome, he thereby stirred up all the Romans against him. Antonius on the other side sent to Rome likewise to accuse him; and the chiefest points of his accusations he charged him with were these: first, that having spoiled Sextus Pompeius in Sicilia he did not give him his part of the isle; secondly, that he did detain in his hands the ships he lent him to make that war; thirdly, that, having put Lepidus their companion and triumvirate out of his part of the Empire and having deprived him of all honours, he retained for himself the lands and revenues thereof which had been assigned unto him for his part.

25 *spoiled*: Despoiled.
*rated*: Allotted.
30 *revenue*: Accented on the second syllable.
31 *'Tis done already, and the messenger gone*: Caesar's extraordinary promptness and efficiency may recall a famous line from Lucan's epic poem *Pharsalia* (II.657), where Julius Caesar is described as 'Nil actum credens, cum quid superesset agendum' ('believing nothing done while anything remained to do').

32 *Lepidus was grown too cruel*: Although based on Plutarch, this sounds unconvincing when said of Shakespeare's Lepidus. This is one of many moments in the play when we do not necessarily believe what one character says of another.

40 *castaway*: Rejected.

52 *ostentation*: Public display.

52–3 *which, left unshown, | Is often left unloved*: Love which is not shown to exist may not exist in fact – or may be thought not to do so.

61 *Being an obstruct*: Since you are an impediment.

66 *nodded*: Beckoned with a nod.

67 *who now*: And they now.

69–75 *Bocchus . . . Lycaonia*: This list of kings is taken from Plutarch.

76 *more larger*: Even longer. The double comparative was a common Elizabethan usage.

79 *withhold our breaking forth*: Restrain me from erupting (into violent or decisive action).

80 *wrong led*: The sense is not very satisfactory, and some editors have emended so that the line reads: '. . . perceivèd . . . were wronged'.

81 *negligent danger*: Danger from negligence.

82 *time*: Present state of affairs.

83 *content*: Happiness.

86 *more dear to me*: Is more dear to me than you.
*abused*: Deceived.

87 *mark*: Reach.

88–9 *makes his ministers | Of us*: Make us their servants.

93 *large*: Licentious, free.

94 *turns you off*: Dismisses you, repudiates you.

95 *potent regiment*: Powerful rule.
*trull*: Harlot.

96 *noises it*: Clamours.

98 *known to patience*: Patient.

III.7

The second movement of the play begins here with the battle of Actium sequence. The battle (September 31 BC) was fought off the west coast of Macedonia.

For his historical details Shakespeare closely follows Plutarch, whose account begins:

> Now after that Caesar had made sufficient preparation, he proclaimed open war against Cleopatra, and made the people to abolish the power and empire of Antonius because he had before given it up unto a woman. And Caesar said furthermore that Antonius was not master of himself, but that Cleopatra had brought him beside himself by her charms and amorous poisons, and that they that should make war with them should be Mardian the eunuch, Photinus, and Iras, a woman of Cleopatra's bed-chamber that frizzled her hair and dressed her head, and Charmion, the which were those that ruled all the affairs of Antonius' empire.

3–19 *Thou hast ... behind*: Plutarch says that 'Antonius, through the persuasions of Domitius [Enobarbus], commanded Cleopatra to return again into Egypt', and goes on to say that Cleopatra bribed Canidius to speak on her behalf to Antony: 'These fair persuasions won him; for it was predestined that the government of all the world should fall into Octavius Caesar's hands.'

3 *forspoke*: Opposed.

5 *Is't not denounced against us*: Hasn't war been declared against me? Cleopatra uses the royal plural; the Romans declared war not against Antony and Cleopatra but against her only. Some editors keep the F reading *If not, denounc'd against vs*, repunctuating it as 'If not denounced against us'. The speech would then mean: 'Even if the war had not been declared against me, why shouldn't I be here in person?'

8 *merely*: Utterly.

8–9 *the mares ... horse*: The mares would carry the soldiers and copulate with the stallions.

10 *puzzle*: Perplex, embarrass with difficulties.

11 *heart*: Mind.

13 *Traduced*: Calumniated, censured.

14 *an eunuch*: The eunuch is Mardian, as Plutarch makes clear.

16 *charge*: Cost, expense.

18 *for*: In the capacity of.

20 *Emperor*: Antony is called *Emperor* three times in this short scene. In this way his stature is insisted on immediately before his fall. (According to Plutarch, Antony had been deprived of his title when war was declared on Cleopatra.)

21–3 *Tarentum and Brundisium . . . Toryne*: These were the two chief ports of south-eastern Italy; Toryne was a few miles north of Actium.

23 *take in*: Occupy.

24–5 *Celerity . . . negligent*: In Plutarch Cleopatra makes light of Caesar's brilliant efficiency: Shakespeare makes her administer a rebuke.

29 *For that*: Because.

30–32 *my lord dared . . . Pompey*: Plutarch mentions both these challenges. Pharsalia, the region where the decisive battle between Julius Caesar and Pompey the Great was fought, was not far from Actium.

35 *muleters*: Mule-drivers.

36 *Engrossed by swift impress*: Hastily brought together by press-gangs.

38 *yare*: Swift, easily manipulated.

39 *fall*: Befall.

43 *Distract*: Confuse.

*most*: For the greater part.

44 *footmen*: Foot-soldiers.

*unexecuted*: Unused.

47 *merely*: Entirely.

51 *head*: Promontory.

57 *power*: Army.

60 *Thetis*: A sea-nymph.

61–6 *O noble . . . foot*: The speech is transcribed, with a few modifications, from Plutarch. A 'captain' cries out to Antony as he passes: 'O noble Emperor, how cometh it to pass that you trust to these vile brittle ships? What, do you mistrust these wounds of mine and this sword? Let the Egyptians and Phoenicians fight by sea, and set us on the mainland, where we use to conquer, or to be slain on our feet.'

62 *misdoubt*: Doubt the existence of, disbelieve.

64 *go a-ducking*: Get drenched in the sea.

68–9 *his whole action grows | Not in the power on't*: His entire strategy has been planned without regard to his real strength.

75 *Carries*: Takes him forward.

76 *distractions*: Divisions, small numbers.

80–81 *With news . . . some*: Things are happening fast and every minute a new development is born. Some editors emend F's *with Labour* to 'in labour', with a consequent idiomatic gain.

III.8

The battle scenes are managed with economy and even austerity. Since Actium was a sea-battle involving thousands of men, it had to be left to the imagination of the audience. There is no hand-to-hand fighting in Shakespeare's dramatization; the use of 'noises off' was therefore particularly important.

3 *whole*: Undivided (not weakened by division).

5 *prescript*: Written orders.

6 *jump*: Hazard.

III.9

2 *battle*: Line of battle.

III.10

0 *the noise of a sea fight*: Exactly what this was on Shakespeare's stage is not certain. It probably involved gunfire from the cannon just outside the theatre – at least when the play was performed at the Globe. See C. Walter Hodges, *The Globe Restored* (1968), p. 82.

1–23 *Naught . . . itself*: Plutarch writes:

> Howbeit the battle was yet of even hand, and the victory doubtful, being indifferent to both; when suddenly they saw the three-score ships of Cleopatra busy about their yard-masts, and hoising sail to fly. So they fled through the midst

of them that were in fight, for they had been placed behind the great ships, and did marvellously disorder the other ships. For the enemies themselves wondered much to see them sail in that sort with full sail towards Peloponnesus. There Antonius showed plainly that he had not only lost the courage and heart of an Emperor but also of a valiant man, and that he was not his own man, proving that true which an old man spake in mirth: that the soul of a lover lived in another body, and not in his own. He was so carried away with the vain love of this woman, as if he had been glued unto her and that she could not have removed without moving of him also . . .

Many plainly saw Antonius fly, and yet could very hardly believe it, that he, that had nineteen legions whole by land and twelve thousand horsemen upon the sea side, would so have forsaken them, and have fled so cowardly; as if he had not oftentimes proved both the one and the other fortune and that he had not been throughly acquainted with the diverse changes and fortunes of battles.

1 *Naught*: Ruin, disaster.

2 *Th'Antoniad, the Egyptian admiral*: Plutarch notes that 'The admiral galley of Cleopatra was called *Antoniad*.' *admiral*: Flagship.

5 *synod*: Assembly (usually used of the gods). Scarus is swearing by all the gods and goddesses at once. *What's thy passion*: What's the reason for your distress?

6 *cantle*: Segment of a sphere.

7 *With very ignorance*: Through utter stupidity.

9 *tokened pestilence*: Plague-spots (announcing imminent death).

10 *ribaudred*: Much discussed and emended; presumably it means something like 'lewd' or 'filthy', perhaps 'rotten with disease'.

12–13 *When vantage . . . same*: Cf. Plutarch: 'the battle was yet of even hand, and the victory doubtful, being indifferent to both'.

12 *vantage*: Chance of advantage.

13 *elder*: Greater.

14 *breese*: Gadfly. Scarus' fury, dismay and horror result in the heaped-up phrases and mixed metaphors of this bellowed announcement. This is a very original variant on the traditional messenger-speech.

17 *loofed*: Luffed (with the head of the vessel turned into the wind, so as to prepare for departure).

18 *ruin of her magic*: Man ruined by her powers of enchantment.

19 *Claps on*: Puts on promptly.

*sea wing*: Means of flight by sea (sails).

*mallard*: Wild drake. Like *cow in June* (14), the word expresses contempt.

26 *what he knew himself*: His true self.

29 *are you thereabouts*: Is that what you're thinking?

*good night indeed*: It's all up.

31 *'Tis easy to't*: It's easy enough to get there.

35 *wounded chance*: Maimed fortunes.

III.11

Plutarch describes Antony's desolation after his flight. First, when Cleopatra, who was in her own ship, 'knew his galley afar off, she lift up a sign in the poop of her ship, and so Antonius coming to it was plucked up where Cleopatra was; howbeit he saw her not at his first coming, nor she him, but went and sat down alone in the prow of his ship, and said never a word, clapping his head between both his hands'. It is a later passage that Shakespeare dramatizes in this scene: '... he returned again to his place and sat down, speaking never a word as he did before; and so lived three days alone, without speaking to any man. But, when he arrived at the head of Taenarus, there Cleopatra's women first brought Antonius and Cleopatra to speak together and afterwards to sup and lie together.'

Shakespeare leaves the location unspecified; it is felt to be vaguely Egyptian, so that editors usually give it as Alexandria.

3 *lated*: Belated (like a traveller who has lost his way after nightfall).

5–6 *Fly . . . Caesar*: Based on Plutarch's account of Antony's solicitude for his followers: 'Then Antonius very courteously and lovingly did comfort them, and prayed them to depart; and wrote unto Theophilus, governor of Corinth, that he would see them safe and help to hide them in some secret place until they had made their way and peace with Caesar.'

8 *show their shoulders*: Turn their backs (in flight).

12 *that*: What.

14 *rashness*: Folly.

17 *Sweep your way*: Clear your path, make things easier.

18 *loathness*: Unwillingness.
*hint*: Opportunity (or perhaps 'suggestion').

19–20 *Let that be left | Which leaves itself*: Leave the man (Antony) who is no longer himself.

23 *command*: The power to command others.

35 *He*: Octavius. Antony is self-absorbed in an internal dialogue and does not at first hear the approach of the others.

36 *a dancer*: Who would wear a sword for ornament.

38 *mad Brutus*: A strange remark, since Marcus Brutus showed no signs of madness, although his ancestor Junius Lucius Brutus pretended in his youth to be simple-minded. (*Brutus* could mean 'stupid'.) Shakespeare may have meant to startle us with the sense that everyone has his own – often surprisingly partial – view of other people. Pompey's earlier references to *the good Brutus* and *the all-honoured, honest, Roman Brutus* (II.6.13, 16) make an obvious contrast.

39 *Dealt on lieutenantry*: Depended on his subordinates to do his fighting for him.

40 *squares*: Squadrons.

41 *stand by*: Stand back.

44 *unqualitied*: Beside himself.

47 *but*: Unless.

49 *reputation*: Honour.

50 *A most unnoble swerving*: Antony takes up Eros' *Most noble sir, arise* (46) and retorts bitterly *A most* un*noble swerving*.

*swerving*: Transgression, lapse.

51–4 *See . . . dishonour*: In his acutely distressed state Antony sees himself as doing something comparably disreputable. 'See how I try to steal away (*convey*) my shame so that you can no longer see it, by brooding on the past and wishing vainly it had never happened.'

53 *looking back*: Looking back at.

54 *'Stroyed*: Destroyed, lost.

60 *beck*: Nod, mute signal.

62 *the young man*: In the year of Actium Antony was fifty-one, Caesar thirty-two.

*treaties*: Terms (for negotiation).

62–3 *dodge* | *And palter*: Shuffle and prevaricate.

63 *the shifts of lowness*: The abject behaviour of those who have been brought low.

67 *affection*: Passion.

68 *on all cause*: Whatever the reason.

69 *Fall not a tear*: Let not a tear fall.

*rates*: Is worth.

71 *Even this*: This alone.

*schoolmaster*: Tutor to the children of Antony and Cleopatra. See the headnote to III.12.

73 *viands*: Solid food.

III.12

Plutarch's account of the exchange of ambassadors between the two sides is worked up by Shakespeare into a weighty episode which occupies this and the next scene. As so often in this play, key roles within individual scenes are given to messengers, ambassadors, go-betweens of various kinds, acting on behalf of masters who seldom have the chance of meeting. Plutarch writes:

> . . . they sent ambassadors unto Octavius Caesar in Asia, Cleopatra requesting the realm of Egypt for their children, and Antonius praying that he might be suffered to live at Athens like a private man, if Caesar would not let him remain in Egypt. And, because they had no other men of estimation about them (for that some were fled, and, those

that remained, they did not greatly trust them), they were enforced to send Euphronius the schoolmaster of their children . . .

Caesar would not grant unto Antonius' requests. But, for Cleopatra, he made her answer that he would deny her nothing reasonable, so that she would either put Antonius to death or drive him out of her country. Therewithal he sent Thyreus one of his men unto her, a very wise and discreet man, who, bringing letters of credit from a young lord unto a noble lady, and that besides greatly liked her beauty, might easily by his eloquence have persuaded her. He was longer in talk with her than any man else was, and the Queen herself also did him great honour; insomuch as he made Antonius jealous of him. Whereupon Antonius caused him to be taken and well-favouredly whipped, and so sent him unto Caesar; and bade him tell him that he made him angry with him, because he showed himself proud and disdainful towards him, and now specially when he was easy to be angered, by reason of his present misery.

4 *pinion*: Pinion-feather.

5 *Which*: Who.

8 *petty to his ends*: Insignificant to his purposes.

10 *To his grand sea*: To the ocean that is its source.

12 *Requires*: Requests.

13 *lessons*: Disciplines. This gives a richer sense than 'lessens', to which it is often emended. But an audience will probably hear it as 'lessens', despite the appropriateness of *lessons* to the schoolmaster who speaks it.

18 *circle*: Crown. The schoolmaster's speeches have a notable eloquence.

19 *hazarded to thy grace*: Dependent on your favour.

21 *Of audience nor desire shall fail*: Shall not fail either to gain a hearing from me or to secure her wishes.
*so*: If.

25 *Bring*: Conduct.
*bands*: (Military) lines.

26 *try*: Put to the test.

27–9 *Promise . . . offers*: Use my authority to promise what she asks; offer in addition anything which you may at the time think effective. This edition keeps F's words; editors sometimes emend, so that the last clause reads 'and more, | From thine invention, offer' or 'add more, | As thine invention offers'.

30–31 *want will perjure | The ne'er-touched vestal*: Need will make the immaculate vestal virgin break her vows.

31 *Thidias*: Shakespeare's name for North's Plutarch's 'Thyreus'; see An Account of the Text.

32 *thine own edict for thy pains*: Your own judgement as to how your services should be paid.

32–3 *which we | Will answer as*: Which (the *edict*) I will obey as if it were.

34 *becomes his flaw*: Carries off his lapse.

35–6 *thou think'st . . . moves*: In your opinion he reveals (of his inner state) through every outward act.

36 *power that moves*: Faculty of mind or body that is put in action.

III.13

1 *Think, and die*: Brood and die (of depression). This is to be Enobarbus' own fate.

3 *will*: Desire, passion.

5 *face*: Appearance, show.
*ranges*: Battle lines.

7 *affection*: Sexual passion.

8 *nicked*: Maimed, emasculated.

9 *opposed*: Were in conflict.

10 *The merèd question*: The sole ground of dispute (or since the verb 'mere' means 'to limit', 'the matter to which the dispute is limited').

11 *course*: Pursue.

15 *so*: If.

16 *us*: Royal plural.

17 *boy . . . grizzled head*: See the note to III.11.62.

20–22 *Tell him . . . particular*: The oddly slack rhythm may indicate that the text is defective; perhaps some words have dropped out. As it stands, it seems to mean the following (with the sense of the second sentence here understood): 'Tell him he is now in the bloom of youth.

But youth is common to all men at some time in their lives. From him the world has a right to expect some proof of personal distinction.' Antony goes on to say that the efficiency of Caesar's government and army prove nothing about his personal qualities, for they exist independently of him.

26 *gay comparisons*: Showy, specious advantages when we are compared. Perhaps there is also a suggestion of 'caparisons', meaning 'external trappings'.

27 *declined*: Past my prime (perhaps also 'having suffered ill fortune').

29 *high-battled*: With great armies under him.

30 *Unstate his happiness*: Lose his happiness by giving up his position.

30–31 *be staged to th'show | Against a sworder*: Put himself on public display in a gladiatorial combat.

32 *parcel*: Part.

34 *suffer all alike*: Decay together.

35 *Knowing all measures*: Having experienced every degree (of fortune).

36 *Answer his emptiness*: Meet in combat one as powerless as he.

41 *square*: Quarrel.

43 *faith*: Fidelity.

46 *story*: History, historical account.

46–152 *Enter Thidias ... gone*: For Plutarch's account of Thidias' visit, see the headnote to III.12.

48 *haply*: Perhaps.

50 *needs not us*: He needs no friends at all, being out of the running.

55 *he is Caesar*: And therefore by definition magnanimous. *right royal*: That's very generous of him. Cleopatra's responses in this and her next two speeches are studiedly ambiguous.

61 *right*: True.

62 *merely*: Utterly.

66 *require*: Request.

71 *shroud*: Protection. The line is two syllables short; perhaps a word has dropped out before *shroud*.

74 *in deputation*: By proxy.

77 *Till from*: F reads *Tell him, from*. The emendation adopted here was suggested by Kenneth Muir in *Notes and Queries* (1961), p. 142.
*all-obeying*: Which all obey.

78 *doom of Egypt*: Judgement on the Queen of Egypt.

80 *If that the former dare but what it can*: If a wise man has the resolution to persist in being wise.

82 *My duty*: A kiss.
*Your Caesar's father*: Julius Caesar; see the note to III.6.6.

83 *taking . . . in*: Occupying, annexing.

85 *As*: As if.

87 *fullest*: Best and most fortunate.

89 *kite*: A slang word for 'whore'.

91 *muss*: Children's game in which small objects are thrown on the ground to be scrambled for.

93, 103 *Jack*: (1) Fellow, knave; (2) substitute (according to the *Oxford English Dictionary*, 'jack' was sometimes 'Applied to things which in some way take the place of a lad or man, or save human labour').

96 *tributaries*: Minor potentates who paid tribute.

103 *again*: Back.

105 *blasted*: Withered, blighted.

107–8 *Forborne . . . women*: Historically, Antony had several children by Octavia.

107 *getting*: Begetting.

109 *feeders*: Servants, parasites.

110 *boggler*: Waverer. The word was usually applied to a restive horse, one given to sudden starting and shying. According to T. R. Henn, however, it here alludes to falconry – to 'the hawk that does not select and keep to one quarry, but turns backwards and forwards from one to another' (*The Living Image* (1972), p. 120).

112 *seel our eyes*: Blind us. In falconry the bird's eyes were sewn up ('seeled') as part of the taming process. Antony, to quote T. R. Henn again, 'like the blinded hawk, stumbles in the filth of the falconers' mews, surrounded by the jeering yard-boys who will see that

she is given no sleep till she surrenders' (*The Living Image*, pp. 120–21).

115 *confusion*: Destruction.

117 *trencher*: Wooden plate.

*fragment*: Leftover.

119 *vulgar fame*: Popular rumour.

120 *Luxuriously picked out*: Lustfully selected.

123 *fellow*: Mean subordinate.

124 *God quit you*: May God reward you! (a phrase used by beggars).

125 *seal*: Token (something which confirms a covenant).

126–8 *O that I . . . herd*: Antony sees himself as a cuckold with horns, and so eligible to take his place among *The hornèd herd*. The *hill of Basan* is mentioned in Psalm 68:15: 'As the hill of Basan, so is God's hill: even an high hill, as the hill of Basan'; and Psalm 22:12 mentions 'fat bulls of Basan'.

128 *savage cause*: Cause enough to run wild.

129–31 *to proclaim . . . him*: To express myself in polite language would be as inappropriate as if a man about to be hanged were to thank the hangman for doing the job neatly.

131 *yare*: Deft, quick.

132 *Cried he? And begged 'a pardon*: Antony jeeringly treats Thidias as a schoolboy who has been flogged for a misdemeanour.

138 *fever thee*: Let (the *white hand* . . .) give you the shivers.

140 *entertainment*: Treatment, reception.

*Look*: See that.

142–3 *harping on what I am, | Not what he knew I was*: Antony cannot accept what he has made of himself.

146 *orbs*: Spheres. See the note to IV.15.10.

147 *abysm*: Abyss.

147–51 *If he mislike . . . me*: Based on Plutarch: '"To be short, if this mislike thee," said he, "thou hast Hipparchus one of my enfranchised bondmen with thee. Hang him if thou wilt, or whip him at thy pleasure, that we may cry quittance."' Plutarch earlier remarks that Hipparchus 'was had in great estimation about

Antonius. He was the first of all his enfranchised bondmen that revolted from him and yielded unto Caesar.'

149 *enfranchèd*: Freed.

151 *quit*: Requite.

152 *stripes*: Weals.

153 *terrene moon*: Cleopatra, the earthly Isis.

155 *stay his time*: Give him time, wait (till he recovers).

157 *one that ties his points*: One who laces up his (Octavius') clothes, a mere valet.

*points*: Tagged laces for fastening clothes.

158–67 *if I be . . . prey*: For Cleopatra's self-defence Shakespeare may have recalled the account in Exodus of the plagues that God inflicted on the Egyptians. These included the plagues of hail and of flies as well as the plague on the first-born. 'I . . . will smite all the first-born of Egypt', says Jehovah (Exodus 12:12); cf. Cleopatra's *The next Caesarion smite* (162) – Caesarion was her first-born child. These biblical resonances may have been felt to lend conviction to Cleopatra's words: hence Antony's *I am satisfied* (167).

161 *neck*: Throat.

*determines*: Comes to an end, melts.

163 *the memory of my womb*: My children.

165 *discandying*: Melting.

*pelleted storm*: Hailstorm.

168 *sits down*: Plutarch has 'Caesar came, and pitched his camp hard by the city'. 'Sit down before' is a military term meaning 'besiege'; this is probably the sense here.

169 *oppose his fate*: Resist his destiny.

171 *fleet*: Are afloat.

*threatening most sea-like*: In a manner as threatening as the (stormy) sea's. Some editors take *sea-like* to mean 'in good sea-going trim'. Perhaps both senses are present.

172 *my heart*: My courage. Some editors read this as addressed to Cleopatra, but it seems unlikely in view of the next phrase.

173 *field*: Battlefield.

174 *in blood*: (1) Covered with blood; (2) in full strength.

175 *chronicle*: Place in history.

177 *hearted, breathed*: Treble-hearted, treble-breathed.

178–9 *when mine hours | Were nice and lucky*: When I was pampered by fortune.

179 *nice*: Pampered, made wanton.

179–80 *men did ransom lives | Of me for jests*: Men bought their lives from me for no more than the price of a joke (as if fighting were a game).

182 *gaudy*: Festive, joyous.

184–6 *It is . . . Cleopatra*: Plutarch writes:

> Cleopatra, to clear herself of the suspicion he had of her, she made more of him than ever she did. For first of all, where she did solemnize the day of her birth very meanly and sparingly, fit for her present misfortune, she now in contrary manner did keep it with such solemnity, that she exceeded all measure of sumptuousness and magnificence . . .

191 *sap in't*: Life in me.

192–3 *contend | Even with his pestilent scythe*: Kill as many as death does in time of plague.

194 *furious*: Enraged to the point of frenzy.

196 *estridge*: Goshawk (a large short-winged hawk; not an ostrich).
*still*: Always.

198 *heart*: Courage.

IV.1

1 *boy*: This was an insult. Shakespeare probably knew from Suetonius' *Life of Augustus* that Octavius was in fact contemptuously called 'the boy' by some of his enemies. Cf. III.13.17 and IV.12.48.
*as*: As if.

3–5 *dares me . . . die*: North's version of Plutarch reads: 'Antonius sent again to challenge Caesar to fight with him hand to hand. Caesar answered him that he had many other ways to die than so.' But in Plutarch's Greek Caesar says that Antony might find many other ways of dying.

6 *Laugh at*: I mock.

7–8 *When one so great . . . falling*: The image is of a hunted animal at bay; cf. IV.13.2–3.

9 *Make boot of his distraction*: Take advantage of his frenzy.

10 *heads*: Chief officers.

12 *files*: Ranks.

14 *fetch him in*: Close in upon him.

16 *waste*: Lavish expenditure.

IV.2

The sequence of short scenes from IV.2 to IV.12 focuses on the last stages in Antony's disintegration. All the incidents are based on Plutarch, but Shakespeare has rearranged them with a view to securing the most effective sequence. The most important departure from Plutarch's order is Enobarbus' defection. In Plutarch it comes before the battle of Actium. Shakespeare delays it until after Thidias' attempted overtures to Cleopatra; indeed it coincides with the night in which music is heard under the earth. Secondly, Antony's successful skirmish, given very little stress by Plutarch, is built up by Shakespeare so that for a brief time it seems a substantial victory. Antony's resurgence of high spirits and final military success are in this way inter-woven with the desertion and death of the man who was closest to him. The final impression made by this brilliant sequence is one of dizzying instability and ultimate dissolution: Fortune is at her most treacherously inconstant, but within the individual personality there are equally volatile shifts of mood.

After Caesar's rejection of Antony's challenge, Plutarch goes on:

> Then Antonius, seeing there was no way more honourable for him to die than fighting valiantly, he determined to set up his rest, both by sea and land. So, being at supper as it is reported, he commanded his officers and household servants, that waited on him at his board, that they should fill his cups full, and make as much of him as they could.

'For,' said he, 'you know not whether you shall do so much for me tomorrow or not, or whether you shall serve another master; and it may be you shall see me no more, but a dead body.'

This notwithstanding, perceiving that his friends and men fell a-weeping to hear him say so, to salve that he had spoken he added this more unto it: that he would not lead them to battle where he thought not rather safely to return with victory than valiantly to die with honour.

5 *Or*: Either.

6–7 *bathe my dying honour . . . again*: Revive my dying honour by giving it a blood-bath. A bath in warm blood was believed to be 'a powerful tonic in great debility from long-continued diseases' (*Oxford English Dictionary*). Of course Antony implies also the other meaning of 'blood-bath': wholesale slaughter, massacre.

7 *Woo't*: Wilt.

8 *Take all*: All or nothing.

13 *kings have been your fellows*: I have had kings as my servants.

21 *Scant not my cups*: Provide liberally.

23 *And suffered my command*: And, like you, also acknowledged me as master.

*What does he mean*: In this incident Shakespeare seems deliberately to insist on an element of mystery or opacity in Antony: Cleopatra's question and Enobarbus' glib reply compel us to make our own interpretation.

25 *period*: End.

27 *mangled shadow*: Hideously disfigured ghost (like the ghost of Hector when he appears to Aeneas in Book II of Virgil's *Aeneid*).

33 *yield*: Reward.

36 *Ho, ho, ho*: Antony attempts to laugh it off.

37 *the witch take me*: May I be bewitched.

38 *Grace*: Herb of grace (but also 'God's grace').

*drops*: Tears.

*hearty*: Loving.

44 *death and honour*: Honourable death.
45 *consideration*: Serious reflection.

IV.3

Plutarch writes, immediately after the passage quoted for IV.2:

> Furthermore, the self same night within little of midnight, when all the city was quiet, full of fear and sorrow, thinking what would be the issue and end of this war, it is said that suddenly they heard a marvellous sweet harmony of sundry sorts of instruments of music, with the cry of a multitude of people, as they had been dancing and had sung as they use in Bacchus' feasts, with movings and turnings after the manner of the Satyrs. And it seemed that this dance went through the city unto the gate that opened to the enemies, and that all the troop that made this noise they heard went out of the city at that gate. Now such as in reason sought the depth of the interpretation of this wonder thought that it was the god unto whom Antonius bare singular devotion to counterfeit and resemble him, that did forsake them.

5 *Belike*: Probably.
10 *Here we*: This is our place.
*An if*: If.
13 *hautboys*: Shawms, medieval reed instruments which would produce an eerie sound under the stage. Cf. *Macbeth*, IV.1.105, where 'hautboys' are heard as the cauldron of the Three Witches sinks.
15 *signs*: Bodes.
17 *the god Hercules*: Shakespeare substitutes Hercules (identified with Heroic Virtue) for Plutarch's Bacchus, whose relation with Antony he has suppressed.
25 *so far as we have quarter*: As long as the period (of our watch) lasts.
26 *give off*: Cease.

IV.4

2 *chuck*: Sweet.
3 *put thine iron on*: Help me on with the armour (of mine) which you are holding.

5 *brave*: Defy.

5–8 *Nay . . . must be*: F assigns these speeches differently; see An Account of the Text.

7 *False*: You have put it on wrong.

10 *Briefly*: In a moment.

13 *daff't*: Take it off.

14 *squire*: Whose duty was to give personal attendance to the knight.

15 *tight*: Skilled.

17 *occupation*: Trade.

18 *workman*: Professional, true craftsman.

19 *charge*: Command.

20 *betime*: Early.

22 *riveted trim*: Armour.

23 *port*: Gate.

25 *well blown*: The trumpets. Some editors take it as referring to the *morning* (26) ('the day is "blossoming" beautifully').

28 *well said*: Well done (a common Elizabethan usage).

31 *check*: Reprimand.

32 *mechanic compliment*: Fussily commonplace civilities.

IV.5

In Plutarch, Enobarbus is mentioned substantially only once, shortly before Actium: Antony

> dealt very friendly and courteously with Domitius, and against Cleopatra's mind. For, he being sick of an ague when he went and took a little boat to go unto Caesar's camp, Antonius was very sorry for it, but yet he sent after him all his carriage, train, and men; and the same Domitius, as though he gave him to understand that he repented his open treason, he died immediately after.

From this brief passage, and from an earlier, even briefer reference (quoted in the note to III.7.3–19), Shakespeare built up the entire character of Enobarbus ('Domitius').

1 *happy*: Fortunate.

2 *once*: Earlier. Cf. III.7.61–6.

4 *revolted*: Deserted.

14 *subscribe*: Sign.

17 *Dispatch*: Make haste (or perhaps 'get it done with').

IV.6

5 *The time of universal peace is near*: Peace was for a time established under Augustus (the 'pax Romana'). Plutarch says at one point: 'it was predestined that the government of all the world should fall into Octavius Caesar's hands'.

6 *Prove this*: If this proves.

*three-nooked*: Three-cornered (perhaps referring to Europe, Asia and Africa).

7 *bear*: Bring forth.

*olive*: Emblem of peace.

8 *charge Agrippa*: Command Agrippa to.

9 *vant*: Van, front line.

10–11 *That Antony . . . Upon himself*: Caesar's remark is in keeping with the more general impression that, since Actium, Antony is essentially in a state of isolation, undergoing a private and subjective ordeal of dissolution.

12–16 *Alexas . . . hanged him*: Plutarch writes of Alexas:

> . . . him Antonius had sent unto Herodes King of Jewry, hoping still to keep him his friend, that he should not revolt from him. But he remained there, and betrayed Antonius. For, where he should have kept Herodes from revolting from him, he persuaded him to turn to Caesar; and, trusting King Herodes, he presumed to come in Caesar's presence. Howbeit Herodes did him no pleasure; for he was presently taken prisoner, and sent in chains to his own country; and there by Caesar's commandment put to death.

13 *dissuade*: Persuade. Some editors emend to 'persuade'.

16–17 *Canidius . . . fell away*: Plutarch writes that after Actium 'Canidius, Antonius' lieutenant, flying by night and forsaking his camp, when they saw themselves thus destitute of their heads and leaders they yielded themselves unto the stronger'.

17 *entertainment*: Employment.

22 *bounty overplus*: Gift in addition.

23 *on my guard*: While I was on guard.

26–7 *Best you safed the bringer | Out of the host*: You had better see that the man who brought it is given a safe-conduct through the lines.

27 *attend mine office*: See to my duties.

30 *alone the*: The only, the greatest.

31 *feel . . . most*: Feel (it) more than anyone else.

32 *mine*: Abundant store.

34 *blows*: Swells to bursting point.

35 *thought*: Melancholy, grief.

IV.7

Plutarch writes:

> Antonius made a sally upon him, and fought very valiantly, so that he drave Caesar's horsemen back, fighting with his men even into their camp. Then he came again to the palace greatly boasting of this victory, and sweetly kissed Cleopatra, armed as he was when he came from the fight, recommending one of his men of arms unto her, that had valiantly fought in this skirmish. Cleopatra to reward his manliness gave him an armour and head-piece of clean gold; howbeit the man at arms, when he had received this rich gift, stale away by night and went to Caesar.

0 *Alarum*: Call to arms.

2 *has work*: Is hard-pressed.

*our oppression*: The pressure on us.

5 *droven*: Driven (an older form of the past participle).

6 *clouts*: Cloths, bandages.

8 *H*: Wordplay on the letter H and 'ache', which was pronounced 'aitch'.

9 *bench-holes*: Holes of a privy.

10 *scotches*: Gashes.

12 *score*: Mark.

15 *sprightly*: High-spirited, cheerful.

16 *halt*: Limp.

*after*: After you.

IV.8

1 *beat him to*: Driven him by blows into.
*Run one*: Let someone run.

2 *gests*: Feats, deeds. The word has a chivalric colouring.

5 *doughty-handed*: Valiant in fighting. Like *gests* (2) the word *doughty* is slightly archaic and romantic.

6–7 *Not as you served . . . mine*: Not as if you were merely obeying orders but as if you were as concerned as I am.

7 *shown all Hectors*: All behaved like Hector (the great warrior-hero of Troy).

8 *clip*: Embrace.

11 *whole*: Well (fully healed).

12 *fairy*: Enchantress (another word with archaic romance associations).

13 *day*: Light.

15 *proof of harness*: Impenetrable armour.

17 *virtue*: Valour.

20 *something*: Somewhat.

21 *nerves*: Muscles.

22 *Get goal for goal of youth*: Keep up with youth point for point.

28 *carbuncled*: Embossed with jewels.

29 *Phoebus' car*: The sun god's chariot.

31 *targets*: Shields.
*like the men that owe*: As becomes the men who own.

33 *camp this host*: Accommodate this army.

34 *carouses*: Toasts.

35–9 *Trumpeters . . . approach*: This military command, delivered in a stentorian parade-ground voice, gives the scene a brilliant climax. The command is of course instantly obeyed. It marks Antony's last heroic moment in the play.

37 *tabourines*: Small drums.

IV.9

The ear-splitting fanfare that concluded IV.8 is followed at once by the hushed silence of night – a carefully judged theatrical effect.

2 *court of guard*: Guard room.

3 *shiny*: Moonlit.

4 *second hour*: 2 a.m.

5 *shrewd*: Bad.

8–9 *men revolted ... memory*: Deserters receive an infamous report in the record of history.

8 *record*: Accented on the second syllable.

12 *mistress*: The moon. He alludes to the moon's supposed influence in inducing mental disease.
*melancholy*: Melancholia.

13 *poisonous damp*: Dampness that induces sickness.
*disponge*: Drop as from a sponge.

15–18 *Throw my heart ... thoughts*: According to current physiology, grief desiccated the heart.

19 *revolt*: Desertion.

20 *in thine own particular*: Yourself.

21 *rank me in register*: Put me down in its records.

22 *master-leaver*: Runaway servant.
*fugitive*: Deserter. As Enobarbus here foretells, he was 'ranked in register' precisely as a deserter by Plutarch (see the headnote to IV.5).

23 *He dies*: Plutarch describes Enobarbus as 'sick of an ague' (see the headnote to IV.5); Shakespeare makes the cause of his death more ambiguous, so that his grief at having deserted Antony seems to assist in hastening his end.

27 *for*: A preparation for.

29 *raught*: Reached, laid hold of.

30 *Demurely*: With a low sound, gently.

31–2 *Our hour | Is fully out*: The period of our watch is over.

IV.10

3 *i'th'fire or i'th'air*: Antony is already fighting in two of the elements, earth and water (land and sea); *fire* and *air* would complete the four elements.

4–9 *our foot ... endeavour*: Some editors believe line 7 incomplete; the missing words may have been to the effect 'Let us go up' (to the hills, from which *we may best discover* ... (8)). Other editors think line 7 essentially complete, taking *Where* (8) to refer back to *the hills* (5); in this case the words *Order ... haven* would be a parenthesis. For the Plutarchan source of these lines, see the first sentence quoted in the head-note to IV.12.

4 *foot*: Infantry.

6 *for*: To put to.

7 *put forth*: Set out from.

8 *appointment*: Equipment.

IV.11

1 *But being charged*: Unless we are attacked.

*still by land*: Inactive on land.

2 *Which, as I take't, we shall*: And I assume we shall be left unattacked.

4 *hold our best advantage*: Take up the best possible position.

IV.12

Plutarch writes:

> The next morning by break of day he went to set those few footmen he had in order upon the hills adjoining unto the city; and there he stood to behold his galleys which departed from the haven and rowed against the galleys of his enemies; and so stood still, looking what exploit his soldiers in them would do. But when by force of rowing they were come near unto them, they first saluted Caesar's men, and then Caesar's men re-saluted them also, and of two armies made but one, and then did altogether row toward the city. When Antonius saw that his men did forsake him and yielded unto Caesar, and that his footmen were broken and overthrown he then fled into the city, crying out that Cleopatra had betrayed him unto them with whom he had made war for her sake. Then she, being afraid of his fury, fled into the tomb which she had caused to be made; and there locked the doors unto her, and shut all the springs of the locks with great bolts; and in the meantime sent unto Antonius to tell him that she was dead.

0 *Alarum afar off, as at a sea fight*: This edition follows F's arrangement. Many editors move this direction to line 3 or, less often, to line 9. In F's arrangement the

battle is joined before Antony and Scarus appear; Antony's first words show that he does not yet know that the fighting has begun. Editors unnecessarily move the direction to a later point on the assumption that Antony's words must correspond to the truth, but the situation gains in irony if they do not. For the noise of a *sea fight*, see the note to III.10.0.

1 *joined*: In battle.
*pine*: Cf. note to 23 below.

3–4 *Swallows . . . nests*: Plutarch mentions this as an ill omen before Actium: 'Swallows had bred under the poop of her ship.'

8 *fretted*: Chequered.

13 *Triple-turned*: From Julius Caesar, from Pompey, from Antony himself.

15 *Makes only wars on thee*: Makes wars on you alone.

16, 25 *charm*: Enchantress, witch.

20 *hearts*: Men (his soldiers).

21 *spanieled*: F reads *pannelled*; editors regularly emend to *spanieled*, meaning 'fawned on me like spaniels'.

22 *discandy*: Become liquid.

23 *this pine*: Antony himself.
*barked*: Stripped bare.

25 *grave*: Deadly.

27 *my crownet, my chief end*: The crown and end of all my activities.

28 *right gypsy*: True gypsy. Cf. the note to I.1.10.
*fast and loose*: A cheating game played by gypsies, who got their dupes to bet whether a coiled rope or trap was fast (fixed) or loose.

29 *Beguiled*: Cheated.

30 *Avaunt*: Begone.

33 *Caesar's triumph*: This is the first reference to the coming triumphal procession through Rome to which Caesar as victor in the war would be entitled. See V.1.65–6 and V.2.109–10 for his intention to lead Cleopatra in his triumph.

34 *plebeians*: Accented on the first syllable.

35 *spot*: Stain, blemish.

36–7 *most monster-like be shown | For poor'st diminutives, for doits*: Like a monster be exhibited to undersized weaklings on payment of their small coins. For *doits* some editors retain F's reading *Dolts*, so that the phrase means 'exhibited to undersized weaklings and fools'; other editors adopt *doits* but interpret *diminutives* as 'small coins'. In favour of *doits* is *The Tempest*, II.2.27–32: 'Were I in England now, as once I was, and had but this fish painted, not a holiday fool there but would give a piece of silver. There would this monster make a man ... When they will not give a doit to relieve a lame beggar, they will lay out ten to see a dead Indian.'

37 *doits*: Coins of very small value.

39 *preparèd*: Grown long for the purpose.

43–5 *The shirt of Nessus ... moon*: Antony recalls the death of his supposed ancestor Hercules (sometimes called *Alcides*). The centaur Nessus gave Deianira, the wife of Hercules, his shirt soaked in poison, assuring her that if she sent it to Hercules it would act as a love-potion. She accordingly sent it, using Lichas as a messenger. When Hercules put on the shirt it burnt him to death; in his agony he hurled Lichas into the sea. The death of Hercules is the subject of Seneca's tragedy *Hercules Oetaeus*, which was probably known to Shakespeare.

47 *Subdue my worthiest self*: Overcome the most heroic part of my nature (that which was most like Hercules).

48 *To the young Roman boy*: The line would be metrically and stylistically improved by the deletion of *young*. Perhaps Shakespeare forgot to remove it after writing *boy*, which makes *young* tautologous.

IV.13

2 *Telamon*: Ajax, who went mad when the shield of Achilles was awarded not to him but to Odysseus.
*the boar of Thessaly*: Sent by Diana to ravage Calydon, and killed by Meleager.

3 *embossed*: Driven to extremity (a hunting term).
*monument*: See the quotation from Plutarch in the

headnote to IV.12.

5 *rive*: Rend, cleave.

6 *going off*: Departing.

10 *bring me*: Bring me word.

IV.14

For Antony's death, Shakespeare follows Plutarch very closely, keeping even the impression of lifelike anticlimax which attends Antony's failure to kill himself at once. He has just received the report of Cleopatra's death:

> Antonius, believing it, said unto himself:
>
> 'What dost thou look for further, Antonius, sith spiteful fortune hath taken from thee the only joy thou hadst, for whom thou yet reservedst thy life?'
>
> When he had said these words, he went into a chamber and unarmed himself; and being naked said thus:
>
> 'O Cleopatra, it grieveth me not that I have lost thy company, for I will not be long from thee. But I am sorry that, having been so great a captain and Emperor, I am indeed condemned to be judged of less courage and noble mind than a woman.'
>
> Now he had a man of his called Eros, whom he loved and trusted much and whom he had long before caused to swear unto him that he should kill him when he did command him; and then he willed him to keep his promise. His man drawing his sword lift it up as though he had meant to have stricken his master. But turning his head at one side, he thrust his sword into himself and fell down dead at his master's foot. Then said Antonius:
>
> 'O noble Eros, I thank thee for this; and it is valiantly done of thee, to show me what I should do to myself, which thou couldst not do for me.'
>
> Therewithal he took his sword and thrust it into his belly; and so fell down upon a little bed. The wound he had killed him not presently, for the blood stinted a little when he was laid; and when he came somewhat to himself again, he prayed them that were about him to dispatch him. But they all fled out of the chamber, and left him crying out and tormenting

himself; until at last there came a secretary unto him called Diomedes, who was commanded to bring him into the tomb or monument where Cleopatra was.

2 *that's dragonish*: That looks like a dragon.

4 *pendent*: Overhanging.

8 *black vesper's pageants*: The spectacular moveable shows of evening. 'Pageants' were originally floats or wheeled stages of the medieval mystery plays. Antony's description may owe something to the new moveable scenery of the Jacobean court masque.

9–10 *even with a thought | The rack dislimns*: As quick as thought, the drifting cloud (*rack*) wipes out. But there is also a wordplay involving the idea of a *body* (cf. 13) being 'dislimbed' – torn limb from limb – on a rack.

12 *knave*: Boy.

19–20 *Packed cards . . . triumph*: Shuffled the cards in Caesar's favour and treacherously allowed him to trump my glory. Antony plays on *triumph*, which in Shakespeare's day could also mean a trump card.

23 *robbed me of my sword*: Unmanned me.

25 *saucy*: Insolent.

26 *die the death*: Undergo the punishment of death.

29 *unto thy hand*: Already for you.

33 *rendered*: Surrendered.

38 *sevenfold shield of Ajax*: Made of brass, lined with seven folds of oxhide.

39 *battery*: Bombardment.

40 *thy continent*: What contains you, what holds you in.

41 *Apace*: Quick.

42 *pieces*: Of armour.

46 *length*: Of life.

48–9 *very force entangles | Itself with strength*: The fiercer the struggle, the more tangled and exhausted he becomes – like a trapped animal. J. Dover Wilson compares Sonnet 23, ll. 3–4: '[Like] . . . some fierce thing replete with too much rage, | Whose strength's abundance weakens his own heart.'

49 *Seal*: Finish (as in sealing a will).

50 *Eros . . . Eros*: The repetition of Eros' name in this scene is very insistent. In classical mythology Eros was the god of love.

51 *couch*: Lie.

52 *sprightly*: High-spirited, lively. (But a secondary meaning – 'ghostly' – may also be present.)

*port*: Bearing, demeanour.

53 *Dido and her Aeneas*: In Book VI of Virgil's *Aeneid*, when Aeneas visits the underworld, Dido refuses to meet her former lover. Antony chooses to recall them simply as famous lovers. But there are further similarities and significant differences between Dido and Aeneas and Cleopatra and himself. Dido, like Cleopatra, was queen over an African realm; but, unlike Cleopatra, she did not succeed in deflecting her lover from his Roman 'duty'. See also Introduction.

*want troops*: Lack followers, retinue.

54 *all the haunt be ours*: Everyone will follow us. (But since everyone there will be ghosts, they will be 'ghost-haunted' too.)

58 *Quartered*: Cut into quarters.

*o'er green Neptune's back*: On the sea.

59 *to lack*: For lacking.

60 *less noble mind*: In apposition with *I* in 57.

61 *our Caesar*: That is, our Roman Caesar.

63 *exigent*: Final emergency, moment of extreme need.

65 *inevitable prosecution*: Pursuit from which there is no escape.

72 *windowed*: Placed as in a window.

73 *with pleached arms*: With hands bound behind him. Another possible explanation, 'with folded arms' (the conventional melancholy posture), seems less likely.

74 *corrigible*: Submissive.

74–5 *subdued | To penetrative*: Humbled with the sense of piercing.

76 *branded*: Exposed with brutal clarity (as with a brand).

77 *His baseness that ensued*: The abject humiliation of the man who followed.

80 *pardon me*: Excuse me from doing it.

83 *precedent*: Former (accented on the second syllable).

86 *worship*: Worth, honour.

87 *Lo thee*: There you are.

98 *by their brave instruction*: By teaching me a lesson in bravery.

98–9 *got upon me | A nobleness in record*: Have beaten me in winning a noble place in history.

104 *Decretas*: In North's Plutarch this character's name is given as 'Dercetaeus'; in F the name occurs twice in the form adopted in this edition, and once as *Dercetus*. The abbreviated speech-prefixes *Decre*. (once) and *Dec*. (three times) also point to 'Decretas' as Shakespeare's preferred form.

107 *his period*: Its end.

113 *enter me with*: Recommend me to.

117 *Sufficing strokes for*: Strokes sufficient for.

122 *Which never shall be found*: A thing that will never happen (that Cleopatra should *dispose with Caesar*).

123 *disposed*: Come to terms.

124 *purged*: Allayed, cured.

133–4 *live to wear . . . out*: Outlive.

136 *To grace it*: By favouring it.

136–7 *Bid . . . and we*: If we bid . . ., we.

IV.15

Plutarch writes:

> . . . and so he was carried in his men's arms into the entry of the monument. Notwithstanding, Cleopatra would not open the gates, but came to the high windows, and cast out certain chains and ropes, in the which Antonius was trussed; and Cleopatra her own self, with two women only which she had suffered to come with her into these monuments, triced Antonius up.
>
> They that were present to behold it said they never saw so pitiful a sight. For they plucked up poor Antonius, all bloody as he was and drawing on with pangs of death, who holding up his hands to Cleopatra raised up himself as well as he could. It was a hard thing for these women to do, to lift him up. But Cleopatra stooping down with her head,

putting to all her strength to her uttermost power, did lift him up with much ado and never let go her hold . . .

0 *aloft*: The staging of the scenes in the monument has provoked much discussion; and whatever is said must be conjectural. It may be, as J. Dover Wilson suggests, that a flat-roofed wooden structure was brought on to the stage; it would be placed over the trapdoor, through which Cleopatra and her maids would enter it. They would then take their places on the roof. See The Play in Performance.

4–5 *we . . . Our . . . our*: Royal plural.

10 *sphere*: In the Ptolemaic astronomy the sun was fixed in a crystalline sphere and, along with the other planets, revolved round the earth. If it burned its sphere, it would fly off into space, leaving the earth in darkness (*darkling*).

11 *varying shore o'th'world*: This is usually taken as a sublime pictorial image – the world seen as an island with an irregular coastline, or possibly a coastline variegated in light and darkness. The word *shore* may, however, be a term of contempt, meaning 'sewer'. 'Common shore' was regularly used for 'common sewer' in Shakespeare's day. Cleopatra would then mean that the world without Antony is nothing but a ceaselessly flowing sewer – just as later, when Antony dies, she finds *this dull world . . . No better than a sty* (61–2). In these concluding scenes there are several other expressions of contempt for the world, which take up Antony's reference, at the beginning of the play, to *Our dungy earth* (I.1.35). (The terms 'common shores' and 'sty' occur in a single scene of *Pericles*, probably written not long after *Antony and Cleopatra*: see *Pericles*, IV.6.174, 93.)

13–31 *Peace . . . friends*: It has been argued, by J. Dover Wilson and others, that Shakespeare made a false start which he then failed to delete. The result, according to this argument, is that we have an unnecessary passage (13–31) and consequently two sets of unnecessary repetitions: Cleopatra's instructions to pull Antony up, and Antony's line *I am dying, Egypt, dying*. Against this, the integrity of the F text has sometimes been defended. It seems, on balance, preferable to hold to the F text, since this is a play uncommonly concerned to render – in some of its scenes, at least – the feel of life as it is lived and especially its tendency to untidiness and anticlimax. That tendency is nowhere more apparent than in this sequence of Antony's death. If the passage objected to by Dover Wilson seems confused and repetitive, that may be exactly what Shakespeare intended.

19 *importune death*: Keep death waiting.

21 *dare not*: She dare not open the gate or descend.

23 *imperious*: Imperial.

25 *Be brooched with me*: Have me as its chief ornament (brooch).

26 *operation*: Power (referring to *drugs*, 25).

28 *still conclusion*: Quietly impassive judgement.

29 *Demuring upon me*: Looking at me demurely (with an irritatingly complacent sobriety).

33 *heaviness*: (1) Weight; (2) sorrow.

34 *Juno's*: The wife of Jupiter; the queen goddess of heaven.

35 *Mercury*: The winged messenger of the gods.

38 *Die when thou hast lived*: That is, don't die until you have lived once again.

39 *Quicken*: Come to life.

42–58 *Give me some wine . . . vanquished*: This is closely based on Plutarch:

> Antonius made her cease her lamenting, and called for wine, either because he was athirst, or else for that he thought thereby to hasten his death. When he had drunk, he earnestly prayed her and persuaded her that she would seek to save her life, if she could possible without reproach and dishonour; and that chiefly she should trust Proculeius above any man else about Caesar; and, as for himself, that she should not lament nor sorrow for the miserable change of

his fortune at the end of his days; but rather that she should think him the more fortunate for the former triumphs and honours he had received, considering that while he lived he was the noblest and greatest prince of the world, and that now he was overcome not cowardly, but valiantly, a Roman by another Roman.

44 *false*: Treacherous.
*housewife*: Hussy (pronounced 'huzzif').

45 *offence*: Insults.

59 *woo't*: Wouldst thou.

64 *garland*: Crown, glory.

65 *The soldier's pole*: The meaning is disputed. Suggestions include 'polestar', 'standard', 'maypole', and, as a possible secondary meaning to one of these, 'phallus'. The first of these seems the best.

66 *The odds is gone*: There is now no difference of value between things.

67 *remarkable*: Wonderful.

72 *but e'en a woman*: Than just a woman (perhaps in reply to Iras' *Empress!*).

73 *such poor passion*: The reference is probably not simply to passionate grief but to *hysterica passio*, a condition common to women, according to medical views current in Shakespeare's time. It was caused by strong passion; its symptoms included swooning. As a woman, Cleopatra is as subject to it as any other woman, irrespective of rank.

74 *chares*: Chores, tasks.

77 *naught*: Worthless, useless.

78 *sottish*: Stupid, foolish.

84 *Good sirs*: Addressed to the women; an Elizabethan usage.

90 *briefest*: Swiftest.

V.1

Plutarch narrates how one of Antony's guardsmen, Dercetaeus, took Antony's sword

and brought Octavius Caesar the first news of his death,

and showed him his sword that was bloodied. Caesar hearing these news straight withdrew himself into a secret place of his tent, and there burst out with tears, lamenting his hard and miserable fortune that had been his friend and brother-in-law, his equal in the Empire, and companion with him in sundry great exploits and battles. Then he called for all his friends, and showed them the letters Antonius had written to him, and his answers also sent him again, during their quarrel and strife; and how fiercely and proudly the other answered him to all just and reasonable matters he wrote unto him.

2–3 *Being so frustrate . . . makes*: Tell him that, since he is so helplessly defeated, his delays are a mere mockery.

5 *thus*: With a naked sword.

14 *breaking*: (1) Destruction, end; (2) disclosure, telling.

15 *crack*: (1) Explosive sound; (2) breach, rift (perhaps 'convulsion').

16 *civil*: City.

19 *moiety*: Half.

21 *self*: Same.

30 *Our most persisted deeds*: What we most persist in doing.

31 *Waged equal with*: Were equally matched in.

36 *followed*: Pursued.

*launch*: Lance.

38 *such a declining day*: A declining day (or sun) such as you have shown.

39 *stall*: Dwell.

41 *sovereign*: Potent.

42 *competitor*: Partner (but see the note to I.4.3).

43 *In top of all design*: In worthiest enterprise.

46 *his*: Its.

47 *Unreconciliable*: In perpetual conflict with each other.

47–8 *should divide | Our equalness to this*: Should sunder us, who were so equally partnered, in this way.

49 *meeter season*: More suitable moment.

50 *looks out of him*: Shows from his appearance.

57 *by some of ours*: From some of my representatives.

63 *passion*: Grief.

64 *greatness*: Loftiness of spirit.

65–6 *her life in Rome . . . triumph*: Her presence alive in Rome in my triumph would make it famous for ever.

74 *hardly*: Reluctantly.

75 *still*: Constantly.

V.2

For his last scene, by far the longest in the play, Shakespeare runs together several occasions which in Plutarch are distinct. The immediate result is a condensation of time: Shakespeare's Cleopatra dies very shortly after Antony; in Plutarch events are more protracted. A perhaps more important difference concerns Cleopatra's emotional state during this final phase in her story. In Plutarch, overwhelmed with grief, she physically maltreats herself: 'she had knocked her breast so pitifully, that she had martyred it and in divers places had raised ulcers and inflammations, so that she fell into a fever withal'; and when, shortly after, Caesar visits her he finds her 'marvellously disfigured; both for that she had plucked her hair from her head, as also for that she had martyred all her face with her nails; and, besides, her voice was small and trembling, her eyes sunk into her head with continual blubbering, and moreover they might see the most part of her stomach torn in sunder'. Shakespeare could make no use of this, or of the account of her visit to Antony's grave; his Cleopatra, who has twice mentioned her *resolution* in IV.15 (49, 90), is an altogether less broken figure, though at the same time her *desolation* (1) is convincingly established. For his conception of her inner transformation, Shakespeare may have owed something to Horace's Cleopatra ode (I.37), especially its last three stanzas:

Yet she preferred a finer style of dying:
She did not, like a woman, shirk the dagger
  Or seek by speed at sea
To change her Egypt for obscurer shores,

But, gazing on her desolated palace
With a calm smile, unflinchingly laid hands on
The angry asps until
Her veins had drunk the deadly poison deep,

And, death-determined, fiercer then than ever,
Perished. Was she to grace a haughty triumph,
Dethroned, paraded by
The rude Liburnians? Not Cleopatra!

(*The Odes of Horace*, translated by
James Michie (1976))

For the rest, Shakespeare closely followed Plutarch, except for Cleopatra's 'dream' of Antony, which was his own invention.

2 *A better life*: The philosophical values of the Stoics are adopted here. The good man (or woman) despised the gifts of fortune and triumphed over adversity by showing resolution or inner constancy. Cf. Antony's words to Eros at IV.14.60–62 and to his other followers at IV.14.136–8.

3 *knave*: Servant.

5 *that thing*: Suicide.

7–8 *never palates more the dung, | The beggar's nurse and Caesar's*: Never more tastes the produce of the mere earth (*dung*), which gives life to all men, whatever their place in society. Cf. I.1.35, *Our dungy earth*.

10 *study on*: Think carefully about.

14 *to be deceived*: Whether I am deceived or not.

15 *That have*: Since I have.

17 *keep decorum*: Do the appropriate thing.

20 *as*: That.

23 *Make your full reference*: Refer yourself wholly (that is, put yourself wholly into his hands).

26 *sweet dependency*: Willingness to be submissive.

27 *pray in aid for kindness*: Ask you to help him in being kind to you.

29–30 *I am . . . got*: I do homage to his good fortune and I formally acknowledge his authority.

29 *send him*: Send him acknowledgement of.

34 *The soldiers approach Cleopatra from behind*: This direction is editorial. The stage business here is unclear and can only be conjectured. Shakespeare may have left it deliberately vague so as to make it adaptable to different stage conditions. What seems to happen is that the soldiers reach Cleopatra from behind, possibly using ladders from the pit up on to the main stage.

41 *Relieved*: Rescued.

42 *languish*: Lingering disease.

45 *well acted*: Duly exercised. But *acted* is ambiguous; it also suggests 'assumed as a role', 'imitated'.

46 *let come forth*: Allow to be displayed.

48 *babes and beggars*: Those to whom 'relief' is usually given.

50 *If idle talk . . . necessary*: If useless words have to be used for once.

51 *This mortal house*: Her body. According to Plutarch, Cleopatra did in fact maltreat herself; see the headnote to this scene.

53 *pinioned*: (1) With arms tied behind, shackled; (2) like a bird with its wings clipped.

54 *once*: Ever.

*chastised*: Accented on the first syllable.

56 *varletry*: Mob.

60 *Blow*: Deposit their eggs on.

*into abhorring*: So that I become an object of disgust.

61 *pyramides*: Four syllables, accented on the second.

62 *extend*: Magnify.

71 *empress*: The title, used by a Roman, implies. considerable respect. Dolabella is flattering Cleopatra.

75 *trick*: Way, habit.

79–92 *His face . . . pocket*: With Cleopatra's 'dream', cf. Lady Percy's elegiac description of the dead Hotspur (*Henry IV, Part II*, II.3.17–38).

79 *stuck*: Were set.

81 *The little O o'th'earth*: F has *The little o'th'earth*. Most modern editors read 'The little O, the earth'. But it

seems essential to keep the very Shakespearian phrase *o'th'earth*; and the likeliest explanation is that a monosyllabic noun has dropped out, so that Shakespeare wrote something like 'orb o'th'earth' (*Coriolanus*, V.6.126), though he is perhaps unlikely to have used 'orb' here, since it occurs four lines later (85). *O*, meaning 'tiny circle', is paralleled in *Henry V*, Prologue 13, 'this wooden O', and, meaning 'zero', 'nothing', in *King Lear*, I.4.188–9, 'an o without a figure'.

82–3 *his reared arm | Crested the world*: A metaphor from heraldry: a coat of arms could have a raised arm as a crest.

83–4 *propertied ... spheres*: As musical in quality as all the spheres (alluding to the Pythagorean doctrine of the harmonious sound created by the movement of the planetary spheres, which was normally inaudible to human beings).

84 *and that to friends*: The meaning required seems to be 'when speaking to friends' and is contrasted with what follows. The text may be corrupt here.

85 *quail*: Make quail.

87 *an Antony it was*: This is F's reading. Most editors adopt the emendation 'an autumn 'twas'. This is plausible, but emendation does not seem absolutely necessary. If it is objected that the F reading does not make sense, it should be remembered that Cleopatra is speaking rhapsodically and with startlingly abrupt metaphors (as the following lines show, for example, *In his livery | Walked crowns and crownets*, 90–91). The idea of Antony as a perpetually plenteous harvest is amply prepared for in *bounty* and *winter*; an audience would understand with no difficulty. For the phrase *an Antony*, cf. II.5.14, IV.2.18 and V.2.99.

88–90 *His delights ... lived in*: Just as dolphins show their backs above the water, so Antony rose above the pleasures that were his element. Dolphins were themselves thought to be highly sensual creatures.

90 *The element*: The sea.

90 *livery*: Service.

91 *crowns and crownets*: Kings and princes.

92 *plates*: Silver coins.

96 *if . . . one such*: If there neither is nor ever was such a man. This reading keeps F's *nor*, and takes the construction to be 'neither [understood] . . . nor'. Some editors emend *nor* to 'or'.

97 *It's past the size of dreaming*: No mere dream could approach it.

97–100 *Nature wants stuff . . . quite*: Nature lacks the material to compete with fancy in the creation of fantastic (*strange*) forms, yet to imagine an Antony would be a masterpiece of conception, natural rather than fantastic, and entirely discrediting the figments of fancy.

99 *piece*: Masterpiece.

103 *but I do*: If I do not.

104 *rebound*: Reflection.

105 *My very heart at root*: To the bottom of my heart.

111–90 *Caesar . . . Adieu*: Shakespeare precedes and follows Caesar's visit to Cleopatra with Dolabella's clear assurances that Caesar intends to make her walk in his triumph. In her interview with Caesar, and particularly in her dealings with Seleucus, Cleopatra is probably deceiving Caesar into believing that she wants to live. Shakespeare leaves room for doubt, but Plutarch's account is unambiguous:

> . . . Cleopatra began to clear and excuse herself for that she had done, laying all to the fear she had of Antonius. Caesar, in contrary manner, reproved her in every point. Then she suddenly altered her speech, and prayed him to pardon her, as though she were afraid to die and desirous to live. At length, she gave him a brief and memorial of all the ready money and treasure she had. But by chance there stood Seleucus by, one of her treasurers, who to seem a good servant, came straight to Caesar to disprove Cleopatra, that she had not set in all but kept many things back of purpose. Cleopatra was in such a rage with him that she flew upon him, and took him by the hair of the head, and boxed him

well-favouredly. Caesar fell a-laughing and parted the fray.

'Alas,' said she, 'O Caesar, is not this a great shame and reproach, that thou having vouchsafed to take the pains to come unto me, and hast done me this honour, poor wretch and caitiff creature brought into this pitiful and miserable estate, and that mine own servants should come now to accuse me; though it may be I have reserved some jewels and trifles meet for women, but not for me, poor soul, to set out myself withal but meaning to give some pretty presents and gifts unto Octavia and Livia, that, they making means and intercession for me to thee, thou mightest yet extend thy favour and mercy upon me?'

Caesar was glad to hear her say so, persuading himself thereby that she had yet a desire to save her life. So he made her answer that he did not only give her that to dispose of at her pleasure which she had kept back, but further promised to use her more honourably and bountifully than she would think for. And so he took his leave of her, supposing he had deceived her. But indeed he was deceived himself.

120 *sir*: Lord, master.

121 *project*: Set forth (accented on the first syllable).

122 *To make it clear*: As to make it seem innocent.

125 *enforce*: Emphasize.

126 *apply yourself*: Conform.

129 *lay on me a cruelty*: Make me look cruel (that is, inflict on me an appearance of being cruel).

134 *may*: That is, may leave, or set out on a journey (for anywhere in the world).

135 *scutcheons*: (Captured) shields.

138 *brief*: Summary.

140 *Not petty things admitted*: Except for trivial items.

146 *seel*: Sew up (see the note to III.13.112).

151 *pomp is followed*: People in high estate are served. *Mine*: My followers.

152 *shift estates*: Change places.

153–4 *does | Even make me wild*: Simply makes me mad.

155 *hired*: Paid for, bought.

158 *rarely*: Exceptionally.

163 *Parcel*: Number off one by one, read out a list of. But this merges with another sense: 'extend', 'augment'.

164 *envy*: Malice.

165 *lady*: Suitable for a lady.

166 *Immoment toys*: Unimportant little things.
*dignity*: Worth.

167 *modern*: Ordinary.

169 *Livia*: Caesar's wife.

170–71 *unfolded | With*: Exposed by.

171 *one that I have bred*: One of my household.

173 *cinders*: Burning coals.

174 *chance*: Fortune.
*a man*: Not a eunuch.

175 *Forbear*: Leave, go.

176 *misthought*: Misjudged.

178 *We answer others' merits*: We are responsible for the faults committed by others.
*merits*: Deserts (good or bad; here bad).

183 *make prize*: Haggle, bargain.

185 *Make not your thoughts your prisons*: Don't think yourself a prisoner, since you are free.

191 *words me*: Puts me off with mere words.

194 *Hie thee again*: Hurry back.

198–203 *Madam . . . this*: Based on Plutarch: Dolabella '. . . did bear no evil will unto Cleopatra. He sent her word secretly, as she had requested him, that Caesar determined to take his journey through Syria, and that within three days he would send her away before with her children.'

199 *makes religion*: Binds me absolutely.

208 *puppet*: Actor in a pantomime. Cleopatra imagines herself and Iras drawn along on a wheeled stage, taking part in an 'Egyptian' tableau.

209 *Mechanic slaves*: Common labourers.

212 *Rank of gross diet*: Smelling of bad food.

213 *drink*: Inhale.

214 *Saucy*: Insolent.
*lictors*: Magistrates' officers. They will be treated by the lictors, so Cleopatra imagines, as ungently as

beadles treated prostitutes in Elizabethan England.

215 *scald*: Scurvy, contemptible.

216 *Ballad us*: Sing our story in ballads.
*quick*: Quick-witted.

217 *Extemporally*: In improvised performances.

220 *boy my greatness*: Reduce my greatness to what an incompetent boy-actor can manage. Shakespeare's Cleopatra was, on the contrary, written for a boy-actor to whose skill and virtuosity these lines implicitly pay tribute.

228 *Cydnus*: See II.2.191–231.

229 *Sirrah*: An address used to inferiors, male or female.

230 *dispatch*: (1) Hasten; (2) finish. Cleopatra plays on both senses.

231 *chare*: Chore, task.

232 *Exit Iras*: This is not in F. Some editors give Charmian an exit too, bringing her back with Iras at the Clown's departure.

233–78 *Here is a rural fellow . . . o'th'worm*: Plutarch writes:

> Now whilst she was at dinner there came a countryman, and brought her a basket. The soldiers that warded at the gates asked him straight what he had in his basket. He opened the basket and took out the leaves that covered the figs, and showed them that they were figs he brought. They all of them marvelled to see so goodly figs. The countryman laughed to hear them, and bade them take some if they would. They believed he told them truly, and so bade him carry them in.

236 *What*: How.

238 *placed*: Fixed.

240 *fleeting*: Changeful. Since the moon 'changed' monthly, it presided over the realm of mutable nature. In choosing to die, Cleopatra is leaving the moon's domain. There is also a possible allusion to Isis, the Egyptian moon goddess, in whose *habiliments* Cleopatra had earlier appeared (see III.6.16–19).

241 *Clown*: Countryman, rustic.

242 *Avoid*: Go.

243–312 *Hast thou . . . stay*: In the period after Actium Cleopatra had investigated the most painless ways of dying. Plutarch writes:

> So, when she had daily made divers and sundry proofs, she found none of them all she had proved so fit as the biting of an aspic, the which causeth only a heaviness of the head, without swounding or complaining, and bringeth a great desire also to sleep, with a little sweat in the face, and so by little and little taketh away the senses and vital powers, no living creature perceiving that the patients feel any pain.

243–78 *the pretty worm . . . joy o'th'worm*: In the scene with the Clown *worm* has three applications: (1) snake, asp (243); (2) the male sexual organ (255); (3) earthworm (270).

247 *immortal*: The Clown's mistake for 'mortal'. But cf. Cleopatra's words at 279–80.

250 *of*: From.

251 *honest*: (1) Truthful; (2) chaste.

252 *lie*: (1) Tell lies; (2) have sexual relations with a man.

253 *died*: Another sexual allusion; see the note to I.2.138.

257 *falliable*: Another mistake by the Clown, presumably for 'infallible'.

262 *do his kind*: Act according to his nature.

264–76 *the worm is . . . mar five*: Shakespeare seems to be making, through the Clown, a detached comment on the powers of sex, which, according as they are used, may be good or evil. The Clown's drily unromantic admonitions sound an astringent note immediately before the play's exalted conclusion.

267 *Take thou no care*: Don't worry.

273 *dress*: Prepare for cooking. There may also be a secondary sense of 'put on clothes'.

274 *whoreson*: Accursed (Elizabethan slang).

280 *Immortal longings*: Longings for immortality.

282 *Yare*: Quickly.

285 *The luck of Caesar*: Octavius was noted for his good

fortune or 'felicity'. Cf. Antony's phrase at IV.14.76, *fortunate Caesar*.

285–6 *which . . . wrath*: The gods give men good fortune in order that they may punish them for having enjoyed it.

286 *after*: Subsequent.

288–9 *I am fire . . . life*: Man was thought to be composed of four elements, two higher (*fire* and *air*) and two lower (earth and water).

289 *baser*: Lower (but also with a contemptuous connotation).

291 *Iras falls and dies*: F has no direction here. Some editors take it that Iras dies simply of grief, but it seems best to assume that she has already applied an asp to herself by the time Cleopatra kisses her. But see the Introduction, p. lxii.

292 *aspic*: Asp.

299 *This*: Iras' death.

300 *curlèd*: With curled hair. Perhaps Cleopatra thinks of Antony as she first met him, *barbered ten times o'er* (II.2.229).

301 *spend that kiss*: Slake his passion on her.

302 *mortal wretch*: Deadly little thing; *wretch*, like *fool* (304), was often, as here, an affectionate term.

303 *intrinsicate*: Mysteriously intricate.

307 *Unpolicied*: Outwitted in 'policy' or statecraft.
*eastern star*: The morning star, Venus.

308 *my baby at my breast*: Plutarch reports that Cleopatra was bitten in the arm. With Shakespeare's version cf. Thomas Nashe's *Christ's Tears over Jerusalem* (1593): 'at thy breasts (as at Cleopatra's) aspises shall be put out to nurse' (*Works*, ed. Ronald B. McKerrow (1904), II.140).

312 *What*: Why.

313 *vile*: Worthless, contemptible. F reads *wilde*, which is possible. But 'vile' was often spelt 'vilde', and 'v' and 'w' were not uncommonly confused, so that the emendation adopted here is not difficult; *vile* seems preferable to 'wild' on grounds of meaning; for other

dismissals of the world, cf. I.1.35 (*dungy earth*) and IV.15.61–2 (*dull world . . . sty*).

315 *windows*: Eyelids.

316 *Phoebus*: The sun god.

317 *Of*: By.

*awry*: Crooked.

318 *and then play*: Alluding to 231–2.

*rustling*: Clattering.

320 *Too slow a messenger*: For once Caesar's administrative efficiency is defective; cf. the note to III.6.31.

322 *beguiled*: Deceived.

324–6 *Is this well done . . . kings*: Based on Plutarch:

> But when they had opened the doors they found Cleopatra stark dead laid upon a bed of gold, attired and arrayed in her royal robes, and one of her two women, which was called Iras, dead at her feet; and her other woman called Charmion half dead and trembling, trimming the diadem which Cleopatra ware upon her head. One of the soldiers, seeing her, angrily said unto her:
>
> 'Is that well done, Charmion?'
>
> 'Very well,' said she again, 'and meet for a princess descended from the race of so many noble kings.'
>
> She said no more, but fell down dead hard by the bed.

329 *Touch their effects*: Meet with realization, are realized.

334 *levelled at*: Guessed at.

337 *simple*: Of humble condition.

344 *like sleep*: As if she were asleep.

345 *As*: As if.

346 *toil*: Net, snare.

*grace*: Beauty, seductiveness.

347 *vent*: Discharge.

*blown*: Deposited (cf. the note to 60). The usual explanation, 'swollen', seems less likely. In the next speech the First Guard explains what the *something* is.

353 *conclusions infinite*: Innumerable experiments.

357 *clip*: Embrace (an amatory metaphor).

359 *Strike*: Touch, afflict.

360 *than his glory which*: Than is the glory of him who.
364 *solemnity*: Ceremonious occasion.

# PENGUIN SHAKESPEARE

**CYMBELINE**
WILLIAM SHAKESPEARE

**WWW.PENGUINSHAKESPEARE.COM**

The King of Britain, enraged by his daughter's disobedience in marrying against his wishes, banishes his new son-in-law. Having fled to Rome, the exiled husband makes a foolish wager with a villain he encounters there – gambling on the fidelity of his abandoned wife. Combining courtly menace and horror, comedy and melodrama, *Cymbeline* is a moving depiction of two young lovers driven apart by deceit and self-doubt.

This book includes a general introduction to Shakespeare's life and the Elizabethan theatre, a separate introduction to *Cymbeline*, a chronology of his works, suggestions for further reading, an essay discussing performance options on both stage and screen, and a commentary.

Edited with an introduction by John Pitcher

General Editor: Stanley Wells

read more

# PENGUIN SHAKESPEARE

**JULIUS CAESAR**
WILLIAM SHAKESPEARE

**WWW.PENGUINSHAKESPEARE.COM**

When it seems that Julius Caesar may assume supreme power, a plot to destroy him is hatched by those determined to preserve the threatened republic. But the different motives of the conspirators soon become apparent when high principles clash with malice and political realism. As the nation plunges into bloody civil war, this taut drama explores the violent consequences of betrayal and murder.

This book includes a general introduction to Shakespeare's life and the Elizabethan theatre, a separate introduction to *Julius Caesar*, a chronology of his works, suggestions for further reading, an essay discussing performance options on both stage and screen, and a commentary.

Edited by Norman Sanders

With an introduction by Martin Wiggins

General editor: Stanley Wells

# PENGUIN SHAKESPEARE

**TIMON OF ATHENS**
WILLIAM SHAKESPEARE

**WWW.PENGUINSHAKESPEARE.COM**

After squandering his wealth with prodigal generosity, a rich Athenian gentleman finds himself deep in debt. Unshaken by the prospect of bankruptcy, he is certain that the friends he has helped so often will come to his aid. But when they learn his wealth is gone, he quickly finds that their promises fall away to nothing in this tragic exploration of power, greed, and loyalty betrayed.

This book includes a general introduction to Shakespeare's life and the Elizabethan theatre, a separate introduction to *Timon of Athens*, a chronology of his works, suggestions for further reading, an essay discussing performance options on both stage and screen, and a commentary.

Edited by G. R. Hibbard

With an introduction by Nicholas Walton

General Editor: Stanley Wells

*Read more in Penguin*

## PENGUIN SHAKESPEARE

*All's Well That Ends Well*
*Antony and Cleopatra*
*As You Like It*
*The Comedy of Errors*
*Coriolanus*
*Cymbeline*
*Hamlet*
*Henry IV, Part I*
*Henry IV, Part II*
*Henry V*
*Henry VI, Part I*
*Henry VI, Part II*
*Henry VI, Part III*
*Henry VIII*
*Julius Caesar*
*King John*
*King Lear*
*Love's Labour's Lost*
*Macbeth*
*Measure for Measure*
*The Merchant of Venice*
*The Merry Wives of Windsor*
*A Midsummer Night's Dream*
*Much Ado About Nothing*
*Othello*
*Pericles*
*Richard II*
*Richard III*
*Romeo and Juliet*
*The Sonnets and A Lover's Complaint*
*The Taming of the Shrew*
*The Tempest*
*Timon of Athens*
*Titus Andronicus*
*Twelfth Night*
*The Two Gentlemen of Verona*
*The Two Noble Kinsmen*
*The Winter's Tale*